God and Politics in Esther

A political crisis erupts when the Persian government falls to fanatics, and a Jewish insider goes rogue, determined to save her people at all costs.

God and Politics in Esther explores politics and faith. It is about an era in which the prophets have been silenced and miracles have ceased, and Jewish politics has come to depend not on commands from on high, but on the boldness and belief of each woman and man. Esther takes radical action to win friends and allies, reverse terrifying decrees, and bring God's justice into the world with her own hands.

Hazony argues that the story of Esther was meant precisely to speak to a generation like ours – one which doesn't tend to see God in the world and isn't waiting for miracles. The biblical God, we learn, is an emergent God, who appears in history and in our lives through those who choose to act, and so build God's kingdom on earth.

This is a thoroughly revised and expanded edition of *The Dawn* (1995), with three controversial new chapters addressing the astonishingly radical theology that emerges amid the political intrigues in the narrative.

Yoram Hazony is President of the Herzl Institute in Jerusalem. He is founder and past president of the Shalem Center, now Shalem College. His books include *The Philosophy of Hebrew Scripture* (Cambridge University Press, 2012) and *The Jewish State: The Struggle for Israel's Soul* (2000). Hazony directs the John Templeton Foundation's project in Jewish Philosophical Theology and is a member of the Israel Council for Higher Education committee on liberal studies in Israel's universities.

God and Politics in Esther

YORAM HAZONY

The Herzl Institute, Jerusalem

CAMBRIDGE
UNIVERSITY PRESS

CAMBRIDGE
UNIVERSITY PRESS

32 Avenue of the Americas, New York, NY 10013-2473, USA

Cambridge University Press is part of the University of Cambridge.

It furthers the University's mission by disseminating knowledge in the pursuit of
education, learning, and research at the highest international levels of excellence.

www.cambridge.org
Information on this title: www.cambridge.org/9781107583450

First edition published as *The Dawn* by Genesis Jerusalem Press, 1995

First Cambridge University Press edition published 2016

Printed in the United Kingdom by Clays, St Ives plc

A catalog record for this publication is available from the British Library.

Library of Congress Cataloging in Publication Data
Hazony, Yoram, author.
[Dawn]
God and politics in Esther / Yoram Hazony, The Herzl Institute, Jerusalem. –
Second edition.
   pages cm
Includes the text of Esther in English and Hebrew.
Includes index.
ISBN 978-1-107-13205-4 (hardback) – ISBN 978-1-107-58345-0 (paperback)
1. Bible. Esther – Criticism, interpretation, etc., Jewish.   2. Politics in the Bible.
3. Esther, Queen of Persia.   4. Bible. Old Testament – History of Biblical events.
5. Jews – Politics and government – To 70 A.D.   I. Bible. Esther. English.
Hazony. 2016.   II. Bible. Esther. Hebrew. 2016.   III. Title.
BS1375.2.H39   2016
222'.907–dc23   2015029113

ISBN 978-1-107-13205-4 Hardback
ISBN 978-1-107-58345-0 Paperback

For Aba
With love

Contents

Preface

Recent decades have seen rapidly growing interest in the book of Esther, both in the popular media and among scholars and theologians. Its plot and characters, theology and political philosophy, are all benefiting from a much-deserved reevaluation. I am pleased to be able to contribute *God and Politics in Esther* to the discussion. I have long considered the Esther story to be an important doorway into the worldview of Hebrew Scripture and of Jewish tradition more generally. In this book, the second in a trilogy of works on the philosophy of the Hebrew Bible that are to appear with Cambridge University Press, I explain why this is so.

My work on Esther began with a challenge many years ago from Rabbi Jay Marcus, to whom I am grateful for commissioning and publishing the earliest version of this book. I am grateful, as well, to Lewis Bateman of Cambridge, who has set the pace for the new storm of academic publishing interest in the area of Jewish ideas. Lew has done perhaps more than anyone else to bring my work to the attention of a broad audience, a debt that I can hardly hope to repay. Thanks, too, to Suzanne Balaban of BMM Worldwide, who has deftly handled publicity for my recent books and added much good spirit to the publishing process besides. I wish to express my appreciation to those who have supported my work on this book, including Michael Murray, John Churchill, and Alex Arnold at the John Templeton Foundation, Barry and Lainie Klein, Seth and Nealy Fischer, Roger Hertog, David Messer, Jack Berger, Bart Baum, Ron Hersh, and Michael Moskowitz.

This book is dedicated to my father, Yehonathan Hazony, whose teachings and ideas are present in each page I write. His ongoing research into the behavior of quantum bodies, and his dissent from accepted theory on this subject despite the hardship of such an unpopular road, is an inspiration to me every day of my life.

Introduction

Ever since the inclusion of the book of Esther in the biblical canon two thousand years ago, there have been those who have asked what place such a work can have in the Bible at all. Their question must be well taken, for at first glance Esther appears to be something very different from what we usually consider to be "biblical." Esther is a tale of kings and queens and evil grand viziers that cannot help but strike one as a romance or a fairy story. Nowhere in its ten terse chapters can one find the cascading moral imperatives of Isaiah and Jeremiah, and even less in evidence are the sober laws of Moses. The term "God" appears nowhere, and one is hard-pressed to find any trace of theology amid the hairpin turns of the tale. Moreover, the Jewish heroes of the story seem to display little piety and negligible concern for Jewish law: Mordechai the Jew guides and advises his cousin, Hadasa, as she hides her heritage, marries a non-Jewish potentate, and, in a realm apparently rife with anti-Semitism, presumably gives up on any aspect of Jewish observance that would betray her past so that she may remain in the royal palace. The book even refers to the young Jewish heroine by the Persian name of Esther, meaning "star" – and the stars were themselves part of the cult of idolatry in Persia – a fact that cannot but suggest assimilation and capitulation to the surrounding civilization.

Yet for all this, when the rabbis of the Talmudic period looked back across Jewish history, seeking to grant it coherence and permanence by assembling its teachings into a canon, they ascribed great significance to Esther as a work concerned with themes relevant to the conclusion of the Bible. Indeed, when the rabbis spoke of the giving of the *tora* to the Jewish people, they argued that it had been accepted not once but twice: Once at Sinai at the beginning of the Bible, and then again at the end, in the time of Esther.[1] And when they considered the eternity of the Bible's teachings, they asserted that there were two portions of Scripture that could never be abolished, the books of Moses and the book of Esther.² And while they taught that the other parts of the Bible could bring an understanding of piety, wisdom, consolation, and greatness, it was only the book of Esther that they thought offered the key to the miraculous.³ To the rabbis, this little story of persecution and court intrigue was something precious, powerful, and exceedingly important.⁴ It was a writing thought worthy of being the Bible's closing words to man – in a sense, God's last words to man.⁵

To begin unraveling the riddle of Esther's meaning, we must first recognize that Esther is a book about exile. That is, unlike most of the other works of the Bible, which depict the Jews in their efforts to come to the land of Israel and build a Jewish nation there, Esther describes a world in which the Jews are distant from their land, their tradition, and their God. When sovereign in the land of Israel, the Jews are confronted directly with questions of national morality: how to govern justly, how to obtain security and peace, how to establish the pious and good society in the face of the terrible obstacles encountered by any realistic appraisal of the proclivities and aptitudes of men. But in Israel, the Jews at least have the advantage of sovereign authority: The government may muster vast material resources and promulgate laws in the service of the public interest; the intellectual leaders may freely study, teach, and write in the pursuit of truth; and the leaders of the spirit may go about inculcating a love of justice and peace among the people. In sum, when sovereign in their own land, the Jews at least possess the power needed to determine and implement an ideal according to their own lights, whether they choose to make appropriate use of this power or not. And it is no coincidence, either, that it was when the Jews possessed this power, living on the land and fighting for it, that they also found themselves directly confronted by their God.

In exile, whether in ancient Persia or in a more contemporary one, Jewish life must somehow persist without the immense resources made available by independent, sovereign power. In exile, the Jews must live in dispersion, their institutions weak, their concerns wandering far from Jewish things, and their politics alienated from every obvious source of cohesiveness, direction, and strength. It is clear at the outset that under such conditions, there is no possibility of freely seeking and implementing any Jewish ideal. To live in a society ruled by others means that the government and the laws are not the product of a Jewish concern for the general public interest, and that they are certainly not the result of an interest in the well-being of the Jews as a nation; that Jewish intellectual endeavors are under constant pressure, whether overt or implicit, to conform to alien norms; and that Jewish leadership, if it is capable and effective, is perpetually viewed with a certain measure of suspicion and even fear – both by the community of non-Jews, and by members of the Jewish community concerned that Jewish success may be interpreted by the gentiles as a challenge to their authority. Thus exile, while never precluding entirely the possibility of Jewish power, nevertheless establishes a formidable presumption against it – a presumption that has ominous theological echoes in the fact that even the most devout come to feel that the way has been lost, and begin to speak, as though in winter, of God having "hidden his face" from his people.[6]

It is to such a setting that we are introduced in the book of Esther. Never before have the Jews experienced anything like it, unless it was in Egypt, a thousand years earlier. Persia is an archetypal oriental tyranny in which the peoples live by grace of the despot's wishes, and in which the physical survival of the Jews implicitly remains an open question, even when, as at the beginning of the tale, the waters seem untroubled. Under these circumstances, the narrative of Esther is faithful to the tenor of the times, seeming to bypass issues of theology and religious observance to cope with the more burning issue of the actual physical survival of the Jews. For this reason, the book of Esther deals first and foremost with the problem of a Jewish politics in exile: how the Jews, deprived of every sovereign institution of power, may nevertheless participate in, and in the last resort make use of, the authority of an alien government to ensure their own vital interests, and in this case their lives. Esther offers its readers a choice between two antithetical conditions – the one being a nightmare of impotence, in which "it was written ... in the name of Ahashverosh the king ... to annihilate, to kill and to destroy all Jews, the young and the elderly, children and women, in one day," and there is nothing to be done; and the other, in which Mordechai the Jew rises to a position of great power with the ability to act in defense of the Jews, being, as it says in the closing chapter, "second to Ahashverosh the king, ... seeking the good of his people and speaking peace to all his descendants." The nature of this utterly political choice – and how it is to be made in practice – is the principal concern and teaching of the book of Esther.

At the same time, Esther also moves to assert itself against another, more subtle opponent, one that had loomed over Persian Jewry for years before Haman had plotted against them. Persia in Esther's time is a cosmopolitan world empire, offering success and wealth to those among the Jewish exiles who will give up on the past and play by its rules. In Persia, as elsewhere, the Jews begin to disappear into the fabric of the empire, some of them changing their names and their attire, and arguing with self-confidence against the possibility and desirability of a continuation to Jewish history. What argument can be made as against these, to a defeated and dispirited Jewry, scattered to the corners of the world and no longer privy to the word of God? In making its political argument, the narrative of Esther consciously responds on these

historical, religious, and theological battlegrounds as well, offering answers
that are among the most daring, and ultimately the most successful, in Jewish
history.

Yet these deadly serious messages tend to be lost when the book is read
today. Its association with the activities now surrounding the festival of
Purim, the Feast of Esther, has rendered such themes obscure, since Esther
is seldom read in a context in which it may be taken seriously on its own
terms. As a consequence, many read the book only in a cursory fashion,
believing that the plot pivots on "coincidence" or "luck." But a closer examination reveals that there are no coincidences in the tale: The political events
leading to the salvation of the Jews of Persia are planned by Mordechai and
Esther, and come to succeed by virtue of their shrewd understanding of the
principles of politics, their courage, and their faith in the face of an apparently godless world. How these elements can work to produce the greatest
of political events, in which "the enemies of the Jews hoped to rule them, but
the situation reversed itself and it was the Jews who asserted rule over their
enemies," is the true tale of Esther, whose teachings demand our attention
and our interest so many centuries later.

PART I

ESTHER 1.1–1.22

I t came to pass in the days of Ahashverosh, the same Ahashverosh who reigned from India to Ethiopia, over 127 provinces, ²in the days when Ahashverosh the king sat on his royal throne, which was in Susa the capital. ³In year 3 of his reign he made a feast for all his princes and his servants, the military power of Persia and Media, the nobles and princes of the provinces being before him, ⁴during which he displayed the riches of his glorious kingdom and the honor of his excellent majesty for many days – 180 days.

⁵When these days had run their course, the king made a feast for all the people present in Susa the capital, from the highest to the most lowly, lasting seven days in the court, in the garden of the king's palace. ⁶There were hangings of white, of fine cotton, and blue, suspended with cords of fine linen and purple from silver rods and marble columns, divans of gold and silver on a floor of alabaster, marble, pearl, and precious stone. ⁷And drinks in vessels of gold, and vessels, each one differing from the others, and the royal wine aplenty, from the hand of the king. ⁸And the drinking was in accord with the law that none should be compelled, for so the king had instructed all the officers of his house, that they should do according to each man's will.

⁹Vashti the queen made a feast for the women as well, in the royal house of Ahashverosh the king. ¹⁰On the seventh day, when the heart of the king was merry with wine, he commanded Mehuman, Bizeta, Harvona, Bigta and Avagta, Zetar, and Karkas, the seven chamberlains who served in the presence of Ahashverosh the king, ¹¹to bring Vashti the queen before the king wearing the royal crown,

to show the peoples and the princes her beauty, for she was fair to look upon. ¹²But Vashti the queen refused to come at the king's command as communicated by the chamberlains, and the king was exceedingly angered, and his rage burned within him.

¹³The king turned to his advisers, who understood the precedents, for such was the king's habit before all who knew law and judgment – ¹⁴those who were close to him being Karshena, Shetar, Admata, Tarshish, Meres, Marsena, and Memuchan, the seven princes of Persia and Media, who saw the king's face, and who sat first in the kingdom –

¹⁵"According to the law, what should be done to Vashti the queen, who has not performed the word of the king as communicated by the chamberlains?"

¹⁶Memuchan said to the king and the princes: "It is not the king alone who has been wronged by Vashti the queen, but all the princes, and all the peoples in all the provinces of Ahashverosh the king. ¹⁷For this deed of the queen will become known to all the women, and their husbands will become contemptible in their eyes, when they tell: Ahashverosh the king commanded that Vashti the queen be brought before him but she came not. ¹⁸And this day, the princesses of Persia and Media who have heard of the queen's deed will be telling it to all the king's princes, and there will be much contempt and anger. ¹⁹If it please the king, let a royal decree be issued, and let it be written among the laws of Persia and Media, so that it should not fail, that Vashti come no more before Ahashverosh the king, and let the king give her royal estate to someone better than she. ²⁰And when the king's edict, which he will issue, is heard throughout his entire kingdom, vast though it be, all the wives will give honor to their husbands, from the highest to the most lowly."

²¹The idea pleased the king and the princes, and the king did as Memuchan advised. ²²He sent letters to all the king's provinces, to every province in its own script and to every people in its own language, that every man should rule in his own house and speak in the language of his own people.

I

Submission and Rule

Esther begins with a party in which Ahashverosh, king of Persia,[1] entertains his princes and legions, drinks himself into a tantrum, fights with his wife the queen, consults with his advisers, and then has his consort humiliated and deposed. The whole sordid scene takes place without mention of the Jews or of their enemies, the subject of the book of Esther, so that one has to ask why the narrative should not have begun with the second chapter or even with the third, when the plot against the Jews breaks into the open. It was this question that moved the rabbis of the Talmud to argue that the Jews of the capital must have been present at the feast, and that something that took place there – either the misbehavior of the king toward the Jews, or their own misbehavior – must have served as the provocation that triggers their subsequent persecution.[2] But the purpose of the party in the book of Esther is not to add to an otherwise dense plot. It is to acquaint us with its host and with the manner in which he rules his empire. It is this empire that inherited those who destroyed the kingdom of the Jews. Dispersed in its midst live their remnant. And one cannot understand what has become of them there, nor whom they will have to fight and why, nor the dangers before them, nor the greatness of their triumph, without first understanding Ahashverosh and his party, and the appetite for rule that throbs there drunk among the revelers from a hundred lands, so that the rabbis said that the Satan danced there himself.[3]

Ahashverosh is the ruler of most of civilization, from Ethiopia to India, and one might think that his time would be taken up with the responsibilities of governing more than a hundred provinces, or of securing them against external threats. Nevertheless, Esther begins by informing us that by the third year of his reign, the principal concern to which he dedicates himself is an ongoing carnival of drinking, which occupies the attention of the political, military, and administrative elite of the empire for no less than six months. Moreover, even the lowest of commoners is given the run of the palace for a week of popular merrymaking, in which they have the chance of a lifetime to drink "royal wine aplenty, from the hand of the king," out of gold vessels, in surroundings of marble and pearl, no less (1.6–7).

The point of this venture is hardly altruism. Ahashverosh pointedly seeks to display "the riches of his glorious kingdom and the honor of his excellent majesty" (1.4) – that is, to create a setting in which the entire empire can see the immense financial and administrative power that he, the king, can muster and dissipate at whim. This is a setting in which gratitude and flattery are lavished upon him from every corner of the empire, a show calculated to heap honor on him, and to create the impression, in the eyes of his subjects, as well as his own, that he is in control of the world.[4]

When we try to understand this Ahashverosh, we have no choice but to suspect that the empire has not yet been suitably impressed with his virtues as a leader – for if he had governed well, there would be little need for such grotesquerie to ensure the people's affections.[5] Yet in the absence of genuine rule, and of actual control over his millions of subjects, he is immensely concerned with the appearance of such rule and of such control. To be more precise, it is the *feeling* of control that he desires. For rule is an appetite, and power is a hunger, which the rabbis compared to a crocodile that would consume the world, and into which one could throw country after country and yet not sate it.[6] Ahashverosh is a glutton for power an empire that is sick with the yearning to extend itself, to swallow others, to control everything. Lacking the talents to secure such power through political prowess and actual leadership, Ahashverosh believes he can move toward the same end by bribing his empire with profligacy and drink. In holding this belief, he is, of course, neither the first nor the last.

The contemporary reader, immersed in the materialism and in the exaggerated estimation of the capacities of human reason that characterize our age, has a difficult time recognizing who and what this Ahashverosh is. We now tend to assume that men are motivated by self-interest, and that reason for the most part suffices to get along with our neighbors and to feed the small stable of our occasionally unruly physical appetites. Absent, on this theory, is any motive for wanting to rule others. And good men, or even most men, are therefore supposed to have no such desire for rule, while the few who are undeniably preoccupied with such things are conveniently considered abnormal. Behavior such as that displayed by Ahashverosh is usually interpreted as a "mistaken" pursuit of "rational self-interest" – as though he and his advisers had reasoned it through and concluded that spending the taxes of the empire in this way would be more prudent than the pursuit of other policy options – without the possibility arising that there might be nothing rational in his motives whatsoever.

Yet this last is precisely the case. The key to the motives of the king lies in recognizing that he is neither rationally self-interested nor, as we see again and again, particularly concerned with the more material desires for money, food, or sexual gratification. The king appears in Esther as a representation of something else, something we are unaccustomed to recognizing in ourselves and others: the appetite for rule, the essential ingredient in the character of every ruler, in this case unenlightened, unchanneled, and unrestrained.

It is worth considering the appetite for rule and control more closely, the better to understand this king and all others. The desire for rule – which the philosophers called *thymos*, and the Jews knew as man's *ruah*, or "spirit" – is a primary aspect of man's nature, the first quality mentioned in the books of Moses with respect to mankind: "God said: Let us make man in our image, after our likeness, and they will rule over the fish of the sea, and over the birds of the skies, and over the cattle, and over all the earth."[7] Every person at all times strives to rule and control that which comprises his world: to find everything in its place as expected; to find his hungers soothed; to find that his friends are trustworthy, his wife faithful, his children obedient; to find others willing to do his bidding; to find those beliefs he holds confirmed and those causes to which he subscribes victorious; to find that his superiors are solicitous, and his opponents, if not utterly vanquished, at least held harmlessly at bay. Such a world is one in which he may move with unlimited freedom, unobstructed and unchallenged, a world of perfect stability and security, physical and emotional. Such a world is a fantasy, but it is one for which man strives from the day he is born, as surely as he strives for physical sustenance. As the appetite for food drives him toward his supper, so too does the appetite for control drive man to rule his world, or if he cannot, to find someone who can rule it in his place and provide him with the stability for which he yearns.[8]

Like all desires, the appetite for rule serves a crucial and life-sustaining purpose when it is held within bounds. It is the spirit that urges that the uncertain, threatening, and challenging be made certain, benign, and beneficial. Every healthy person experiences the tides of the spirit in some measure: self-confidence, dedication, enthusiasm, magnanimity, and a sense of purpose when control and rule are at hand; anger, fear, jealousy, guilt, and aimless depression when they are lost. Together, these feelings map the boundaries between that which has already been achieved and that which has not, allowing man to build his life from one achievement to the next, driving him to extend the frontiers of the controlled, of that which is as it "should" be: to invest in shelter for winter, to resolve a difficult problem, to uncover a lost object, to master an elusive skill, to invent a much-needed device, to excel in one's profession, to win a recalcitrant love, to save a drowning child, to defend against a threat to one's life, to right injustice.

And there are also men of exceptional spirit, in whose soul all of these passions and more appear not so much as events but as cataclysms, as eruptions of sensation, direction, and strength, and who are capable for this reason of achievements on a scale that others can hardly imagine. In this regard, the Bible speaks of "men of spirit" – administrators such as Joseph, warriors such as Caleb and Joshua, and artists such as Betzalel, to name a few[9] – the most outstanding of individuals, whose tremendous desire for rule is directed by reason or the command of higher authority toward tasks of which only they are capable.[10] For in all things, greatness requires two characteristics: an exceptional spirit, which provides a man with the power, dedication, intensity, and boldness needed to control, to order, to achieve, and to build; and reason – whether that of superiors or advisers, or his own – which provides man with right and consistent aims toward which he can divert the power of the spirit.

When it is not so directed, however, the exceptional spirit becomes a monstrous growth, whose eruptions drive the individual in arbitrary or ill-conceived directions, consuming all that stands in its way without being of profit to anyone: A man will be an overly spirited fool, given over to excessive excitements regarding the objects of his desire, to childish dependence on those who pander to these fetishes, to paranoid overreactions at the slightest hint of weakening in his rule, and, above all, to uncontrollable humiliations and rages when he feels that he has lost control – which in turn lead him to every kind of desperate action to restore it. Such a man is Ahashverosh, king of Persia, who, for want of the feeling of power over others, devotes half a year of his life to filling the nobles and commoners of his empire with drink, showering them with gifts, and boasting to them of his wife, that they might better recognize his greatness.

And being such a man, Ahashverosh is the archetype of the political ruler: All spirit, he will do anything to feel that he has control over others. But having little reason of his own, he has no positive conception of what to do with this rule, applying the full force of his authority in whatever direction will make him feel most in control at a given moment. The result is that despite having vast powers at his disposal, and occasionally making forceful use of these powers, Ahashverosh is at all times reacting to the pressures and manipulation of those around him – as is the state itself.[11]

With this in mind, let us return to the king's party. In the entire stew of ostentation, excess, and flattery that comprises the description of the feast, perhaps the most interesting detail is the liberty that the king accords the merrymakers: "And the drinking was in accord with the law that none should be compelled, for so the king had instructed all the officers of his house, that they should do according to each man's will" (1.8). That the king had seen fit to issue such an order itself indicates how unusual it was for his government to concern itself with the will of his subjects. The presumption, of course, was that if one were invited to a royal feast lasting six months, one came; and if one were given wine to drink in abundance, one drank wine in abundance – and the king's officers would ensure that this was the case. The great rabbinic exegete R. Levi emphasized the point by suggesting that normally the officers would have preferred to kill a guest rather than let him offend the king by abstaining: "They had a great flagon and would pour out of it for every individual. Even if he died, even if he went insane, they would not let him be until he had drunk all of it."[12] In this figure, Persia is the party, and the king's officers are themselves the flagon, pouring the king's rule down the throats of his subjects, even unto insanity, even unto death.

Ahashverosh, however, makes an instructive exception. He knows that he may demonstrate his power by issuing commands and having them obeyed, yet he senses that he can achieve more by granting a small measure of freedom. For the spirit seeks a control over others that is not sated by mere physical obedience. Certainly, Ahashverosh wants to feel that his subjects fear him and will do his bidding. But he wants much more: To truly feel he controls his people, he needs to rule their emotions first and foremost. He needs for them to love and respect him, and to desire his rule. There is no better way of gaining the gratitude of others than by using power to bestow liberty – for this means granting a gift of power to another. For those whom Ahashverosh has invited into his palace, accustomed as they are to submitting to the wishes of the king, this microscopic, one-time grant of power can win their gratitude as no material gift can. It is no coincidence, either, that the material gift of choice is alcohol, an agent whose action is directly on the spirit, "releasing inhibitions," "steadying the nerves," "making the heart merry," all of these affectations deriving from a chemically enhanced sense of power and control.[13]

The climax of the festival, and of Ahashverosh's show of power, is his flaunting of Vashti the queen before the people. Her husband merry and drunk, the queen is to be escorted out by his servants "to show the peoples and the princes her beauty, for she was fair to look upon" (1.11).[14] We are told nothing of their relationship other than this. But on the basis of Esther's treatment later on, we may surmise that there is not much to it. The queen is cloistered away in a distant corner of the palace, constantly subjected to a grueling regimen of treatments to improve her appearance, texture, and scent, and able to see the king only when it pleases him to summon her. And when she appears in public with him for the first time during six months of festivities, it is not as his partner in ruling, nor as his partner in life, but as another accouterment in his demonstration of total power: The empire is to admire her object beauty and to be impressed that the king has – as the Talmudic scholar Rav depicts Ahashverosh as saying – such a "vessel" for his "use."[15]

But Vashti prefers not to serve this purpose and refuses to appear, exposing his weakness before the princes and nobles, and even before the commoners of the empire. One can hardly think of a greater humiliation: For six months, he has devoted himself to the systematic elaboration of his control, seeking to extract gratitude and honor from every man whom it is within his power to reach, a meticulously orchestrated show of omnipotence. And yet on the last night, at the last moment, he is proven impotent in his own house before the eyes of the throng he has labored so long to impress. In a moment, Ahashverosh is transformed into an object of laughter, and control over his world slips through his fingers.

Anger is the emotion of the spirit that moves men to muster all of their energies and facilities and focus them on the reassertion of control. In a situation of helplessness, one can expect to feel an enduring shame; but where there is the possibility of recourse, the result is rage. Thus behaved Pharaoh, when time and again he felt himself defeated, but then out of shame was born anger once more ("Pharaoh's heart hardened"), and he turned to re-enslave the Jews whom he had been forced to liberate.[16] Here, too, Ahashverosh seeks a way of reasserting his power, and he turns demonstratively to the assembled princes and wise men, as they hold back smiles of pity and embarrassment, and asks them to name that punishment which they would find fitting for publicly humiliating the king of all the Persians and Medes.

Ahashverosh's move is a masterstroke. At once he turns his personal shame into an issue of state, with himself at the helm of an entire empire that has been insulted, inviting those assembled to join him in doing justice and reestablishing the honor of the king. And at least one among their number is ready to seek favor by helping Ahashverosh escape the trap he has set for himself. Memuchan, one of the seven princes of Persia and Media sitting in the first rank, hastens to point out that the interest of the princes, and indeed of all men in the kingdom, is identical to that of the king: "It is not the king alone who has been wronged by Vashti the queen, but all the princes, and all the peoples in all the provinces of Ahashverosh the king. For this deed of the queen will become known to all the women, and their husbands will become contemptible in their eyes ... and there will be much contempt and anger" (1.16–18).

With this, Memuchan takes up the king's cause, turning the royal family's domestic spat into an empirewide battle of the sexes, with Ahashverosh representing all men against the constant challenge presented by the women in their homes. He assures the king that, far from laughing at him, every man in his kingdom is in sympathy with him, since women, following the queen's lead, will leave no man safe from similar humiliation in his own home. Now Memuchan, who "knows the precedents," decrees what must be the punishment for a wife who challenges the authority of her husband: "That Vashti come no more before Ahashverosh the king, and let the king give her royal estate to someone better than she" (1.19). The queen should be stripped of all property, position, and honor, and forever banished from the sight of the king.

For challenging the power of the king, Vashti is doomed to remain a widow to a living husband, deprived of every material or emotional asset she has or could have for the rest of her life; nothing is to remain save her life itself.[17] Such a complete annihilation of the person of the queen, publicly forcing her into permanent, complete, and degraded submission, should be seen as the natural consequence of a deed such as hers. In this way, avers Memuchan, "when the king's edict, which he will issue, is heard throughout all of his kingdom, vast though it be, all the wives will give honor to their husbands, from the highest to the most lowly" (1.20).

Memuchan therefore offers the king a response calculated perfectly to reassert his battered sense of his own power: Ahashverosh will at once (i) prove to Vashti and all his kingdom that he alone rules, and absolutely; (ii) annihilate the queen's challenge to his control by ensuring that she is never in a position to shame him again; and (iii) cement the adherence, gratitude, and honor of the people by promulgating a decree that amounts to a gift of power to every adult male in the kingdom – that same gesture Ahashverosh wished to achieve through the free drinking of the king's wine. Thus vindicated by law and handed back the leadership of all Persia, Ahashverosh responds enthusiastically. The king issues the decree as proposed, publishing it in every language and in every province, "that every man should rule in his own house" (1.22).

With this, "the rage of Ahashverosh the king ... subsided" (2.1). He has for the moment regained his precious, perfect control over his home, his kingdom, and his world.

But for the more sober among the onlookers, it is impossible to feel at ease with the abrupt termination of the queen's reign, and with the leer of juvenile satisfaction that creeps across the king's features when the deed is done. In this moment, the intoxication of the festivities dissipates, leaving an unobstructed view of the partymaster and of the forces that move him. Gone is the king's pursuit of his subjects' affection, gone the flattering gifts of freedom and power. It becomes clear that the person of the king is a fiction, a name and a face, under which riots the crocodile spirit, devouring until it controls. Where is his reason, that he might consider and reconsider his own interest, before destroying his wife the queen for a passing slight? Where is his reason, that he might consider and reconsider the interests of his empire, before feeding pieces of it to the reptile in his breast, devouring until it controls? But the ruler is not reason, but something else. For those who recognize this, the party is a revelation, and the harbinger of far worse to come.

PART II

ESTHER 2.1–2.23

After these things, when the rage of Ahashverosh the king had subsided, he remembered Vashti, and what she had done, and what had been decreed against her.

²The king's youths, who attended him, said: "Let fair young virgins be sought for the king. ³Let the king appoint officials in all the provinces of his kingdom, that they may gather together all the fair young virgins to Susa the capital, to the house of the women, to the custody of Hegai the king's chamberlain, keeper of the women, to be given their ointments. ⁴Let the young woman who pleases the king be queen in Vashti's place."

And the idea pleased the king, and he did so.

⁵Now in Susa the capital there lived a Jew whose name was Mordechai, the son of Jair, the son of Shimi, the son of Kish of the tribe of Benjamin, ⁶who had been exiled from Jerusalem among those expelled with Jechonia, king of Judah, who had been exiled by Nebuchadnezzar, king of Babylonia. ⁷He had raised Hadasa, that is Esther, his uncle's daughter, for she had neither father nor mother. The young woman was beautiful and fair to look upon, and when her father and mother had died, Mordechai had taken her for a daughter.

⁸It came to pass that when the king's commandment and his law were heard, and when many young women were gathered together to Susa the capital, into the custody of Hegai, that Esther was also brought into the king's house, into the custody of Hegai, keeper of the women. ⁹The young woman pleased him, and she found grace before him, and he hurried to give her her ointments and her special rations, and the seven maids chosen to be given her out of the king's

house, and he advanced her and her maids to the best place in the house of women. ¹⁰Esther had not made known her people and her kindred, for Mordechai had instructed her that she not tell. ¹¹Every day, Mordechai would take a walk past the court of the house of women, to know how Esther fared and what was to be done with her.

¹²Now when each young woman's turn came to go in to Ahashverosh the king, after she had been twelve months under the regimen for the women – for such were the periods of anointing, six months with oil and myrrh, and six months with sweet odors and other women's ointments – ¹³this is how the young woman would come to the king: Whatever she requested would be given her to bring with her from the house of the women to the king's house. ¹⁴In the evening she would come, and in the morning she would go to the second house of the women, into the custody of Sha'ashgaz, the king's chamberlain, keeper of the concubines, and she would come in to the king no more, unless the king desired her and she was summoned by name.

¹⁵But when it came the turn of Esther, the daughter of Avihail, the uncle of Mordechai, who had taken her for a daughter, to go in to the king, she requested nothing other than what Hegai the king's chamberlain, keeper of the women, advised – and Esther found favor in the eyes of all who looked upon her.

¹⁶Esther was taken to Ahashverosh the king in his royal house in the 10th month, that is Teveth, in year 7 of his reign. ¹⁷The king loved Esther more than all the women, and she found grace and favor in his eyes more than all the virgins, and he placed the royal crown on her head, and made her queen in Vashti's place. ¹⁸Then the king made a great feast for all his princes and his servants, the feast of Esther, and he granted the provinces a remission in taxes and gave out gifts from the king's hand. ¹⁹And when the virgins were gathered together again, and as Mordechai sat in the king's gate, ²⁰Esther did not reveal her kindred or her people, as Mordechai had instructed her, for Esther did as Mordechai instructed her, just as she had growing up.

²¹In those days, while Mordechai was sitting in the king's gate, two of the king's chamberlains, Bigtan and Teresh, from those who kept the door, were angered and sought to lay hands on Ahashverosh the king. ²²The matter became known to Mordechai, who told it to Esther the queen, and Esther reported it to the king in Mordechai's name. ²³The matter was investigated and it was found to be true, and they were both hanged from the gallows, and it was written in the book of chronicles in the presence of the king.

2

Political Favor

Three years and more have elapsed since the king's humiliation and his angry banishment of the queen,[1] and Ahashverosh begins to remember Vashti with longing. The immutability of Persian law and his own pride standing in the way of reconciliation, Ahashverosh accepts the urgings of his attendants to search for "someone better than she."[2] It goes without saying that such a one should be more concerned with the king's wishes and less with her own than her predecessor, so there is no point in advertising. It is not ambitious volunteers that Ahashverosh seeks. Instead, the order goes out for the king's officers to conscript the most attractive virgins from every corner of the empire, so that the king may have a taste of each in turn until he finds one to his liking.

Among his other failings of character, it transpires that Ahashverosh likes forcing himself on women, a fact that within context comes as little surprise. Nothing offends the spirit so much as sexual cravings, which in and of themselves constitute overwhelming evidence of need, lack of control, and powerlessness. Because sex provides proof of such manifest need, sexual relationships naturally paint every individual at his or her most vulnerable. This is why the longings of love are so easily transformed into rage, which arises in the effort to reassert the control lost when desire is confronted with rejection.

Ahashverosh has already suffered the consequences of allowing a woman to assert her own will in a relationship, and it is likely that fear of repeating the mistake – perhaps even a fear of women – has been responsible for the lengthy delay before he is prepared to return to the field. When finally the king does decide to reenter the arena, he makes sure that the game is rigged so that, as with his six-month winefest aimed at winning the favor of the nobles, he believes he cannot lose. The virgins are not asked whether they wish to love him. They are merely to submit, each inexperienced girl alone facing the might of the empire, giving up her own hopes and dreams and her own loved ones, and daring not object for fear for her life. Moreover, her submission on the single night of her exposure to him is guaranteed, for if she in any way incurs his displeasure, she is doomed to spend the rest of her days in childless imprisonment or worse. As for Ahashverosh himself, he is protected from rejection as no man has ever been: He has never seen her before and will never see her again unless he wills it, and there is no one who will ever find out what takes place between them on that night. Nor must he fear that another in the kingdom will be told in the dead of some night, years hence, that he was a better man than the king, for she will have no other man. In such a relationship, the person of Ahashverosh is elevated to absolute mastery, while hers is essentially annihilated. It is the perfected institutionalization of rape, in which the king's will is the only will, his power the only power. Whether or not others have succeeded in implementing Memuchan's decree in their own families, Ahashverosh, at least, has hit upon a way in which he may completely "rule in his own house."

Into the king's dragnet falls a Jew named Mordechai, and his orphaned cousin Hadasa, whom he has raised since childhood. We know little about Mordechai – only that he is a Jew, and descended from those who were "exiled from Jerusalem among those expelled with Jechonia king of Judah, who had been exiled by Nebuchadnezzar, king of Babylonia" (2.6). The narrative is not concerned to tell us about Mordechai's personality or personal biography and concentrates only on this, the central point: that being a Jew, he has been stripped of his own nation and capital city, and has lost his own king and any capacity to wield power in his own defense.[3] That is, his position with respect to the king and the empire is essentially no different from that of the virgins. The Jews, like the virgins, have been forced to give up everything of independent value to them and are, it seems, powerless before the will of the state and its ruler.[4] Only one echo of a fact escapes the anonymity in which Mordechai is cloaked: the fact that this Jew lives not in "the town of Susa," where the Jewish quarter was located (3.15, 8.15), but in the midst of "Susa the capital" (2.5), the fortress that was the center of Persian power and the focus of every effort to control it, direct it, or wield it.[5]

On the surface, it appears that Mordechai's dealings with the authorities are straightforward. Persia accepts only submission, and submit to its will he does. When confronted with the demand that he deliver the girl, he acquiesces, understanding that whatever might be the terrors and degradation of the night with the king and its aftermath, these cannot justify drawing the king's anger and courting death. Thereafter, Mordechai instructs that she not make known her people and her kindred (2.10, 2.20), although hiding her identity as a Jew will guarantee that she must make sacrifices in religious observance to maintain the facade.[6] What is more, although he has raised her with the Hebrew name of Hadasa, he counsels her to go by a Persian one in the court: Esther, meaning "star."[7] And since Esther "did as Mordechai instructed her, just as she had growing up" (2.20), it appears that passivity is her own strategy as well: It is her submissiveness, along with the fact that she is "beautiful and fair to look upon" (2.7), that makes her the favorite first of Hegai, the eunuch in charge of the women, and then of the king himself. In Esther, the king has finally found a dispirited poppet who could be the answer to his dreams of domination.

Yet an incident related immediately after the account of Esther's bid for the throne makes it clear that this view of Mordechai's relationship with Persia is mistaken, and that the lessons Esther learned from her cousin were in fact of a very different nature. The narrative relates that by the time of the festivities surrounding the coronation of the new queen, and probably long before then, Mordechai had been in the habit of "sitting in the king's gate" (2.19), the receiving area of the citadel, in which the supplicants of the empire waited for an audience with the king or tried to obtain one when they had business. In the absence of any sort of legislature or assembly, all of the most important politics of the empire were of necessity conducted there. Of course, those who make it their business to "sit" in the king's gate are no more inert than those today who have a "seat" in parliament, and the obvious inference is that Mordechai was by this time a known figure, deeply involved in the intrigues of the court.[8] Thus when a conspiracy is hatched to assassinate the king involving members of his own bodyguard, Mordechai is sufficiently trusted, or else sufficiently skillful at bartering rumors and bribes, to be able to obtain reliable information concerning the plot, including the identities of the conspirators. (His talents in this regard appear again later when he passes Esther inside information from a supposedly private conversation between the king and his vizier [4.7].[9]) Once in possession of this intelligence, Mordechai tips off Esther, who takes it to the king, thereby setting off an investigation that results in the conviction and hanging of two members of the guard (2.21–23).

Mordechai thus purposely places himself in a position in which he can be privy to sensitive information, and then, on his own initiative, risks himself in order to take sides and influence the political struggles of the empire. Now, none of this is in any sense submissive. Instead, it reminds us that there are in fact three possible courses of action in the face of a regime such as that of Ahashverosh: resistance, submission, and active support of the despot. From the role Mordechai plays in foiling the conspiracy, it is difficult to avoid the conclusion that he prefers not the second course but the third.

Incongruous though this seems at first blush, Mordechai's reasoning is sensible. Ahashverosh's rule may be egregious in many respects, but it is for the time being not overtly hostile to the Jews. This is not to say that Persia is clean of anti-Semitism; just the opposite is true.[10] And it is precisely because of this widespread antagonism toward the Jews that Mordechai is willing to accept

Ahashverosh's relatively benign authoritarianism as the best of the available evils. There is no reason to think that any regime that might follow the over-throw of the king would be any better, for Jews or for anyone else, and there is every reason to believe it could be worse, particularly as Mordechai is familiar with the actual conspirators. Where the only alternative to bad government is something worse, there exists no reason to choose resistance. There is no value in risking death where nothing will be gained by it.

Submission is the easiest option. Men tend to abdicate from making deci-sions, from taking actions, from bothering and troubling. To become an imple-ment in the hands of others, to let the light of the spirit go out, this is an option that Mordechai could have exercised from the very beginning – not seeking to disguise Esther's lineage, not coming every day to inquire after her well-being since all was lost, not making his presence felt in the court day in and day out, and certainly not coming to the rescue of the tyrant who had stolen his adopted daughter from him. Such is the course taken by most men at most times, beat-ing the path of least resistance on the assumption that this way will draw the least attention and result in the least trouble.

But much as one may wish to misunderstand this point, the truth is that in politics at least, the path of least resistance is never likely to be the path to the least trouble. Even under the most serene circumstances, there is never any cer-tainty that the menace accommodated by submission today will not become something even worse on the morrow; and one may cast an eye at history and conclude that the eventual appearance of this something worse is even prob-able – and how much the more so in a viper's nest such as the court of Susa. Mordechai understands that with Esther in the clutches of Ahashverosh, and with himself and the entire Jewish people similarly powerless before the king, to follow his every order in passive submission is simply to wait for the fall of an axe that must come sooner or later.

The only recourse is to attempt to accumulate some measure of power that can be used for defense when the necessity arises. To the Jews of the quarter and many others, such an enterprise must have seemed chimerical. With their people scattered across the face of the earth, the idea of mounting a defense against anything must have appeared preposterous. Mordechai, however, lived in another world. In the political thicket of the capital, power might be elu-sive, but it was there to be had if one were willing to learn its rules and play its game: In Susa, even the weak could become powerful if they secured the king's willingness to use his authority in their favor – as politicians say, to "gain favor" with him, or to "gain influence" with him.

Ironically, there is virtually no way that this can be accomplished through passive submission to the king's commands. Countless are those whose flac-cid spirits crave the rush of power in their chest, even if it be someone else's power. For this reason, a man such as Ahashverosh is invariably surrounded by a thousand flatterers seeking to serve, whose sole virtue is that they part like warm butter before the knife of his will. But these the ruler can always replace with others just like them, so he values them little and develops no special interest in retaining them. As soon as they fail in something or begin expecting something significant in return for their services, they become more trouble than they are worth, and the king quickly disposes of them.

Of immense value to the king, on the other hand, are those who are not submissive, but who initiate action so that his will be done. To understand the difference, one need only consider the assassination attempt that Mordechai succeeds in aborting. Mordechai receives no instructions from the king. He is independently alert to the king's interest, and is willing to employ his judgment and talents in the king's service unbeknownst to Ahashverosh himself – in a situation fraught with risk, in which assisting him means siding against would-be killers who may rule the empire by morning, and in which only independent and immediate action can be of any use. No number of obedient sycophants could have sufficed to save the king under such circumstances.

Passive obedience offers the king the use of another body; Mordechai's activism offers him the use of a mind. The king has millions of bodies at his command, as many as he needs for virtually any task. He lacks not body, nor spirit, but mind: The king's own consciousness, even if he were the wisest of men, is incapable of knowing all that must be known for effective rule, of paying attention to all that must be attended to, of deciding all that must be decided, of giving all the orders that must be given, of ensuring that all these orders are carried out. And the question of whose mind is to watch over the king's interest in those times, places, and situations in which he himself is unable to be present and to know, decide, and issue commands hounds every ruler from the first moment of his reign. What he needs are men who will be "second to the king" (10.3), acting in his stead but for his benefit: men who, if forgotten for an hour or a year, will have done all that he would have willed them to do and more. By watching to see who is actively taking initiative to ensure that his will is done, the king can learn whose interests he may profitably consider his own, and he comes to rely on such individuals as a matter of course. It is these whom the king truly appreciates, and it is these who would truly harm him if they withdrew from his service. For both of these reasons, it is to them that he may be willing to grant substantial favors and real influence.

Thus while there is certainly no love lost between Mordechai the Jew and the despot whom he may never have met, he acts to save the king's life, endangering himself to demonstrate that when the worst has come to pass, there is at least one individual upon whom the king can truly rely. Mordechai cannot know for certain that something will come of this, but under the circumstances, only such efforts to gain power through the favor of the king offer a chance of success.

Let us consider two biblical precedents for Mordechai's approach to building up Jewish power through the painstaking work of accumulating political favor, precedents to which we will have cause to return at different junctures in the narrative: Joseph, who had risen to be vizier to Pharaoh in Egypt a thousand years before; and Daniel, who, according to the account in the book of Daniel, had been slated to reach a similar position in the Persian court under Darius, several decades before the story of Esther takes place.[11]

Joseph had begun his political career in the society of his eleven brothers as an intelligence gatherer for his father Jacob, whose control over his independent and sometimes violent sons had been slipping with age. Scenes immediately preceding Joseph's appearance in the narrative suggest a deterioration into anarchy, with two of the older brothers massacring the inhabitants of an entire town against their father's objections, and another sleeping with one of his father's wives.[12] Lest the point be missed, the rabbis elaborated on the situation, suspecting the brothers not only of sexual misconduct, but of tormenting the younger brothers by referring to them as slaves and of perpetrating unspeakable cruelties against the animals in their care.[13] In this context, it is apparent that Joseph's struggle against his brothers is from the start an attempt to reassert discipline on behalf of his father: "The lad was with the sons of Bilha and the sons of Zilpa, his father's wives, and Joseph brought his father their evil report."[14] The natural consequence is that he wins his father's favor, as expressed in the infamous gift of the striped coat: "Now Israel loved Joseph more than all his children because he ministered to him in his old age, and he made him a striped coat."[15] By demonstrating that his own will can be relied upon as a second to his father's, Joseph wins increasing influence and authority – and the hatred of his rivals among the brothers, who eventually decide to destroy him by selling him into slavery.

But far from being destroyed by being enslaved in Egypt, Joseph flourishes in an environment in which he can apply his uncanny skills. He throws himself into active pursuit of the interests of a series of masters, each of whom responds just as his father Jacob had, despite the fact that he is a slave and a foreigner, the epitome of powerlessness. Thus with regard to Potiphar, captain of Pharaoh's guard, who buys Joseph from the traders, we are told: "His master saw that the Lord was with him and that the Lord made all that he did prosper in his hand. And Joseph found favor in his eyes and served him, and he made him overseer of his house, and all that he had he put in his charge."[16] Later, Joseph similarly ingratiates himself with the keeper of the prison to which he is sent as a ward, and ultimately he makes the same inroads with Pharaoh himself – applying his cunning to reaching

high office, buying much of the land in Egypt for the royal estate, and levy-
ing unprecedented taxes for the benefit of the king.[17] And because of the
investment he has made in winning favor in the Egyptian court, Joseph is
able to use his authority to assist the Jews, feeding them and sheltering them
at Pharaoh's expense during years of famine that could easily have destroyed
them all.[18]

Daniel, too, is well equipped with the kinds of traits that might make him a
favorite of the Babylonian and Persian kings who are his masters. Like Esther
and Joseph, he is attractive in appearance; he can interpret dreams after the
fashion of the idolaters as Joseph can; and he has various other skills and
knowledge as well.[19] But none of these could propel him to the top of Persian
politics unless he shared with Joseph an understanding of what it means to
be "second to the king," applying these exceptional talents to protecting the
king's interest, which he in fact does: "As for me, in the first year of Darius
of Media, I stood up to support him and to strengthen him."[20] When Darius
promotes him to prominence, it is to a panel of triumvirs intended to watch
over (and spy on) the empire's officials "so that the king should have no loss."[21]
Obviously, such a position is one of great trust, reserved only for those known
to be able to pursue the king's interest selflessly and with enthusiasm. And
Darius is not disappointed. Daniel quickly "became distinguished above the
triumvirs and governors because of the exceptional spirit that was in him," and
so thoroughly does he win Darius' trust that he decides to appoint him vizier.
Moreover, Daniel's service to Darius succeeds in turning the Persian king to a
course favorable to the Jews, which results in his issuing an edict granting official protection to the Jewish faith.[22]

Joseph stands as the prototype of the Jewish second to the king, whose
model clearly informs the careers of Daniel, Mordechai, Esther, and others in
imperial Persia centuries later.[23] But it is Esther, once she has been stolen out
of her family and deposited in Ahashverosh's house of women, who proves to
be the most gifted subsequent practitioner of Joseph's art.[24] With her arrival
in the precincts of the palace, the narrative relates that she immediately begins
to gain the favor of those around her, beginning with Hegai, the keeper of the
virgins. According to the literal meaning of the Hebrew, "Esther made good,
in his eyes" (2.9), as a result of which he is kind to her, advances her in the
sequence of maidens who will come in to the king, and gives her the best of the
facilities available. Later, as she gains in confidence, we are told that she "found
favor in the eyes of all who looked upon her" (2.15). And finally, as Joseph
was loved more than all his brothers, "the king loved Esther more than all the
women, and she found grace and favor in his eyes more than all the virgins,
and he placed the royal crown on her head, and made her queen in Vashti's
place" (2.17).

Concerning Esther's personality and motives prior to ascending to the throne, the narrative is sparse. But in the one place where it bothers to explain why everyone is so taken by Esther, it is clear that it is not beauty that is driving her success, but an understanding of the workings of political favor much like that which dictates Mordechai's moves in the court. The scene in question concerns Hegai, the keeper of the women, whose responsibility it is to ensure that the young women brought in to the king night after night are at the pinnacle of their attractiveness. In order to bolster their confidence and allow each some measure of personality, they are permitted to take with them whatever accouterments and accessories may catch their fancy for their one night with the king: jewelry, flowers, musical instruments, food, and gifts. Esther's response is captured in a single, essential verse: "When it came the turn of Esther ... to go in to the king, she requested nothing other than what Hegai the king's chamberlain, keeper of the women, advised – and Esther found favor in the eyes of all who looked upon her" (2.15).

There can be no appreciating this statement without considering Hegai himself, a man whose life's work is catering to the sexual caprice of the king. The significance of this fact can be understood by recalling that Pharaoh, irritated at his wine steward and baker, had thrown both into prison and then ordered the baker hanged.[25] Hegai may have had a particular affection for certain young women over others, but it is a mistake to think that such considerations would have altered his professional behavior where his livelihood and his life itself were at stake. Hegai's only real concern is to please the king with a suitable bride as quickly as possible and so avert the imminent danger that Ahashverosh will become impatient with his work, or otherwise offended by it, and fly into a rage. His rapidly advancing Esther after being impressed with her is therefore not a gesture to her, but a career move of his own: The sooner the king has found his queen, the better. In this regard, there is a tension between the women outfitting themselves in accordance with their own wishes when going in to the king – which may have been the custom in the house of women well before his time – and his own interest in putting on the best possible show.

In her dealings with Hegai, Esther succeeds because she has learned well from her cousin. Rather than doing what the others do, Esther makes it clear to Hegai that she considers him to be the expert and that his interest is identical with hers. Far from being passive, she makes it her business to understand what it is he wants, and seeks ways to advance his will with the active support of her own. This is the meaning of "she requested nothing other than what Hegai ... advised – and Esther found favor in the eyes of all who looked upon her." Esther finds favor with all who have power over her, just as Joseph had in Egypt, by convincing them that in all her doings, she seeks their interest.[26] The rabbis of the Talmud used different metaphors for explaining this, with R. Judah comparing Esther to a sculpture that a thousand people can look upon, each seeing something that he personally admires.[27] Similarly, while the narrative suggests that a foreign wife who raised one's children in an alien tongue is a particular sign of dishonor and lack of control, R. Eleazar suggested that Esther put others at ease to such a degree that every man mistook her for a member of his own people.[28] R. Joshua ben Korha takes the argument to the extreme, claiming that Esther was not really physically beautiful at all – and that the attraction to her was exclusively the result of this appeal.[29]

When Esther finally comes to the king, it is this ability that turns the trick and makes her queen. By this point, Ahashverosh has had his fill of submissive young women who receive him as the trauma that he is, and of more assertive ones who remind him of Vashti by insisting on doing things their own way. When Esther comes to him, she looks first for what he desires, and makes sure he obtains all he wishes and more. And it is difficult to escape the conclusion of some of the rabbis that on this first night, this concern finds its expression in rather sensual terms: "If he wanted to find in her the taste of a virgin, he found it; if the taste of a married woman, he found it."[30]

But it is equally clear that Ahashverosh's yearning to replace Vashti cannot have been driven principally by his sexual appetite. Had his melancholia been sexual, his harem should have sufficed to treat it. His problem is, not surprisingly, one of the spirit, one of lack of control. For despite his abusive behavior toward her, Vashti had, it seems, offered the king a certain security that his other "vessels" and playthings had not been able to replace. Evidently a strong woman, the queen had been not only something to show off and to relieve his hungers. When she was not resisting him, Vashti had apparently been a personality capable of increasing the king's sense of self-worth through the reassurance that one such as she could love him, of soothing the pangs of his spirit by offering him stability – crucial functions of love that are too often believed to be appropriate only to a mother figure. And it is here, more even than in the sexual, that Esther's personality truly shines. She understands that in the relations between man and woman, no less than in politics, the limp submission of doing what one is told, while superficially appearing to grant power, in reality grants very little. The feeling of power over others is greatest when one feels control over something of independent worth, someone who might have resisted fiercely if he or she had so desired, but who chooses to be of service. Independent action rather than submission is thus the turnkey to love, just as it is to political favor. By giving Ahashverosh her initiative and the active use of her strength in pursuit of his interest, Esther bestows on the king a gift of power – precisely that for which he has so desperately longed and for which he is immediately willing to make her queen.

Of course, in choosing against resistance and submission, and in favor of active support of the despot, both Esther and Mordechai open themselves to the charge that they have been blinded by their concern with ends rather than means; that they have corrupted themselves, prostituted themselves; that all this truck with tyrants constitutes a willful collaboration with evil, and that no good man should be involved in such endeavors, much less a good Jew. To be sure, Esther's concerted effort to actually become queen by means of her bedroom manner ranks rather high on the scale of collaboration, and Mordechai's saving the life of this Ahashverosh is only somewhat more tolerable. For if the king is such a villain, who would want to help him in achieving his desires? If this is the meaning of political favor, then perhaps such favor is immoral, a descent into degradation and pollution? As the medieval exegete Rashi suggests, Mordechai's entry into the world of government and political favor meant that he neglected *tora*, the study of what is righteous and holy.[31] If this is what Esther and Mordechai must do in order to succeed, would it not be better to refuse, to abstain, to die rather than play according to rules dictated by impure men?

Since politics is the pursuit of the possible in this world, impure and corrupt though it is, to answer this question is to pass judgment on politics itself. And later on in the tale, once Mordechai and Esther have achieved a degree of political success and find themselves forced to determine which Persians should live and which should die, the question of the legitimacy of political means for the Jews, and for all moral men, is to return again in force.

PART III

ESTHER 3.1–3.15

After these things, Ahashverosh the king promoted Haman, the son of Hamedata the Agagite, and advanced him, and set his seat above all the princes who were around him. ²And all the king's servants who were in the king's gate bowed and prostrated themselves before Haman, for the king had so ordained concerning him, but Mordechai did not bow nor prostrate himself.

³The king's servants who were in the king's gate said to Mordechai: "Why do you violate the king's commandment?"

⁴It came to pass that when they spoke to him day in and day out and he did not listen to them, they told Haman, to see whether Mordechai's words would stand, for he had told them that he was a Jew. ⁵When Haman saw that Mordechai did not bow nor prostrate himself, Haman was filled with rage. ⁶But it was disdainful in his eyes to lay hands on Mordechai alone, for they had revealed to him Mordechai's people, so that Haman sought to annihilate all the Jews throughout the entire kingdom of Ahashverosh, the people of Mordechai.

⁷In the 1st month, the month of Nisan, in the year 12 of Ahashverosh the king, they cast the pur, that is the lot, before Haman, testing day by day and month by month, until they reached the 12th month, the month of Adar.

⁸Then Haman said to Ahashverosh the king: "There is a certain people scattered and dispersed among the people in all the provinces of your kingdom, and their laws are different from those of other peoples, and the king's laws they do not keep, so that it is of no benefit for the king to tolerate them. ⁹If it please the king, let it

be written that they be destroyed, and I will weigh out ten thousand talents of silver into the hands of those who have charge of the business, to bring it into the king's treasuries."

[10]The king took his ring from his hand and gave it to Haman, the son of Hamedata the Agagite, the persecutor of the Jews. [11]And the king said to Haman: "The silver is given to you, and the people, to do with them as you see fit."

[12]The king's scribes were called on the 13th day of the 1st month, and it was written according to all that Haman had commanded, to the king's satraps, and to the governors who were over every province, and to the princes of every people, to every province in its own script and to every people in their own tongue, in the name of Ahashverosh the king and sealed with the king's ring. [13]And the letters were sent by courier to all the king's provinces, instructing to annihilate, to kill, and to destroy all the Jews, the young and the elderly, children and women, in one day – on the 13th day of the 12th month, the month of Adar – and to take their property for plunder. [14]Copies of the document to be given out as law in every province were distributed to all the peoples so that they might prepare themselves for that day. [15]The couriers went out in haste at the king's behest, and the decree was given out in Susa the capital. And the king and Haman sat down to their drink, but the town of Susa was left in turmoil.

3

The Enemy

Since men are free, politics can never deal in certainties, but only in probabilities. This means that while everything may depend on the political move of a righteous man, even his best calculations cannot prevent the worst if someone else has prepared better and has struck with greater skill. And so it is in Esther: Mordechai's interference in the attempt on the king's life – intended to gain him favor with the king and his advisers – instead plays into the hands of another, who has for years been moving, probing, pressing for just such an opportunity. And in providing him with this opportunity, Mordechai also ensures the ruin of his own hopes of gaining influence with the king, instead bringing himself into open confrontation with Ahashverosh's court.

The investigation of Ahashverosh's closest servants reveals that Mordechai's information had been correct. Two of these servants had indeed conspired to murder the king, and the results of the inquiry bring about their arrest and subsequent execution. Others among the king's officials are exonerated, but not without damaging his trust in them and, consequently, their capacity to perform their duties. Additional conspiracies are considered possible, but the king's advisers and the princes of the empire disagree as to where the threat may lie, and few of them are themselves above suspicion. Thus while the immediate danger may have passed, it is clear that the effects of the attempted coup cannot so quickly be repaired. Like Vashti's insubordination, the treachery of his trusted officers leaves Ahashverosh exposed, before the kingdom and in his own eyes: While he presumes to possess the power to rule the known world, it becomes apparent that he cannot even tell what is happening in the palace at Susa. And just as Vashti's rebellion leads him to reassert himself by deposing and banishing her, so too does the rebellion of the king's servants lead him to take drastic action to grind them all under heel. He responds to the chaos with the imposition of a figure he believes will be able to restore order and inspire awe in other would-be conspirators: Haman the Agagite, before whom, Ahashverosh decrees, the entire political leadership of the empire is expected to pay obeisance:

> After these things, Ahashverosh the king promoted Haman, the son of Hamedata the Agagite, and advanced him, and set his seat above all the princes who were around him. And all the king's servants who were in the king's gate bowed and prostrated themselves before Haman, for the king had so ordained concerning him (3.1–2).

The appointment and the heavy-handedness with which it is abruptly imposed cannot have been popular. The many advisers of the court and the princes and governors of the empire, each immersed in his own efforts to win the support of the king and gain influence over his government, suddenly learn that they have to humble themselves before the new vizier – someone with whom they are certainly familiar, but whose upstart position in the court is evident from that fact that he had not even been worthy of mentioning as one of the king's advisers at the party a few years earlier. Mordechai himself considers the appointment and the way it has been carried out to be an outrage and cannot reconcile himself to it. When confronted with the demand to prostrate himself before the vizier, he refuses to obey – "but Mordechai did not bow nor prostrate himself" (3.2). And when asked to explain himself by the other courtiers, he defiantly declares that it is because he is a Jew:

> The king's servants who were in the king's gate said to Mordechai: "Why do you violate the king's commandment?" It came to pass that when they spoke to him day in and day out and he did not listen to them, they told Haman, to see whether Mordechai's words would stand, for he had told them that he was a Jew (3.3–4).

Haman, enraged in turn, moves to eliminate this first threat to his authority – by ordering the massacre, eleven months hence, of every Jew in the empire (3.6).

Why does Mordechai refuse to obey the decree of the king? Nothing in Jewish law or custom forbids a Jew to bow before a ruler,[1] and there is every reason to presume that when in the presence of Ahashverosh in earlier years, Mordechai had indeed bowed to him, as had everyone else in the empire. Indeed, Esther herself goes so far as to fall to the floor before the king in supplication later on in the story (8.3). What is the difference between bowing to Ahashverosh, which is done without hesitation, and bowing to the vizier, for which it is worth endangering everything? The meaning of the book of Esther turns on there being a compelling answer to this question. For without such a reason, we can hardly consider Mordechai a hero for later saving the Jews from destruction – since it was his own stubbornness that drew Haman's ire in the first place, making an enemy of him and bringing on the decree of annihilation. Rather than being the savior of the Jews, Mordechai should in this case be regarded as the culprit by whose intransigence the Jews are nearly annihilated root and branch.[2]

Mordechai's public resistance to Haman's authority strikes a dissonant chord in another way: It contradicts everything that he has come to stand for throughout the first seven years of Ahashverosh's reign. Until this point, Mordechai obscures his identity as a Jew and advises Esther to do the same, seeking only to be accepted at the king's gate and to be taken into the confidence of the king and his advisers. As for acts of Jewish identification on his part, whether in public or in private, we hear nothing. Neither Esther's intermarriage nor anything else is able to inspire him to leave the path of accommodation and resist the government, and certainly not to violate the king's laws and embark on an open confrontation with his officials. Suddenly, we are told that he disdains to offer respect to the new vizier and refuses to assist in the consolidation of his rule by contributing to the public's acceptance of him. He challenges the king as well, in effect denying that Ahashverosh has the authority to elevate Haman in such a way. Most important, Mordechai determines that if this battle is to be fought, he must fight it as a Jew, and he proceeds to announce what has not been known to many of the courtiers until now: that he is a Jew, and that this, somehow, is the reason for his collision with the vizier.

On the surface, it is as though Mordechai has recanted everything he has ever believed about his relationship with the Persian state. But Mordechai has not changed: It is Persia that has changed. To make sense of the revolution in Mordechai's behavior, we must first understand the revolution that has taken place in the king's government, and the meaning of the coming to power of this vizier, this Agagite.

4

The King's Men

Haman's installation heralds a dramatic shift in the nature of government in Persia. What had been a state whose actions were driven by the hazardous buffoonery of the king's need to feel powerful now embarks on a purposive effort to impose total political rule through terror and violence. An unpleasant but tolerable regime becomes one of injustice and idolatry. How does Mordechai come to believe that such a change in the motives of the state has come about?

While the narrative is once again sparse, we know several important facts about Haman's meteoric rise in the Persian court:

   (i) Ahashverosh promotes Haman "after these things" (3.1) – that is, as an immediate result of the attack on his life in the previous episode;
  (ii) The king sets Haman "above all the princes who were around him" (3.1), when prior to this we hear of the prominence and importance of "the seven princes of Persia and Media, who saw the king's face, and who sat first in the kingdom" (1.14); and
 (iii) The king commands "all the king's servants who were in the king's gate" (3.2) to prostrate themselves before Haman – in effect ordering the entire political leadership of the empire to humble itself before him.

The force of these innovations seems clear enough. Until this time, the narrative describes Ahashverosh's government as being open to influence from numerous directions, and Ahashverosh himself as respecting and relying on a large cast of nobles and attendants to provide him with advice and direction. This is particularly evident in that Memuchan, the least of the seven princes present at the king's table, is permitted to speak before the others and to advise the king on a matter as personal as the fate of his queen; as well as from the fact that the search to find a new royal consort is instituted at the urging of an anonymous clutch of assistants referred to only as "the king's young men" (2.2). One must suspect that these two examples bespeak a far larger cast of individuals who have the king's ear in the early stages of the story, and this should not be surprising. The ruler of even the smallest country, and certainly of an empire, must make educated decisions on a vast range of subjects: on war and foreign relations, financial policy and taxes, religion and education, law, internal government and the maintenance of the power of the state, as well as on a host of local issues affecting the appeasement and functioning of every individual province, not to mention the management of the king's personal properties and the administration of his own royal person. Issues as sensitive as the king's personal security and his search for a wife are matters that must be delegated to knowledgeable individuals whose opinions he is likely to treat as decisive. On every subject, the king must have trusted opinions, and preferably more than one, to allow him to hear out the different aspects of an issue and make the best possible decision.

Indeed, the narrative goes out of its way in the first two chapters to stress that prior to Haman's elevation, it had been the king's habit to seek advice from all whom he believed to have an understanding of law and justice (1.13) – and to list by name no fewer than *eighteen* of Ahashverosh's advisers and servants who had a measure of influence on his decisions: seven advisers on law and policy, seven administrators of the court (whom we know to play a pivotal role in policy as well from Harvona's crucial interjection at the climax of the story), two security men, and two royal matchmakers. And all of these are in addition to the throng of courtesans and politicos such as Mordechai who shift about the king's gate looking for some service to render.

In this maelstrom of voices competing for favor, trust, attention, and control, the elevation of Haman constitutes not merely the promotion of one voice at the expense of the competition, as usually happens when one adviser proves himself to be more able than others. After the attempt on his life, Ahashverosh is frightened – and what frightens him in particular is the tumult and confusion that is the political storm constantly taking place around him. He sees that he does not understand the aims of many of those princes, advisers, lawyers, officers, and servants pushing to be close to him. While most may be innocent of criminal intent, they all look to him much as had the two security men before their betrayal: constantly maneuvering and plotting, shifting and challenging and pressing their points of view. Who knows which ones are benign and which ones lethal? Who could know?

Terrified by the implications of this perpetual battle for power, with him at the center, Ahashverosh's instinct is identical to that of countless other utopians and totalitarians. He determines to end history. By positioning Haman above all others, Ahashverosh seeks to terminate the politics of the court, rendering all his servants silent and harmless by making them answerable to a single

enforcer whose capacity to terrorize will be unquestioned.[1] The fact that the
court is prostrating itself before a relative newcomer is all the better for humiliating the rest of the courtesans and emphasizing the power of the king to do
as he pleases. This was a point the rabbis stressed by asserting that the vizier
had previously been a barber[2] – lowly and servile, but with the unquestioned
capacity to slit the throats of the mighty. We arrive at the same conclusion if we
suppose that Haman was a brutally successful provincial governor, brought in
to do the same work on the court. In either case, it is clear that Haman brings
to the service of the king a quality he lacks – the methodical purposiveness and
direction of the razor, which will cut all that is uneven down to the stubble.
Whether one is a prince on the ruling council of Persians and Medes, a courtier
of long standing, or a commoner, the new rule is intended to crush all aspira-
tion and place all in order, so that henceforth Ahashverosh will have to hear
only one trusted voice: Haman's. And the narrative reflects this new reality
by literally silencing everyone else. After the vizier's installation, no opinion
is recorded in the palace other than those expressed by Haman, and none of
the king's other advisers and servants is even worth mentioning by name.[3]
Moreover, from his subsequent acquiescence in Haman's plot to murder the
Jews, it is clear that the king is deadly serious in his intention to distance himself from all other advisers and to listen only to the one. As Ahashverosh is in
love, so he is in politics: Just as he had extinguished the will of his queen and
instituted in her place a system of dealing with women only through silent
compulsion, so too would he now extinguish the will of his servants and institute in their place a system of dealing with the empire only through silent
compulsion.[4]

   Yet stunning as may have been the king's decision to elevate Haman above
all his advisers – and his subsequent decision to remove the signet ring from
his own hand and place it in Haman's keeping, symbolically delegating to him
all of his authority (3.10) – it remains unclear why all this should have been so
difficult for Mordechai to accept. For what possible difference could it make
whether absolute authority was exercised by Ahashverosh or by his vizier?

   The Talmud touches on the question of what Mordechai believed was fundamentally wrong with the new arrangement when it examines the arguments
he must have made to rally opposition to Haman's installation and to his decree
against the Jews, which follows no more than a few weeks later. According to
Rav, Mordechai argues that: "Haman has raised himself above Ahashverosh."[5]
On this reading, Mordechai attributes criminality to Haman's behavior from
the outset – claiming that through his machinations he has succeeded in usurping the authority of the king. This may well have been an argument that could
have stirred up the Persians against the new vizier, but it suffers as a motive
for Mordechai himself, not least because it is false. At no point in the narrative

does Ahashverosh actually lose control over Haman, although he does fear this possibility. The vizier never makes a move without the king's permission from the day he takes office to the very end.[6] What is more, this line of argument fails to resolve the central question of Mordechai's motive for resisting Haman. For if the vizier were merely taking the king's place as the absolute authority in the realm, why should Mordechai have treated him any differently from Ahashverosh or any other despot?

A second opinion cited in the Talmud, however, cuts deeper into the matter. According to Shmuel, Mordechai's problem with the installation of the vizier is that: "The king below has prevailed over the king above."[7] In other words, Ahashverosh himself has set the state on a new and evil course, arrogating to himself authority that rightly belongs only to God.

But what does this mean? What authority does God claim over non-Jewish states, or over any state? And what does it mean for a king such as Ahashverosh to prevail over God?

The point of departure here is that God concerns himself with the peoples of all nations, as he tells Jonah with reference to the Assyrian city of Nineveh: "Should I not be concerned for Nineveh, for this great city, in which there are more than one hundred twenty thousand people, who do not know their right hand from their left, as well as much livestock?"[8] Although God is at times forced to repay wrongdoing with destruction, his standpoint is nonetheless one of concern for the men of all nations, whose well-being he desires and demands of those who can affect it. Foremost among these, of course, are the rulers of nations, in whose hands are placed the lives of so many others. When these rulers earnestly pursue the good of their people, God and his servants stand up to strengthen them, as Daniel "stood up to strengthen" Darius. From this we see that a ruler who seeks the good of his subjects does God's will. As Jeremiah said of Josiah, king of Judah: "Did he not … do justice and righteousness? Then it was well with him. He judged the cause of the poor and the needy. Then it was well. Is this not to know Me? says the Lord."[9] Thus all nations should be ruled for their well-being: The ruler who strives for this serves God himself, even if he is an idolater such as Darius. The ruler who does not rebels against God, raising his arbitrary desires above those of the King above.

All this is common to the entire Jewish tradition, as far back as the destruction of Sodom for its cruelty and oppression, at the beginning of the books of Moses.[10] What is new in the book of Esther is that it was composed in a later age, during roughly the period when Greek philosophers were seeking structural theories for how to produce the "best regime" – attempting to assess, for instance, whether one produces a better state by structuring it as a monarchy, so that ultimate authority is in the hands of one man, or as a democracy in which authority is given to the many (having experienced both, they advocated monarchy). Esther, too, speaks to its time by bringing the search for structural explanations to the classic Jewish problem of the difference between good and evil rule. It suggests that the state, never too highly regarded in the biblical tradition, remains tolerable to the extent that it remains open to the competition of views, as represented by the eighteen advisers surrounding Ahashverosh at the beginning of the story. What brutalizes the state is the inclination of the powerful to shut out the competing voices that must be heard if one is to reach a judgment that is at all reasonable. Shutting out these voices, the government becomes nothing better than a clique of arrogant men sitting down to revel in their power while the people suffer from their decisions: "The king and Haman sat down to their drink, but the town of Susa was left in turmoil" (3.15).[11]

Let us consider more closely at how this works to explain the difference between the good state and that which "prevails over the king above."

It was Plato who first spoke of the state as a ship, and this metaphor is instructive. For it makes no difference who is captain or how he has attained this position. If he is a poor navigator, the ship sinks.[12] Of course, this is true with regard to the individual, as well: If he is a poor navigator, he will just as surely bring about his own personal ruin. But unlike the individual, the decisions of the state affect the lives and deaths of millions, and so it is all the more important that the state, which has no mind or will of its own, be piloted by the best possible reasoning. The ruler must issue laws, judgments, and decisions in response to every situation and question that arises, and in principle, all of these must be correct. Thus while the state rules, its purpose is to rule well, and the best state is one in which the ruler correctly understands what course is required and so can use his authority to implement this truth.

The Greek affinity for monarchies was based on the belief in the possibility of a virtuous and scholarly king, who, being a philosopher as well as a ruler, would be able provide the state with the wisdom necessary to flourish. But the philosopher-king was a type that the Bible would have considered rather unlikely. Instead, the biblical tradition held rulers in general – and there is no reason to think that this assessment should be restricted only to monarchy – to be much like Ahashverosh: a great deal of spirit and very little brain. Left to his own devices, he would always be short of knowledge, and lacking as well in reason to weigh this knowledge. The ruler was thus expected to be capricious and deadly, although subject to substantial improvement if advised by men able to direct him properly: "The wrath of a king is angels of death, but a wise man will placate it."[13]

On the face of it, it may seem that all one needs to establish just rule is a king willing to be told what to do, and a single, highly competent adviser who is capable of unambiguously discerning the true goals of the state. But the Jewish tradition discounts this possibility as well, because it is more or less impossible to find such an adviser: According to R. Johanan, each person grasps reality from a different perspective, so that no one man can ever understand the whole truth of any matter by himself: "Every word that went forth from the Lord was fragmented into seventy languages."[14] Thus not even something as unequivocal as a communication from heaven can help being fragmented into scores of different perspectives when perceived by different men, each with his own "language" for interpreting the world.

One need only recall the story of the tower of Babel – on which the theory of the "seventy languages" is apparently based – to recognize the far-reaching political implications of R. Johanan's theory. According to the books of Moses, the earliest people did have a simple and unambiguous understanding of what was good policy for their state, such as every government desires: Their goal was to erect an all-encompassing metropolis in Mesopotamia for the entire human race, centered around a tower reaching to heaven, and this project was considered feasible because all men were united in supporting it – being "of one language and unified words." The implication is that mankind would have succeeded had God not "scattered" the builders, saying: "Let us go down and confound their language, that each will not be able to understand what the other is saying. So the Lord scattered them from there across the face of the land, and they ceased to build the city."[15] In the view of R. Johanan, the reason that the Mesopotamians ceased to construct their united city was not that they simply could not understand the literal languages being spoken; they could have used interpreters. Rather, the account of the tower depicts the creation of different worldviews, each dictating its own understanding of reality – each man with his own "language" so that he has difficulty in appreciating the views and interests of his neighbor. What prevents men from unified political action is therefore the existence of the "seventy" perspectives, which ensure that every proposal seeming good to some will be unacceptable to others.[16]

In the book of Esther, however, the aim is assumed to be for the ruler to recognize the existence of these different perspectives and to approximate just rule by seeking out advisers who can, each of them, provide him with a part of the true picture. That these perspectives will contradict one another is obvious, as the rabbis envisioned God informing Ahashverosh, who wished for all his citizens to be silent and simply to love him: "Two men seek the hand of the same woman. Can she marry both of them? ... So two ships lie in the same harbor, one waiting for a north wind, the other for a south wind. Can the same wind carry them both together?"[17] And precisely because the differing political perspectives contradict, one adviser may never suffice for the king in practice. Each one, fighting to advance his own sectarian interest, is also the bearer of information as to what is happening in the empire and advice as to what should be done. And while all these minor truths and half-truths clamoring against the others may be a nuisance and a menace to the king, each constitutes a small part of the answer as to what must be done in the empire. It is the role of the ruler, if he is to understand the condition of his state and its needs, to hear these and attempt to weigh each against the other.[18]

The narrative in Esther does not propose that Ahashverosh approaches this ideal, but it does make a related argument: It suggests that for all his detestable personal traits, the actual evil that the king can do is kept reasonably in check so long as he is surrounded day and night by a range of advisers representing various perspectives that he has no choice but to take into account – if only because he wishes to impress them all so that he may harvest their apprecia-tion. The main exposition of this point is the episode of Vashti's banishment. The king has been driven onto a towering spire of rage as a result of being pub-licly embarrassed by a member of his court. And yet for all this, Ahashverosh actually succeeds in abusing his power to a rather inconsequential degree. After all, what really happens? The queen is tossed out of court, and a foolish but on the whole benign edict is issued informing Persia that wives should obey their husbands.[19] A real catastrophe – such as a decree of death for wives who disobey their husbands – is avoided, and the reason for this is clear: "The king consulted with his advisers, who understood the precedents, for such was the king's habit before all who knew law and judgment" (1.13). In the worst case, the decision as to what is to be done is made while the drunken and outraged king is surrounded by advisers and servants, standing symbolically before the watching eyes of the entire empire, whose reactions must be taken into account. Almost always, one of these advisers is clever enough to help him down with-out damaging himself or the empire irreparably, and if this one were to stray much too far from a tolerable solution to the crisis, his proposals would for the most part be blocked by those of the others.[20]

This system is very far from ideal of a state whose rulers have the tools to find its true course, being in fact no more than its mediocre shadow. But it nonetheless stands in stark contrast with the rule of Ahashverosh through Haman, whose "advice" represents not even such a mediocre approximation of the truth, but a scant one-seventieth of the truth – in most cases necessarily a lie. Ahashverosh now rules a state that cannot even hope to approximate true policy, since it is structurally prevented from doing so. There is now only one person whom Ahashverosh must try to impress, whose appreciation he must concern himself over. For this reason, the most fateful decisions will now be made in private, without consulting anyone else or taking any other inter-est into account. Ahashverosh, out of fear and laziness, assumes for himself the prerogative to rule the state not in accord with what is truly for its ben-efit. Rather than being the captain whose role is to pilot his ship among the shoals of reality, he chooses to steer by some other method with the purpose of achieving some other goal. And in so doing, he sets his own will with regard to the government of the state above that of God: "The king below has prevailed over the king above."

And the evil when such a deed is done does not remain abstract. When, under the reign of Haman's advice, offense is once again taken because of the rebellious behavior of a member of the court, the result is radically different from what we saw the first time around, in the case of Vashti's insubordination. This time, it is not Memuchan, implicitly balanced by the potential reactions of the other princes and the rest of the servants and the throng, who provides the reasoning to instruct the king's appetite for rule. This time, the machinery of the state accepts the perspective of one man, unbalanced and untempered, and the result is an unbalanced and untempered eruption of evil:

> Then Haman said to Ahashverosh the king: "There is a certain people ... and their laws are different from those of other peoples, and the king's laws they do not keep, so that it is of no benefit for the king to tolerate them. If it please the king, let it be written that they be destroyed." ... The king took his ring from his hand and gave it to Haman, the son of Hamedata the Agagite, the persecutor of the Jews. And the king said to Haman: ... "Do with them as you see fit" (3.8–11).

5

Idolatry

Yet there is something more to Mordechai's refusal to prostrate himself than these political considerations alone. After all, the refusal to bow is traditionally a Jewish expression of religious faith: Jews do not refuse to bow before kings or their viziers. Jews refuse to bow before idols. Are we then to understand that Mordechai believed the vizier somehow to be an idol, that he had made of himself a god?

When the rabbis retold the story of Mordechai's refusal, they understood that such was indeed the case, writing, for example, that the new vizier had affixed an idol to his tunic: "Was Mordechai just looking for quarrels, or just being generally disobedient to the king's commands? The fact is that when Ahashverosh ordered that all should bow down to Haman, the latter affixed an idolatrous image on his breast for the purpose of making all bow down to the idol."[1] The Talmud also cites the opinion of R. Huna, who was even more direct: "What had Mordechai seen that he picked a quarrel with Haman? It was for this reason, that he had made himself an object of worship."[2] The argument is that Mordechai's assault on the installation of the new vizier is not only a reaction to a current political event. In taking up this political cause, Mordechai the Jew joins into in a far broader Jewish war, already in progress a thousand years and more; and Haman, while certainly the purveyor of an immediate political evil, is also the latest champion of that same philosophical and religious horror that Judaism had come into existence to fight in the time of Abraham. If we are to fully appreciate the Jews' war against the vizier, a war that opens with a man who will not bend, and closes with the deaths of a substantial part of the fighting power of Persia, we must understand the idolatry against which the war was fought.[3]

Judaism and idolatry are irreconcilable opponents, for Judaism is the rejection of the servitude to idols and false gods. Thus R. Johanan argued: "Anyone who repudiates idolatry is called a Jew."⁴ And historically, at least, this was the case: Judaism arose from within the blast furnace of Mesopotamian and Egyptian idol worship in the time of Abraham as a reaction against what was then considered civilization. But R. Johanan was not only referring to the distant past. The rabbis considered the battle of Abraham against all of Mesopotamian thought to be that of Mordechai in Persia as well: "Why is he called a Jew [i.e., a man of Judah], surely he was a Benjaminite? Because he declared the unity of God's name before all mankind, as it is written, 'But Mordechai did not bow nor prostrate himself before him.' "⁵ Thus the opposition to Haman was itself understood by the rabbis to be tantamount to "declaring the unity of God's name," the central tenet of Jewish belief.

We usually understand *idolatry* to refer to the making of figures, from clay or metal, wood or stone, that represented gods – or that were themselves considered gods – whose pleasure and grace were thought necessary to obtain human good: sustenance, fertility, victory, peace. Frequently, there were men who claimed to have the ability to provide these things, and these men were referred to as gods, or else as the representatives of the gods, as well. Everywhere in the ancient world there were men who were idols just as surely as there were statues that were idols. In both cases, the good of human beings and of nations was to be achieved by appeasing these gods, whereas suffering and evil were supposed to result from incurring their displeasure. Of course, since each people generated its own idols in accordance with local ideas, there was a virtually unlimited range of theories as to what gods were appropriate for human worship and what human behaviors were pleasing and displeasing to these deities. Some gods would exercise their influence in return for food and wine, others enjoyed parties and entertainment, and yet others appreciated the sacrifice of produce and beasts. There were gods that appreciated orgies and bestiality. And there were those whose pleasures centered on human blood, on the hearts extracted from living men, or on children sacrificed by their parents to the beating of drums.

Since the evil in idolatry was so great, it is difficult to understand why men found it good. But idolatry was actually the result of a positive human desire to ascertain the causes of suffering and ameliorate them. Before idolatry, there was only helplessness – the belief of an infant who falls but knows neither the reasons for his hurt nor any way of preventing his suffering from recurring. Idolatry was the first intellectual endeavor of humanity as it rose above the immediate and visible in search of effective means for treating its afflictions. As Rava ben R. Isaac related of a certain idolatrous temple, its intention was for good, although the results were heinous: "Whenever the world is in need of rain, the idol appears to its priests in a dream, saying: 'Kill me a man and I will send rain.' They kill a man for it, and rain really does come."⁶

Why should such a report of the efficacy of idolatry have been preserved by the rabbis? The point presented here for our consideration is that idolatry was not a perfect falsehood, such as one would have if these shameful murders were committed and the rains did not come. On the contrary, the obstinate persistence of idolatry derived precisely from the element of truth that was in it: They would kill a human being, and the rain would in fact come. And from the perspective of the idolater, the relation between the two events appeared effective, undeniable, and true. The flaw lies not in the idolater's willingness to accept simple falsehood as the truth, but in his unwillingness to consider causes and effects other than the most local ones that are visible to him from within his own severely limited perspective. The idolatrous farmer believes that his need for rain can be alleviated through murder because no other causes for rain are considered beyond the most local one, which is his own actions (and those of his priest); likewise, the idolatrous farmer believes that his need for rain can justify murder, because no other effects are considered beyond the most local one, which his own betterment (and that of his priest). This means that at its core, idolatry comes into being and persists in the world only due to human arrogance: Idolatry arises from the belief that the local truth of one's own perspective comprises truth as a whole – that one-seventieth of the truth is the truth itself, when a broader view will reveal that, in the end, this one-seventieth amounts to a barren lie.

The example provided by Rava ben R. Isaac also touches on a second infirmity that haunted the world of the idolaters: So dark were the demands for the destruction of property, sex crimes, mutilation, and murder made by the false gods of antiquity that their overall effect was not to ameliorate suffering but to embitter human life. Often enough, what these gods demanded in exchange for empty promises of well-being was the release of the vilest human inclinations, to the pleasure of some among men and the ruin of society as a whole. And it was just this disregard for idolatry's other, overall effects that transformed it into a menace to the well-being of all its practitioners and their environs. As the rabbis argued, the ultimate end of every idol was that it came to life in order to spit in its master's face.[7]

Both in thought and action, the system of the idolaters was what we refer to in today's terms as moral relativism: the belief that in every place and time, human suffering is governed by *local* truths relevant to each place and each people and ultimately emanating from the perspective and will of local, individual human beings.[8] The prophets of Israel denied the effectiveness of such local prescriptions, as well as of the desirability and permissibility of acting on the basis of such claims. Instead, they insisted that the appearance of evil is governed by *universal* principles determined by the nature of man and of the creation itself. For this reason, the first three commandments given by God at Sinai are a comprehensive rejection of the relativistic epistemology of the idolaters and their multitude of local gods, with their local truths. As we read:

   (i) I am the Lord your God;
  (ii) You will have no other gods beside me;
 (iii) I, the Lord your God, am a jealous God, visiting the sins of the fathers upon the children to the third and fourth generation of those that hate me,
 (iv) but showing mercy to thousands of generations of those that love me and keep my commandments;
  (v) I am the Lord your God who brought you out of Egypt, out of the land of bondage;
 (vi) You will not make yourself a carved idol;
(vii) You will not bow down to them and serve them.[9]

These first claims serve as the substructure upon which the first general laws of morality were built: that righteousness consists first of seeking the good of man – respecting his life, family, property, dignity, right to respite, right to privacy, and right to justice, these being the remaining seven of the ten commandments; and that evil is everywhere a consequence of the fact that mankind ignore these principles, doing what appears right in their own eyes according to their own local perspective.

It is therefore no surprise that the pagan gods and their human beneficiaries saw every Jewish demand as either theft or warfare: Jewish insistence on the existence of generally applicable rights was a theft of their own prerogatives, and Jewish resistance to ways of the idolaters was a slave rebellion by those who refused to understand that they were rightly the slaves of some god-king or other. This is why the collision of Moses and his universal God with the will of Pharaoh serves as the archetype for the war that the emergence of Judaism brings into history. Moses comes to Pharaoh – a full-fledged pagan deity in his own right, whose will is truth for an entire civilization – and orders him, in the name of principles whose force is upon all men, to cease the merciless servitude of the Jews:

> Afterward Moses and Aaron went in and told Pharaoh: "So says the Lord, God of Israel: Let my people go that they may celebrate me in the desert."
>   Pharaoh said: "Who is the Lord that I should obey his voice to let Israel go? I know not the Lord, nor will I let Israel go."[10]

Pharaoh had, in the name of his own divine will, pursued every evil against the Jews, up to and including the slaughter of their children whom he understood to be his possessions. Moses' response in this passage is that of universal right settling accounts, and this is indeed what is enacted in the subsequent narrative: Egypt is torn asunder by a relentless war of wonders that destroys its water supply, its livestock, and its grain and finally slaughters its children before returning to more conventional war and eliminating Pharaoh's armed forces. And while the ferocity of the attack may leave some uneasy today, this was understood by ancient Jews to be the only method of doing business with idolatry: The God of Israel promised to return evil unto the third and fourth generation of those who hate him – that is, against all living members of any society that is governed by villainy.

Nor is the Jewish war against idolatry limited to periodic resistance against king-idols and their states. From the time of Abraham, the Jews claimed the right to establish a society on earth free from the pollution of idolatry. And while it may have been impractical for the Jews, "the fewest of peoples,"[11] to wage war against the pagan empires of Egypt and Mesopotamia, they did claim for themselves a small patch of land along the trade route between the two superpowers, where they were able to serve as a bone in the throat of the entire idolatrous world. In the land of the Jews, idolatry – the belief in the absence of general standards of right and wrong, and thus the source of evil – is to be driven from the land. No prisoners are to be taken, no inquiry is to be made into their ways, no treaties are to be signed with them. And the reason for this is explicit: "For every horror that the Lord hates have they done for their gods. Even their sons and their daughters have they burned in fire for their gods."[12]

There is little in our own experience that can approach the circumstances being described here, or the war that the Jews are expected to wage against idolatry. Certainly, even contemporary democracies engage in "unconditional" war; the nuclear targeting doctrine of "countervalue" warfare also aimed to destroy the largest possible number of the civilian population, including children and the aged, all in the hope of ending war more quickly.[13] But the purpose of the wars against idolatry was not to protect Jewish lives by ending the war more rapidly. It was to protect the Jewish people, and ultimately all of mankind, from an idea – an idea that, once accepted, duped men and drugged them to moral insensibility, justifying in their minds every conceivable darkness. Idolatry was amnesia, and against it Judaism strove to make men remember: that murder was evil, that perversion was evil, that right was a tree of life to those who embrace it, that wrong would bring certain ruin. Idolatry would teach the Jews to forget, and to forget meant their end as Jews, as individuals and as a people. And in the theology of Judaism, in which the human race could be elevated above the morass of endless depravity only if some would take it upon themselves to believe in this elevation and fight for it, the end of the Jews and their mission would mean that all of humanity was doomed.

Hence the famous dictum of Resh Lakish: "The Holy One, blessed be he, spoke to the works of creation, saying to them: If Israel accepts the *tora*, you will exist, but if not I will return you to chaos and void."[14]

As the Jews entered Canaan in the time of Joshua, the eradication of the amnesia of idolatry was therefore considered the bedrock upon which civilization and civil life itself were to be based – and every human urge was suspected of being a threat to the memory that the Jews were to fix in their heads. For this reason, the Jews were forbidden to allow the children of the idolaters to remain among them lest they come to love them and become influenced by them; they were forbidden to make any use whatever of religious treasures, lest they come to use them as the idolaters had; they were told not even to inquire as to the nature of idolatry once it was destroyed. The war of the Jews against idolatry was total, a war of survival that was, at its heart, a war to uproot the disease of moral relativity from the world. No wonder, then, that when in a later age the rabbis sought to explain what it was that had made Abraham worthy of being the first Jew, they supposed that as a boy he had smashed the idols that his father had made. For them, the essence of Judaism is what Nietzsche, in a later time, called "philosophy with a hammer" – the smashing of the idols.[15]

It is in this context that Mordechai's war against Haman and his followers must be understood. So long as Ahashverosh had made decisions in consultation with a broad range of advisers, there was reason to hope that the laws and actions of the Persian state would tend toward at least the roughest approximation of a tolerable settlement among the competing perspectives, interests, and truths in the empire. Haman's installation, however, eliminating as it did the action of interests other than his own, suppressed the search for a greater truth on the part of the state. Henceforth, Persian policy would be defined by the perspective and desires of a single man, Haman. Since it would be his desires rather than truth which would now determine right and wrong for much of mankind, his elevation transformed him (and Ahashverosh, as well) into a usurping god, a pretender to knowledge and power he did not have, an idol. Mordechai refuses to bow because he recognizes that to serve Haman's whim would be akin to serving the Canaanite gods – in principle, and, as quickly becomes clear, in practice as well.

6

Disobedience

Most of the early leaders among the Jews were individuals whose confrontation with idolatry began from a position of weakness: The false gods wielded state authority. They commanded armies and police, gave orders, and were obeyed. And where there was no hope of military resistance, the role of the Jew was to fight by other means. The biblical account of the story of the Jews therefore closes with the repeated disobedience of Mordechai and Esther, through which the Jews are saved from annihilation – much as it begins with the disobedience of Shifra, Pua, and Jocheved, through which the Jews were saved from enslavement to Pharaoh. In between, the narrative depicts over a thousand years of nearly continual willingness to abrogate law and state authority in order to do what is right.

Remarkably, this message of Jewish resistance to state idolatry and injustice has been consistently misread or ignored by those who have sought to characterize the Bible as a book of submission. Such interpretations are invariably built around Abraham's supposed willingness to sacrifice his own son Isaac at God's command. This reading distorts the story of Abraham at Moria, which is not concerned to demonstrate Abraham's obedience, but rather his faith that "God will see to the sheep for an offering," and so deliver the boy.[1] But in any case, the call to serve God, which is surely an authentic biblical teaching, does not turn the Bible into a book of submission before human authority. Indeed, it is the exact opposite. For God's will in the Bible can be considered equivalent to what today is referred to as the higher law or universal justice. To equate obedience to the dictates of justice with obedience to injustice is to miss the point of the entire Bible, which is that the individual must obey only the dictates of moral truth, even (and especially) when these violate the laws of the state.[2]

46

In all of antiquity, the Bible is the only document that consistently advances the fundamental ideas that are today known as "civil disobedience," unequivocally articulating the familiar principles that were then alien to virtually the entire world: that there is a standard of right and wrong that transcends the decrees of the state; that the state has no right to rule if it rules unjustly; that conscience and not the state must be the ultimate arbiter of the actions of every man; that individual disobedience is justified and obligatory in the face of state injustice; and that resistance and even the overthrow of the state is justified and obligatory in cases of unbearable tyranny. Indeed, the biblical narrative consists in large part of explicit indictments of both Jewish and gentile governments for the injustice of their laws and the unjust behavior of their rulers – accounts in which those who act independently and offer resistance are invariably the heroes. By looking at this tradition more carefully, we may more fully understand what is meant by the decision of Mordechai the Jew to continue the way of his people – the people of the book, and therefore the people of disobedience.

The biblical account of the emergence of the Jews begins with the flight of Abraham, the first Jew, from the Mesopotamian city of Ur, in the very heart of the civilized world – a flight that ends with Abraham's determination to make his life anew, at the age of seventy-five, as a herder of goats and sheep on a patch of land he finds along the trade route to Egypt, the underdeveloped and culturally irrelevant wilderness of Canaan. The narrative itself tells us little about the reasons for Abraham's escape from the civilization of the Euphrates River basin.[3] Yet it is clear from his turbulent stay in Egypt, which ends in a hasty retreat, that there is no love lost between the Hebrew patriarch and the great Nile civilization, either. It is therefore no sudden distaste for the particular fads of Mesopotamian culture, no warrant for his arrest in the hands of the Mesopotamian authorities, that drives him to break with the world he had known his entire life. Instead, he cashiers the glory of the world empires of his day because he believes that in this way he and his descendants, and the rest of the world as well, would be blessed.[4] He had come to the conclusion, after years of bitter turmoil, that in Mesopotamia and Egypt, nothing resembling the blessing he wished for his children could be found. And one need only consider the civilizations from which Abraham escaped in order to begin to understand that he was right.

For more than a thousand years before Abraham, the Nile and Euphrates rivers had given rise to the most advanced cultures mankind had known. The unparalleled might of these two rivers had been harnessed for massive irrigation projects and a flourishing waterborne trade, allowing the rise of the Sumerian empire and its successors in Mesopotamia and of Egypt of the Pharaohs. Both empires, like those of China, India, and Persia, engaged in public works on an unprecedented scale to increase the land available for farming, engaging their entire populations as slaves for periods of weeks or months when important projects were under way. The enforced management of millions of people was a form of taxation, and necessitated the establishment of a huge bureaucracy capable of keeping records of the entire population and its contributions to the public weal. Needless to say, it also enabled the spectacular enrichment of the king and his family, as well as requiring the creation of a colossal military apparatus capable of enforcing the labor tax and defending the developed areas against nomadic peoples, who coveted the wealth and power that had been amassed in the river valleys.

The social consequences of such wholesale organization of men were of the first degree. In order to bring an entire empire into the service of building mammoth physical structures such as the pyramids in Egypt and the Chinese Great Wall, every source of fear and authority that could be devised had to be brought to bear in securing beastlike submission – even where, as with these undertakings, this submission would mean the inevitable ruin of a certain portion of the race. To coerce the bodies of every person capable of physical labor, the king would employ a vast police apparatus, relying for information on the bureaucracy that tracked his legions of internal informers. While these tentacles of the state coerced the body, men's minds too were brought under heel by a religious system that ordained that the will of the gods was identical to the will of the ruler: The king was himself a descendent of the gods and their principal servant, wherever he was not himself an essential deity in the pantheon. Law issued by the ruler was therefore a reflection of the unchallengeable law of the universe and had to be obeyed on pain of earthly hell, which was a down payment for what was coming after death. Direct evidence of the divine powers of the state was provided by the official priesthood, who generally maintained a monopoly on all science, astronomy, engineering, and mathematics. Besides the intimidation inherent in this complete control of wisdom and knowledge, these skills were applied to the erection of gargantuan towers and astronomical observatories, connecting the state to the heavens in a way that was obvious to any with eyes to see. The priesthood itself was on the payroll of the state, thus ensuring that it played its role. Under such systems, religion was nothing more or less than the cosmic ideology of the government, the intellectual and spiritual mortar that fused the masses into a single tool in the hand of the state by reassuring that obedience meant salvation and disobedience rightful and inevitable agony.[5]

It follows, of course, that there was not much discussion of a right to disobedience in the ancient world. Neither in Egypt, nor in Mesopotamia, nor anywhere else did mankind bother to struggle, as later thinkers did, with questions of what limits there might be to what the state may require of men. And the notion that there might be a right of the individual to dissent against unjust government was without foundation in the thought of any people.⁶

This is the world from which Abraham found no choice but to become a refugee. He turned his back on the slave labor and terror gods of Mesopotamia, staking his claim to an undeveloped patch of hill ground in Canaan where he could shake off the yoke of the state. Unlike the heroes of other ancient narratives, the figures of the books of Moses are therefore neither royalty nor nobility. Nor, after the fashion of modern literature, are they democratic figures near the bottom of the social structure. Instead, Abraham and his descendants are shepherds, nomads who view civilization from the outside, looking down from the hills at the doings of society and state as they chart their own independent course through the wilderness. The splendor and lies of urban life are of little worth to them; even less so the beast life of the farmers in the valleys, living out their days in toil that these lies may be fed. For in Canaan, Abraham and his people have found what is more precious to them than all else, political and ideological independence: political independence in that they live as nomads, ungoverned, their labor and their property and their actions unregulated and untaxed by anyone other than themselves; ideological independence in that their vantage point and the freedom and dignity of their work allow them to gaze long and deep into the sky, focusing on what truly matters – the proximity of all men to danger, error, and death, and the consequent responsibility they must take for discovering the true course and acting on it.⁷

The degree to which the Bible values conscience as the core of such political and moral independence is dramatized perhaps most forcefully by the fact that the biblical heroes do not, as should be expected, tend to submit passively even to the will of God: Abraham, the first Jew and the prototype of subsequent Jewish values, is depicted as a man with the conscience and strength to challenge God himself. When God intends to destroy every man in Sodom, Abraham argues: "Will not the judge of all the earth do justice?" – and God himself hears him out. Moses, the archetype of a Jewish national and religious leader, argues with God and alters the course of his judgments. Indeed, in case the message is somehow to be missed, the books of Moses inform us that the very name of the Jewish people, Israel, is derived from this most crucial of qualities, the ability to struggle with the world as it has been decreed: "Your name will no longer be Jacob, but Israel, for you have struggled with God and with men and have prevailed" – *Israel* meaning "will struggle with God." What in other cultures would have been sacrilege is thus elevated into a national symbol and the crux of Jewish belief: the refusal of the shepherd to accept the order of the universe as it has been decreed, and the demand of his conscience to know why it cannot be improved.⁸

It can come as no surprise that a people whose tradition so strongly emphasizes the need to contend even with God in matters of justice gave rise to a long history of men and women unwilling to be intimidated by the pretenses of human institutions. Indeed, the tone with respect to earthly rulers is set in the first scriptural reference to them, the description of the Mesopotamian ruler Nimrod: "He began to be mighty on the earth. He was a mighty hunter before the Lord."[9] – that is, a man of spirit, power, and violence. The narrative then presents the results of the accumulation of vast powers in the hands of the Mesopotamians and their empire: "They said: Come, let us build a city, and a tower reaching to the sky, and we will make a name for ourselves, lest we be dispersed across the earth."[10] From the perspective of the shepherd, the establishment of the great and tyrannical world empires is in its essence vanity, the pursuit of glory and power to no productive end; other than the erection of huge monuments of ego and stone at incredible expense, there seems to be little good in it. In the end, God is depicted as dividing them into disparate nations and scattering them abroad. The fate of all states built on the quest for fame and power is understood to be dissension and dissolution.

This suspicion of states and rulers is a common thread running through the entire Bible, beginning with the stories of the patriarchs. Indeed, with uncanny consistency, each new figure in the narrative is almost immediately introduced to readers in terms of his resistance to the state. Thus other than his actual arrival in Canaan, the first event we learn of in Abraham's life is his resistance to the will of the Egyptian Pharaoh, whom he has reason to fear will murder him to take his wife.[11] A similar account introduces Isaac as well, and later, when he finds his father's wells being destroyed by a Canaanite king, we are told that he resists the rulers by redigging one well after another.[12] Likewise, when Jacob and his sons travel back to Canaan, the first event of interest to the narrative is his peaceable purchase of a plot of land on which to encamp, only to have his daughter Dina raped by the local prince – an outrage that prompts Jacob's sons Shimon and Levi to then destroy the inhabitants of the town.[13] Perhaps most tellingly, it is as a result of the Hebrew shepherds' greatest misdeed, the plot to murder their brother Joseph, that they receive the ultimate punishment: They are forced to give up their nomadic life and come under the totalitarian rule of the Egyptian Pharaoh.

Like the other stories of the books of Moses, the account of Israel in Egypt immediately opens with an act of resistance to the state: The Egyptians have come to fear the strength of the foreign Jewish population, and Pharaoh determines to submit the Jews to slavery – the making of bricks with which he can build his edifices – in order to strip them of the capacity to resist him. Having done so, he then summons the Jewish midwives and orders them to kill every male child born among the Jews, the intention being to absorb the women into the Egyptian population and so eliminate the Jews as a people. But the mid-wives, Shifra and Pua, refuse the command:

> But the midwives feared God and did not do as the king of Egypt com-manded, keeping the children alive.
> And the king of Egypt called in the midwives and said to them: "Why have you done this thing, keeping the children alive?"
> And the midwives said to Pharaoh: "Because the Hebrew women are not like the Egyptian women, but vigorous, and they give birth before the midwives can arrive."[14]

Seeing that the midwives will not cooperate, Pharaoh seeks a different method of enforcement, ordering that his entire people participate in slaugh-tering any Jewish boy that is born. Jocheved, a woman from the tribe of Levi, decides she must resist the law, giving birth in secret and hiding her son for a full three months as the killing of the other babies takes place all around her. When finally she cannot hide the child any longer, she sets him adrift on the Nile, hoping for a miracle. And she receives one: for Pharaoh's daughter, finding the ark and pulling the screaming baby from the water, immediately understands what has happened and decides that she, too, will risk her life for the child by violating her own father's decree – in so doing, according to the rabbis, becoming a Jew because she renounces her servitude to the idol in order to do what is right.[15] Jocheved's daughter Miriam is also implicated: Standing by the river and watching the entire scene, she asks Pharaoh's daughter whether she would like a Jewish wet nurse for the child. She brings Jocheved, who cares for the boy until he is weaned and adopted by Pharaoh's daughter as a son.[16]

It is by means of this conspiracy that two Jewish women and an Egyptian princess together abrogate the Egyptian law and manage to save a single Jewish boy: Moses. Neither does the narrative leave any question as to what kind of an education the Levite child received from Pharaoh's daughter. Before we learn anything else about Moses as a grown man, we find that he, too, is unafraid to shatter the Egyptian law for the sake of what he believes to be right:

> It came to pass that when Moses was grown, he went out to his brothers and saw their suffering; and he saw an Egyptian man beating a Hebrew man, one of his brothers. He looked this way and that, and when he saw that there was no man, he slew the Egyptian and buried him in the sand.[17]

Although raised in Pharaoh's court, there is no question that Moses retains his shepherd's eye for resistance, and it is this, no less than his upbringing as a leader among the Egyptian nobility, that prepares him to become the first political and religious leader of the Jews as a nation – and the one who will lead them to revolution.

Having fled Egypt for fear of the king's anger, Moses becomes a shepherd like his forefathers. It is while tending his flock in the wilderness that he has his first encounter with God, an encounter that sends him back to Egypt seeking an end to the enslavement of his people. The grueling rounds of Moses' confrontation with Pharaoh – each punctuated with the demand the Egyptian king "let my people go, that they may serve God" – are the mold from which is cast the entire subsequent tradition of the Hebrew prophets and the unprecedented belief in their authority to castigate the holders of state power. Of course, the Jewish slaves are not necessarily built for such a bruising battle, and their leaders even blame Moses for the wrath Pharaoh visits upon them.[18] Nevertheless, Moses does not end up with sole responsibility for the revolution when it comes: Before the Jews gain their freedom from Egypt, on the night of the last plague, Moses requires that every one of them publicly return to his shepherd past – trampling on the Egyptian law by slaughtering a sheep, a god to the Egyptians, roasting and eating it "so that nothing remains of it in the morning," and then smearing its blood on the doorposts of the house for all to see. It is made clear, moreover, that only those who do so can expect salvation and freedom.[19] Thus disobedience, by which Moses came into the world, also becomes the act by which each Hebrew slave turns his back on the state of the oppressor and accepts the higher law that makes him a Jew.

This suspicion of ruling authority continues to pervade the thought of the Jews even once they have entered Canaan and have no choice but to wield political power themselves. The first effort on the part of the people to erect a centralized state fails because Gideon, whom they have chosen to be king, refuses to take part, declaring: "I will not rule over you, nor will my son rule over you, but the Lord will rule over you."[20] Only after further generations of civil war and humiliation on the battlefield does the determination of the Jews to establish a strong centralized state such as those of other nations reach an irresistible pitch, and even then the people find themselves opposed by the prophet Samuel, who objects to the state on account of the oppression that will inevitably follow from such an accumulation of power.[21]

Although the Jews ignore Samuel's warning, crowning Saul as the first king of a united Israel, the spirit of his critique is accepted nonetheless. From the outset, the Jewish tradition of opposition to government ties the king's hands, making absolute rule impossible. The books of Moses themselves had laid down laws specific to the Jewish king, limiting his right to amass wealth and luxury and insisting that the duration of his rule was dependent on his adherence to God's law.[22] And in subsequent accounts, the narrative repeatedly emphasizes the Jews' rejection of the decrees of their own kings when they deemed them unjust. In one famous scene, Saul orders his men to fast in preparation for battle with the Philistines and threatens death should anyone disobey. When his son Jonathan is found to have violated his decree, Saul orders that he be executed for transgressing the king's orders. But the soldiers of Saul's army reject his authority to have such a thing done:

> Jonathan told him, saying: "I tasted some honey with the end of the staff that was in my hand; therefore I must die."
> Saul said: "So will God do and more. For you will surely die, Jonathan."
> And the people said to Saul: "Is Jonathan to die who has brought this great victory to Israel? Absolutely not. As God lives, no hair will fall from his head, for he has done God's work today." So the people rescued Jonathan, and he was not killed.[23]

And disobedience to unjust use of authority was not only a fact of Saul's relations with his people. It was an institution of Jewish life throughout the period of the Jewish kings – the institution of the prophet, an entire class of individuals whose role it was to declare God's message in opposition to the actions of the king, his servants, and the official priesthood. Despite the establishment of a Jewish kingdom, the prophets continued the heritage of moral resistance that had been bequeathed to the Jews by their forefathers, bringing their oratory and rage to bear on any act of state that in their view undermined the cause of justice.

In some cases, as in Nathan's famous accusation against David – who had taken another man's wife and then arranged to have him die in battle – the intention was to bring the king's behavior back into line.[24] But on occasion, the independent moral authority of the prophet was used for full-blown resistance amounting to revolution. When Saul's rule becomes intolerable, it is the prophet Samuel who declares David his successor, in effect setting out to overthrow the ruling line.[25] The prophet Elisha goes further, pronouncing Jehu the new king during the villainous rule of Jehoram and his mother Jezebel, thereby touching off the execution of the royal family and the eradication of the entire priesthood of Ba'al from Israel.[26] And when the prophet Jeremiah believes that Jerusalem is about to be razed because of the suicidal policies of Zedekia's government, he goes so far as to call for the people to disobey the law and go over to the Babylonian enemy so that something may be saved.[27]

The biblical history of the Jewish nation closes with the exile of the Jews into Babylonia and then Persia, a turn of events that might have been expected to temper Jewish enthusiasm for uneven fights with authority. Yet it is remarkable that the books describing this period are as unabashed as their predecessors in advocating disobedience: In the book of Daniel, three Jewish leaders in the exile – Hanania, Mishael, and Azaria – brazenly defy the law of Babylonia that requires them to prostrate themselves before a gold statue that Nebuchadnezzar has erected.[28] Daniel himself later refuses a similar order to worship the Persian king Darius.[29] The book of Esther is even more aggressive, sanctioning not only the violation of unjust laws, but repeatedly establishing the effectiveness and importance of abrogating other laws in the pursuit of right, as called for by modern theories of civil disobedience.[30] It turns out that Mordechai's repeated refusals to bow before Haman (3.1–2, 5.9) are only the opening rounds in a campaign that includes an illicit court appearance by Mordechai in mourning attire (4.1–2), his certainly illegal incitement of Esther to go before the king unsummoned despite the prohibition against approaching the king (4.8), and Esther's two separate decisions to break this law and come before the king to plead for her people (5.1–2, 8.3–4).[31]

The theme of disobedience to the law of the state is especially striking when argued against a backdrop of God's apparent absence, as it is in the book of Esther.[32] It is one kind of act of faith to take on the power of the state when one suspects God will save the day in the end. It is something else again to insist on provoking confrontation with the state when such assistance seems unlikely to come. Faced with the overwhelming power of the empire-idols that had enslaved the earth, one could easily have concluded, as the early Christian thinkers did, that it is better to submit in this world and triumph in the next.[33] Yet it is one of the great achievements of Mordechai's disobedience that it was able to demand the continuation of Jewish activism in an era in which man had begun to feel himself suspiciously alone as he stood before his oppressors. Even under the bitterest days of Roman subjugation, when Jerusalem lay in ruins and the land was filled with the bodies of the fallen, the rabbis continued to preach Mordechai's message of disobedience, arguing that power and rule on earth, no matter how vast, cannot grant sovereignty, which is the right to command – a right that ultimately rests only with the individual (or the state) when guided by truth. Thus R. Simlai argued that it was nothing less than independent sovereignty that was granted every individual at Mt. Sinai, where "six hundred thousand ministering angels descended and set two crowns on the head of every individual of Israel, one for action and one for understanding."[34] Moreover, they completely rejected the possibility that one had a right to use this individual independence and sovereignty to withdraw from the world as called for by non-Jewish philosophies of the time: "If someone says: Why should I concern myself with the troubles of society, bother with men's controversies, and listen to their voices? Peace be unto you, my soul. One such as this is destroying the world."[35]

7

Joseph

Judaism is a rebellion against the authority of the ruler to establish what is right according to the weight of his interests and the perversity of his whims. But the biblical texts are without illusions: The Jewish effort, during the period of the judges, to live without central government and with only God as king ended in misery and failure. Even Abraham, the shepherd-idealist, could not survive without to some degree learning to manipulate men, their states, and their wars.[1] And while he withdrew from civilization to lead a purer, truer life, the fact is that in times of famine – and there was threat of starvation in Canaan in every generation from Abraham's arrival until the Jews finally resettled in Egypt – it was to the wealth and technology of Egypt that he and his followers turned time and again in order to survive. While the goal was ever to bring heaven to earth, it rapidly transpired that to do this one would of necessity have to deal with the ways in which things are done on earth. And this meant collaboration with the very state idolatry that Judaism rejected.

The inevitable incursion of the state-idols into the idyll of the Jewish shepherds in Canaan is the subject of the Joseph story in the books of Moses, which serves as a touchstone for all subsequent Jewish discussion on the topic. Three other books of the Bible – Daniel, Nehemia,[2] and Esther – address themselves to the question of Jewish power under foreign empires, all of them being more or less explicit responses to the story of the descent of the Jews into Egypt in the time of Joseph and its consequences.

In Genesis, we are told that the patriarch Jacob had twelve sons, who begin their lives as shepherds in the tradition of their fathers. Together, they form the first Jewish society, which will serve as a prototype for the house of Israel for all time. Like every society, it has its own intricate politics, with no fewer than five of the brothers aspiring to inherit leadership of the clan from their father: Reuben, Shimon, Levi, Judah, and Joseph. Of these, Joseph is the youngest, yet by the time he is seventeen, it becomes clear that he is possessed of very special traits. He has a particular talent for using the ways of worldly power – appearance, favor, influence – to gain what his status as the youngest and weakest cannot give him. The narrative speaks of how Joseph "shepherds his brothers," serving as his father's agent in his efforts to control them, and so wins the favor of his father, who "loved him more than all his other children" and gives him special gifts.[3] He is also physically attractive, which boosts the appreciation of those who appreciate him, as well as his own vanity.[4] Moreover, Joseph reports being visited by dreams in which he and his brothers are binding sheaves of grain, their sheaves prostrating themselves before his, and in which the stars and the heavenly bodies prostrate themselves before him. To these the brothers retort in hatred: "Would you indeed reign over us? Would you rule over us?"[5]

Joseph's dreams reflect what the brothers might otherwise have guessed: that Joseph sees them not as shepherds, as nomadic and independent agents, but as farmers, members of a vast structure of earthly power in which their lives depend on the protection of rulers who provide sustenance and arms – a power structure in which it is his talents, and not theirs, that are essential. As it turns out, there is no small measure of realism in this view, and the Jews, too, will have to come to terms with this fact. Moreover, Joseph's desire for control derives, at least in part, from a desire to impose truth and peace on the relations of disunity, violence, and disrespect that have come to mar the life of the clan with the decline of their aging father's authority.[6] Unlike Jacob, however, the brothers are incapable of digesting these crucial aspects of Joseph's message. To them, their younger brother, with all his manipulations and his dreams of rule, is everything that their fathers rejected. He is like a Babylonian, an Egyptian. Even the interpreting of dreams is not a Jewish custom but a science of the Egyptians.[7] As R. Levi argues, when the brothers say, "Look, here comes the dreamer," what they are really driving at is "Here comes the one who would ensnare them into serving foreign overlords."[8] It is therefore with no small pleasure that they take the first opportunity to tear the cloak of his authority off of Joseph, sell him to a caravan of traders, and send him where they believe he rightly belongs: Egypt.

In Egypt, Joseph does indeed thrive, rising rapidly in every task assigned him by Potiphar, the Egyptian officer who has purchased him. At first it seems as though all he must do to succeed is apply his formidable talents, and all will be well. But it soon turns out that this is not the case – that there is a fundamental contradiction between the ways of power and the purist ideals on which Joseph was raised. Such a crisis first appears in the Joseph story in the episode in which he is subjected to the advances of Potiphar's wife. When it becomes clear that she cannot be deterred, Joseph is faced with the decision of his life. Everything he has worked for and achieved stands to be destroyed if he refuses her, and yet to accept her is to sacrifice the most basic teachings from his father's house. As taught in a parable of the school of R. Ishmael, Joseph's father appears to him in the window over Potiphar's bed, saying: "Your brothers will have their names inscribed upon the stones of the priestly garments [in the future Jerusalem] and yours among theirs. Do you wish to have your name erased from among theirs in order to be called a patron of harlots?"[9] More than this, to accept her means to allow the immediate exigencies of power to dictate right and wrong, and therefore to become just as the Egyptians are, doing everything in the service of their empire-idol. This is the meaning of the dictum of R. Avin that Potiphar's wife had an idol over the bed to which she struggled to bring Joseph. In that moment, the quest for power itself stood to become the god in whose service he worked.[10]

Potiphar's wife confronts Joseph with the dilemma faced by his great-grandfather Abraham: Succeed according to society's standards by adopting its values, or smash the idol and become a failure and a laughing-stock. At this moment, Joseph evidences the exceptional strength that is in him, and he succeeds in resisting.[11] If the price of power is adultery, we believe him to be saying, this price is too high, and his career comes to a wretched close in an Egyptian dungeon. For long years he rots in the pit, his life ruined.

In later rabbinic literature, this painful triumph over the Egyptian temptress is understood as a representation of what Joseph had to endure throughout his entire subsequent life. Thus in one vivid dialogue, Joseph is depicted as trying to fend off Potiphar's wife, only to find that it is Egypt itself that is seeking to seduce him:

> She said to him: "Yield to me." He said: "No."
>
> She said: "I will have you imprisoned." He said: "The Lord frees the captives" (Psalms 146.7).
>
> She said: "I will bend your proud posture [with slavery]." He said: "The Lord raises up those who are bent down" (Psalms 146.8).
>
> She said: "I will blind your eyes [with idolatry]." He said: "The Lord gives sight to the blind" (Psalms 146.8).
>
> She offered him a thousand talents of silver to yield to her, "to lie with her, to be near her" (Genesis 39.10). But he would not listen to her: Neither "to lie with her" – in this world; nor "to be near her" – in the world to come.[12]

Since Joseph does succeed in remaining a Jew to the end of his days, and one whose children themselves stay Jews and become leaders in Israel, the rabbis recognize this first spiritual victory as being symbolic of his far greater achievement of wielding power in Egypt and yet using it in the service of his people. It is thus the refusal of Potiphar's wife that, according to R. Johanan in the name of R. Meir, earns Joseph his place as a Jew: "From this was he worthy to be made a shepherd."[13]

Yet this sanguine assessment of Joseph's life was not accepted by the rabbis unanimously. Among the great commentators were those who claimed that Joseph's behavior in Egypt was flawed, criticizing his adoption of an impressive series of Egyptian customs ("Why did Joseph die before his brothers? ... Rabi said: Because he embalmed his father"[14]); his willingness to allow his servitude to Egypt to dishonor the Jewish patriarch who was his father ("In the opinion of the rabbis: Nearly five times did Judah say: 'Your servant, my father,' 'your servant, my father.' Yet he [Joseph] heard it and kept silent"[15]); and the arrogance of rule that disfigured his character even as an adult (R. Judah also said in the name of Rav ... : Why did Joseph die before his brothers? Because he conducted himself with rulership"[16]). They referred to Joseph as "bones," the symbol of living death in exile;[17] and as a cask of wine that had been emptied of its contents.[18] Even an ostensibly supportive commentator remarks that Joseph's great achievements as a Jew take place in private.[19] And these unflattering statements come on top of the criticism leveled against Joseph by the books of the Bible dealing with Persia, all of which considered his performance in Egypt to be in one way or another troubling.

The reason for the ambiguity in the tradition is that, despite Joseph's survival as a Jew, it is far from clear what lessons he actually draws from the years lost in Pharaoh's prison. For the truth is that the story of Potiphar's wife, in which Joseph sacrifices all he has gained of earthly power to triumph as a Jew, does not repeat itself. If anything, the opposite seems to be the case: Never again does Joseph refuse the order of a superior, and nothing he does for the rest of his life works in contravention of his own increase in power – and that of the god-king he serves. It is almost as though his encounter with Potiphar's wife is also his last stand as a shepherd, and the lesson he draws from the dungeon is that to be an idealist in Egypt is untenable.

It is true that Joseph's work in the service of Pharaoh ultimately prepares Egypt to survive seven years of famine, apparently saving the Jews and all of Egypt from starvation. But from the viewpoint of the shepherd, there is a horrible sense in which everything is lost here. For Joseph's life's work becomes the construction of the Egyptian house of bondage, an idol such as Abraham had sacrificed everything to reject. Dying in political triumph, ruler of the world as he had dreamed as a boy, the narrative nevertheless posthumously hands Joseph his punishment for having collaborated with idolatry: It is two centuries and more before his final, Jewish wish is granted and his bones are brought out of Egypt to be buried in Shechem in the land of his fathers. In the meantime, the idol he has himself assisted in building goes about flaying the flesh from the backs of his children and their descendants – until Moses, raised amid the idolatry of the Egyptian court, follows in the steps of his forefather Abraham, becoming a shepherd, returning to God, and destroying the work of Joseph's hands with a stick.

The bitter ironies of this tale are endemic to the thought of the earliest Jews: Yes, mankind might have perished but for the successes of this idol-state, and a Jew might save his people and save the world by building the greatest empire-idol of them all. The Joseph narrative, for all its miserable ambiguity, makes clear that while the empire-idol is the source of spiritual death, it is also the fount of physical life – and hence its allure. Without Joseph's Egypt, there would have been no Jews. But what kind of salvation is it to return to the house of bondage, serve it, build it that others may serve it, and in so doing increase the suffering and idolatry in the world? Is this not evil itself?

The argument in this direction is so strong that the three later Persian political writings, all of which in principle defend Joseph's decision to go into the service of Egypt, are nevertheless at pains to reject various decisions Joseph makes in trying to come to terms with his servitude.

In Daniel, the argument against Joseph is that he erred in adopting Egyptian ways in order to gain favor and the power this entailed.[20] According to this way of looking at things, there is no need for the Jew to make even the smallest compromise on any of his principles to advance in a foreign court, because political success depends directly on scrupulous observance of traditional Jewish ritual and faith. Thus keeping kosher miraculously makes Daniel and his fellows stronger and more handsome than those who eat the meat served by the Babylonian king, and their refusal to follow state laws that conflict with Judaism is of no consequence: The death penalty miraculously fails to work when applied to Jews, and a swift demise awaits those who attempt to enforce it.[21] The secret to success is therefore piety in its most obvious form: Sacrifice nothing of the law, and salvation will come from heaven – without much waiting or speculation required to see it.

In Nehemia, there is no miraculous reconciliation between Jewish piety and political interest, and so no criticism of Joseph for having compromised his outward Jewishness to gain power. Rather, the criticism is that having gained power, Joseph failed to use it to do right. Thus Nehemia, in a position similar to Joseph's as a close adviser of the king of Persia, uses his influence to allow the Jews to return to the land of Israel and rebuild their autonomy and military power in Jerusalem, whereas Joseph appears loath to approach Pharaoh to ask for his people's freedom.[22]

Even more stunning is Nehemia's rejection of the manner in which Joseph ruled in Egypt. Since Joseph always understands his role to be advancing the interest of his master, he has no compunction about taking advantage of the years of bitter famine to extort land and livestock from the starving populace and ultimately to reduce the Egyptian people themselves to slavery, all in exchange for grain that he had previously taken from them in taxes. As we are told:

> So Joseph bought all the land of Egypt for Pharaoh, for every Egyptian sold his field, because the famine prevailed over them, and the land became Pharaoh's .... Then Joseph said to the people: "Behold, I have bought you and your land this day for Pharaoh. Here is grain for you, and you will sow the land. And it will be that at harvest times, you will give a fifth to Pharaoh, and four-fifths will be your own ...."
>
> They said: "You have saved our lives."[23]

Nehemia, having arrived in Jerusalem, discovers that the analogous situation has been taking place in the land of Israel: The Jewish landholders have been lending to the populace so that they may survive the famine and the king's taxes and then foreclosing on the land and driving the people into poverty and slavery. When he hears of it, however, he is outraged:

> I reprimanded the nobles and the rulers ... and I held a great assembly against them. I said to them: "We have redeemed our brothers, the Jews who were sold to the gentiles, as best we were able. Will you now sell your brothers, or have them sold to us? ... I likewise, and my brothers and my servants, have lent them money and grain. I pray you, let us release this debt. Restore to them, I pray you, even today, their lands, their vineyards, their olive yards and their houses, as well as the interest on the money, the grain, the wine and the oil, that you exact from them."
>
> They said: "We will restore them. We will require nothing of them. We will do as you say."[24]

Thus Nehemia avoids the utopianism of Daniel in which every political goal may in fact be achieved without compromising anything. But rejected as well is the premise of the Joseph story, in which the statesman is inevitably the servant of the state-idol and its values, a taskmaster in the construction of the house of bondage. In Nehemia, the Jew may use the politics of a foreign empire to achieve what is right, provided he can move beyond the exclusive concern for the king's interest and exercise his own will with the power he has attained.

But what if one is not already the king's adviser? What if one is far less powerful – as Joseph and Daniel were at the beginning? We know nothing of how Nehemia rose to power, and herein lies a profound question: Is Joseph right in compromising so much to become Pharaoh's vizier? Is Daniel right in compromising nothing whatsoever to become Darius' vizier?

In the middle ground between them is the standpoint adopted in the book of Esther. Mordechai accepts Joseph's claim that if the Jews wish to survive the famine, they must have a friend in Egypt. This is precisely why he chooses not to live in the Jewish quarter but in the fortress of Susa, the "Egypt" of the Esther story, downplaying his Jewish identity and spending his time in the pursuit of power in the court of Ahashverosh. He believes in doing the work of the world, and he does it according to its own rules. This is why the rabbis taught that "the descendants of Rachel are alike in the miracles they experience and in their greatness" – the descendants of Rachel being Joseph, Mordechai, and Esther.[25] Both narratives contemplate a significant sacrifice in terms of the outward signs of one's Jewishness in order to achieve greater ends; and in both cases, due to the talents of these figures, the result is indeed great political achievements.

Yet in refusing to obey the king's order to bow down before Haman, Mordechai too denies the necessary conclusion of the story of Joseph in Egypt – that one either refuses to enter the court as a servant of the king, or else becomes an instrument of the king's will in all things. For Mordechai, the elevation of the vizier to exclusive power represents a line beyond which one cannot continue serving the master without losing everything, a line beyond which no Jew, and indeed no man, should go. True, the Jew can and must compromise, obey, and bend to gain power that can be used for good. But in the end, salvation can never come from gaining power, only by *expending* the power that has been gained to alter the course of events. If this is true, then the power to bring redemption can come only through rejecting Joseph's road, as Mordechai does, and traversing the road of Moses and Abraham, which is the road of disobedience and war.

8

Amalek

Beyond the insinuation of idolatry, the narrative sends a second, unmistakable signal that the introduction of Haman into the story is a red-flag event, a point of no return beyond which there is no choice but to drop every pretense of political accommodation and fight. For Haman, we are told, is an Agagite. Writers have argued over whether Haman is supposed to be a literal descendent of Agag, king of the Amalekites, who had led them against the Jews in the first years of the Israelite kingdom five centuries earlier, or whether the reference is intended to be figurative. But in either case, the association is clear and the narrative stresses it in various ways so that it cannot be dismissed. Mordechai himself is introduced as being a Benjaminite, a great-grandson of Kish, and therefore a relation of Saul, son of Kish, who became the first king of the Jews and united them in the war against Agag.[1] Moreover, the war against the Amalekites itself goes back even further, dating from the first days of the Jews in the desert, when Amalek harassed the liberated slaves without mercy. The result is that Haman is not merely "the enemy of the Jews" because of his determination to murder them, nor is he simply an anti-Semite, although this is also the case. Haman the Agagite is heir to a conflict that has been with the Jews from the day they left Egypt and became a people.

The exodus of the Jews from Egypt is the central figure around which all of later biblical and Jewish history is built: To do God's will, Israel must leave "the house of bondage," where they have been enslaved to the will of arbitrary men, and strike out into the wilderness of Sinai in search of a truth and a law that derives from something higher than this. Only once they have attained such a truth and such a law is it possible to proceed, armed now with both freedom and knowledge, to the land of the promised redemption.

This message is one of eternal hope for the Jews and for all mankind, and yet it is hardly one of optimism. Having left Egypt amid signs and wonders, the Jews find themselves very far from utopia. The books of Moses relate that immediately upon arriving in the wilderness, the entire project is threatened with ruin by two challenges that hound the Jews throughout the years to come, and throughout the millennia to come. The first is internal to the camp of the Jews: the loss of nerve and embitterment against the physical hardship that must be endured – the lack of water, and then the lack of food, and then the lack of water again.[2] The second is external: the ambush by the Amalekite fighters who fall upon the freed slaves – untrained in bearing arms, burdened by their women, their aged, and their children and exhausted from the desert – slaughtering them without mercy.

In both cases, the narrative reports that the Jews are saved from certain death by a miracle, and yet there is a difference. The hardship that comes of physical duress is inevitable. Every great struggle is fraught with difficulty; were it not, it would hardly be worth remembering. But the difficulties imposed by the war waged on the Jews by Amalek are not inevitable. They are the choice of men, and the judgment of the biblical narrative against the men who chose to become such persecutors is harsh. The books of Moses promise an eternal war against Amalek until the very name of this people is obliterated from under heaven: "And the Lord said to Moses: I will utterly blot out the remembrance of Amalek from under heaven …. Because the Lord has sworn by his throne that the Lord will wage war with Amalek from one generation to the next."[3]

There is clearly something greater here than meets the eye. Most marauding desert tribes are in no sense eternal, nor do they boast either the merits or the demerits necessary for God to bother vowing to wage war against them. Moreover, while the Amalekites are certainly idolaters, the imperative to war against them is even more brutal than that decreed against the Canaanite nations: The Canaanite idolatries are to be eliminated from the land of Israel so that they should not be a snare to the Jews, but those who flee the land will be spared. Here there is no mention of idols, no mention of snares, and no mention of the land. Instead, Amalek is to be warred against "from one generation to the next," wherever they may be found "under heaven," until not only they but their memory as well is "blotted out." Who are these men?

A more direct expression of what is at stake is found in Deuteronomy, where Moses tells the story of the Amalekite attack at Refidim a second time:

> Remember what Amalek did to you along the way, when you had come out of the land of Egypt. How he met you along the way, and attacked your rear and all those who were faltering behind, and you were faint and weary, and he feared not God. Therefore, when the Lord has given you rest

from all the enemies about you in the land which the Lord your God has
given you for an inheritance to possess it, you will blot out the memory of
Amalek from under heaven. Forget not.[4]

Here the text enumerates three aspects of the events at Refidim to explain the
relentless stance to be taken by the Jews against Amalek for all time: First,
Amalek attacked those who were worst off. Second, Amalek attacked when
it was clear that the Jews were powerless to fight. And third, Amalek did not
fear God.

Thus it is not merely the fact that Amalek made war against Israel that
earned them the eternal enmity of the Jews. For there may be many reasons
to kill when a force of many thousands is marching through the desert.
Wars are fought against rival powers to eliminate them as a threat, or to
despoil them, or to enhance one's own reputation. But in all of these cases,
the Amalekites should have sought to engage the Jews as a military force,
attacking the best men and the least tired in order to destroy them as a
threat, or take them and their possessions into captivity, or gain in stature
for having demolished a formidable power. But in none of these instances
should they have wished to pursue the course they did, cutting down "those
who were faltering behind" – widowed women burdened with children, the
old and the sick. Having drenched the sands of Sinai with the blood of the
weak and the helpless, they would be no closer to removing a threat, no
closer to taking spoil, no closer to glory. What could possibly be the purpose
of such a crime?

One answer, of course, could be that there is no purpose beyond the pleasure
involved, beyond the sensation of unrefined liberty that is the spring of cruelty.
There are those in the world who need no excuse to taste of this and so enjoy
the anguish of the other.

But even if this is part of the picture, Amalekite tactics are more likely to
have been directed toward another purpose. The territory of the Amalekites
was in the Negev, in the southern reaches of the land of Canaan. If the Jews
were to make their way directly across the wilderness of Sinai, it would be the
land of Amalek that they would enter first. The threat to Amalekite interests
was overt, and the Amalekite response methodical: They kill the weak in order
to induce the Israelite political and military leadership to give up on the possibility of a more serious fight and back off. For when one attacks the weakest
members of society, this is an attack on the leadership and on the soldiers as
well – not on their bodies, but on their spirit, their sense of rule, and therefore
on their ability to fight. Damaged enough in early rounds of applied terror,
even the most physically powerful opponent may be made to feel that control
is lost and that further engagements will bring worse – even that capitulation

and "peace" are preferable to further confrontation. The most basic method of terror warfare even today is just this: the use of applied cruelty against innocents, the more efficiently to forestall the need for direct military engagement.

And there is good reason to think that Amalekite terror worked precisely as intended. For while the Jews do manage to win by a miracle in their first engagements with Amalek deep in Sinai, the price of battle is high: When twelve representatives of the Jewish leadership subsequently cross into Canaan to gain an understanding of the forces they will have to challenge, "whether they are strong or weak, few or many,"[5] the result is a complete collapse of nerve. Still feeling the lashes dealt them by a few detachments of Amalekite fighters far from Canaan, the extrapolation to full-scale war is for them simply inconceivable. They gape at the might and fortifications of Amalek in the south, of the Hittites, Jebusites, and Emorites on the central mountain ridge, and of the Canaanites in the plains and valleys, and the majority of them return with spirits crushed, unequivocally and absurdly reporting: "All the people that we saw in the land are men of great stature .... We were in our own sight as grasshoppers, and so we were in their sight."[6]

There are, it is true, a few men of unquenched spirit among the Jewish leaders – Caleb from the tribe of Judah and Joshua from the line of Joseph are named – who are adamant that the strength of the Canaanites is exaggerated, saying: "Let us go up and possess it, for we are certainly capable of it."[7] But their voices fail to carry the day, and the leadership, supported by most of the people, insists on withdrawal rather than war. And once this position is staked out, the incredible conclusions are quickly drawn. Judging themselves unable to enter the land, the Jews decide they have no choice but to capitulate further and return to slavery in Egypt: "Why has the Lord brought us to this land, to fall by the sword, and that our wives and children should be prey? Would it not be better for us to return to Egypt? ... Let us appoint a leader and return to Egypt."[8] The taste of blood at the hand of Amalek has done its work. The Amalekites have gained themselves peace from the Jews for forty years and more – during which time they continue their abominations at leisure, while the Israelites, restrained from returning to Egypt by Moses, wait out their qualms in a desert purgatory of their own devising.[9]

In this dreadful episode lies the basis of the Jewish God's war against Amalek from generation to generation. Amalek's wrong is in its insistence on savaging those least capable of defending themselves, whether for the pleasure in it, or because it is the least strenuous method of asserting Amalekite control and bringing Jewish military power to its knees. An invalid or a child is for Amalek a tempting target, precisely because they are no threat to him at all. And once he is willing to ask what good may come of destroying these, he inevitably finds satisfactory answers. In so calculating, Amalek pursues his own ends, whatever these may be, without any threshold to stay his hand. Amalek concerns himself with no consequences other than those that a mismove in the shifting contest of earthly power can produce. In the language of the books of Moses, Amalek "fears not God" – and so brings himself into collision with the thought of the Jews, in which to "fear God" is considered a cornerstone of the entire structure of the law and of civilization itself, as the books of Moses demand: "And now, Israel, what does the Lord your God require of you, other than to fear the Lord your God?"[10]

Yet contrary to what might be inferred, the difference between the man who fears God and the one who fears not is not necessarily emotional at all – that is, not necessarily a matter of being afraid. Rather, what is of greatest significance is that those who fear God behave differently toward their fellow men, as is evident from the other uses of this expression in the books of Moses: "You will not curse the deaf, nor place a stumbling block before the blind, and you will fear your God."[11] And: "Love the stranger, for you were strangers in the land of Egypt. You will fear the Lord your God."[12] Similar verses associate the fear of God with respect for the aged, and with the refusal to engage in fraud, the abuse of one's bondsmen, or extortion from those who have taken on loans.[13] All these cases are the same: One may easily harm another who is dependent and weak – the deaf, the aged, the farmer, the slave. A person who "fears God" will recognize a limiting line that he may not cross, while one who "fears not God" will recognize no such line, as suggested by Abraham's infamous assessment of the city of Gerar: "Surely, there is no fear of God in this place, and they will kill me to have my wife."[14]

The disagreement here is not only over whether moral delimitations are recognizable in the nature of the world. It is more profound than this. What Amalek represents is the oldest position in moral philosophy: the denial that, on balance, there is anything to fear about any moral line that might be drawn, since it is strict adherence to evident personal or political interest that rewards most handsomely – the thesis that "crime pays." In contrast, the position of the Jews is that moral boundaries are not only recognizable, but dangerous: that is, that the violation of such a limiting line in one's behavior is itself, on balance, sufficiently imprudent that it must be feared, in effect making life within the confines of moral limiting lines a matter of personal and political interest in this world – the thesis that "crime does not pay."

This remarkable claim is the subject of a parable of the rabbis to the effect that Amalek and Jethro the Midianite, Moses' father-in-law, both served as advisers to Pharaoh, each one beginning from a position of enmity toward the Jews. "But when Jethro beheld that God had blotted out Amalek both from this world and the next, he felt remorse and repented."[15] The suggestion here is that various desert tribes in and around Canaan, Midian included, actually accepted moral norms such as those of Amalek, thereby qualifying any of them to serve as mentors to Pharaoh, whose morally undelimited understanding of his political interest leads him to murder Jewish children at birth. (The midwives Shifra and Pua, on the other hand, are distinguished from Pharaoh in their unwillingness to participate in the slaughter, despite their obvious interest in obeying the law, "for they feared God."[16]) What leads to Jethro's rejection of the position of Amalek – and so to the rabbinic suggestion that he became a convert to Judaism[17] – is not revelation, but prudence: So long as moral claims are aimed at convincing him that he must sacrifice his interest in this world to secure his position in another, he can easily deny the existence of any other world. It is only the recognition that the paradigm of Amalek ultimately brings destruction to its adherents in this world, as well, that can move a pragmatist such as Jethro to think that moral limits must be feared at all.

It is some such process of reasoning that, the rabbis suggest, must bring a non-Jew such as Jethro to approach Moses in the narrative in Exodus and present him with what becomes the Jewish alternative to government according to the Amalekite-Pharaonic paradigm: "Take from among the entire people men of strength, who fear God, men of truth, hating illicit gain, and place them over them."[18] Here, as well, the reason for the demand that the rulers "fear God" is apparent: that they should be unwilling to abuse those in their charge for their own self-interest.

It is important to note that the books of Moses themselves also address the question of the superiority of the Jewish paradigm over the Amalekite one from the perspective of non-Jewish wisdom. The position of such wisdom is represented by the conjurer Bilam, "the man whose eyes are open,"[19] who is commissioned by an ornery Moabite king to curse the Jews. Bilam, however, comes to examine the situation for himself and finds that, regardless of what the desert kings may wish, there is an actual truth to the matter, and it is the opposite of that which they decree. With regard to Amalek, he concludes: "The beginning of all nations is Amalek, but his end is eternal annihilation"[20] – meaning that in all the world, the powerful have always begun from Amalekite premises; but in the end, these prove themselves only to be destructive. With regard to Israel, he concludes: "He has beheld no iniquity in Jacob, and has seen no perversity in Israel .... How goodly are your tents, O Jacob, your dwelling places, Israel .... God brought him up from Egypt, as the horns of the wild ox is God to him, he will devour his enemies among the nations."[21] Far from being a sacrifice of personal and political interest, Bilam urges that the fear of God among the Jews provides them personal well-being as individuals and translates as well into tremendous strength in the confrontation with Israel's external enemies. To "the man whose eyes are open," it is Judaism that is the path to self-interest, and Amalek the path to self-destruction.

The figure of Amalek therefore stands as the anti-Jew, caught up in the most false and destructive of idolatries: the belief that the pursuit of power is the only proper justification of human action, and that the power-idol – more correctly, the human spirit itself as idol – suffices to justify all human action in its pursuit.

Herein lies the distinction between Amalek and other idolatries to which the Jews stand in eternal opposition. As a general matter, idolatry is the subjugation of moral valuation to standards dictated by partial truths deriving from a local, and therefore essentially arbitrary, perspective. As such, every idolatry is evil in principle, even where it seems perfectly benign. One can imagine a tree or a star or a man-god whose adherents are not obliged by its dictates to commit perversity and violence; perhaps they are obligated to do good. Such a theology is an evil and a snare because it denies that the same moral norms are everywhere in force (that "God is one") and so permits all manner of evil in principle. But it is nevertheless possible that its disciples are "God fearing" in the biblical sense – as indeed some pagans in the books of Moses appear to be.[22] They know some version of right and wrong, and they fear to do wrong according to what they know.

In Amalek, we find the reverse case. We have no idea what gods ruled over the Amalekites. None are named, and for all we know, there may have been none at all. What we do know is that whatever gods may have belonged to Amalek, as a people they did not fear any moral boundaries established by them. Unlike even the most depraved of the idolaters of Canaan, they respected no limits on their desire to control all as they found fit.

What is frightening is to recognize how difficult this idea is to uproot – or rather, how difficult it is to implant the belief in moral limits that must be feared if man is to live. This is the reason that, while the commandment to blot out Amalek from the world is stressed again in Deuteronomy, so too is the ominous warning not to forget to do so. The irony, of course, is that God's promise to annihilate the memory of Amalek from the earth is to no small degree undermined by his promise to war against Amalek for untold generations.[23] Like hunger and thirst, there is a sense in which Amalek, although fit to be eradicated in every generation, is nevertheless eternal. Just as man tends to turn away from what he must do to avoid hunger and thirst as soon as he is sated, so too does the willingness to set limits on his behavior erode when he feels safe and is not faced with the consequences. And we know from our own experience, too, that those who deny all limits are forever finding the beautiful words, the high phrases, and the slippery and diseased thoughts needed to strengthen this beast in others, to make them appreciate and approve, and to pull them along and down, men and nations, into their abyss.

Not lightly is Haman referred to over and over as "Haman, the enemy of the Jews." For in his pursuit of power without limit, and in his willingness to destroy all the Jewish people, "the young and the elderly, children and women," so that he might have his way with Mordechai, he repeats precisely the first crime of the Amalekites, who "attacked your rear and all those who were faltering behind" to have their way with the Jews. In so doing, he proves himself to be a true Agagite – whose struggle to eradicate the Jews by bleeding the defenseless among them had begun in the desert wastes a thousand years before he was born.

9

Anti-Semitism

More than a century has passed since the term "anti-Semitism" was invented as another way of referring to hatred of Jews. Today it has come into wide use, yet it conveys as little as it ever did. It still takes no more effort to explain that one "hates Jews" than it does to ascribe "anti-Semitism" to him; and the Jews, of course, were never actually hated for being Semitic, that is, a people of Middle Eastern origin. But the failure to have found a more meaningful name for the disease only reflects on how little we understand it. Some have said that anti-Semitism is a byproduct of Christianity, yet it has haunted Islam from its very foundations. Some have believed it is to be matter of religious persecution, although the Nazis made it a matter of race. And some have argued that it arises from ignorance, yet it has claimed many of the most brilliant minds in history. Anti-Semitism is everywhere, and no race nor creed nor time seems impervious to it. Every people rises and falls, except the Jews. And no hatred has ever been so great, so abiding, and so permanent as the hatred of the Jews. What does it mean?

The Jewish people came into being with anti-Semitism. Indeed, the first time in history that we encounter the Jews as a people, it is amid the rage of an enemy and his plot to destroy them:

> The children of Israel were fruitful and increased abundantly and multiplied and grew exceedingly mighty and the land was filled with them. Now there arose a new king over Egypt who knew not Joseph. He said to his people: "Behold, the people of Israel are more and mightier than we. Come, let us deal wisely with them lest they multiply and it come to pass that when any war should chance, they also join our enemies and fight against us and go up out of the land." Therefore they set taskmasters over them to afflict them with their burdens .... But the more they afflicted them the more they multiplied and grew, and they were mortified on account of

the people of Israel …. And Pharaoh charged all his people saying: "Every son that is born will you cast into the Nile, and every daughter will you keep alive."[1]

This passage is from the opening lines of Exodus, telling us of Pharaoh's hatred for the Israelites living in Egypt, of his decision to undertake a final solution to his Jewish problem. The account of this first decision on a final solution is startling in its prescience, its component parts all too familiar to us. We read that:

(i)   The Jews have attained remarkable success in a foreign land, Egypt.
(ii) Pharaoh assesses the Jews to be "more and mightier than we," although this is clearly absurd.
(iii) Pharaoh fears that the Jews will fly out of his control, rebelling, siding with his opponents, and fleeing Egypt.
(iv) The continued growth of the Jews is received by the Egyptians with horror – "they were mortified."
(v)   Pharaoh decides on a preliminary effort to reduce their strength by imposing special taxation of forced labor.
(vi) Finally, he determines to annihilate the Jews altogether through the slaughter of their male children and the absorption of their women into the Egyptian population.

At first glance, the entire account makes little sense. Successful as the Jews may have been, Pharaoh's assertions to the effect that the Jews had grown more powerful than all Egypt are preposterous. The Nile River basin was one of the great centers of population in the world, its people numbering in the millions. Moreover, nothing in the narrative suggests that any of the Jews had the slightest training in warfare. We are therefore left with the conclusion that Pharaoh and his people were drawn to slaughter the Jews among them, despite their being perfectly good slaves, without any cause at all. And this despite Pharaoh's efforts to couch his argument as though it were a rational, strategic calculation.

The key word for understanding what was taking place among the Egyptians is *vayakutzu* – "and they were mortified" because of the Jews. The Hebrew word has the connotation of being stung, or stabbed by thorns – "and they were stung on account of the Jews." The response to the success of the Jews and their growth is not one of actual fear, but a burning, stinging rage that consumes the Egyptians all the more as their repeated efforts to subjugate them meet with failure. It is this same hatred that we find in the book of Esther, when the vizier's sensation of perfect control is marred by his inability to control the Jew: "All the king's servants who were in the king's gate bowed and prostrated themselves before Haman, for the king had so ordained concerning him. But Mordechai did not bow nor prostrate himself .... When Haman saw that Mordechai did not bow nor prostrate himself, Haman was filled with rage" (3.2,5). And just as the fact of the multiplying Jewish children continues to prick at the Egyptians every time they consider it (the text in Exodus speaks of the growth of the Jews no fewer than nine consecutive times), so too does Haman's pain and hatred deepen upon every encounter with Mordechai:

> Haman went out that day happy and in high spirits, but when Haman saw Mordechai in the king's gate, how he neither stood nor stirred before him, Haman was filled with rage against Mordechai. Haman restrained himself and returned to his house, and he sent for his friends and for Zeresh his wife. Haman recounted to them the glory of his riches, and the great number of his sons, and everything in which the king had promoted him and elevated him above the princes and servants of the king .... "Yet all this is worthless to me, so long as I see Mordechai the Jew sitting at the king's gate" (5.9–11, 13).

It is this stinging in Pharaoh's spirit, and in that of Haman, increasing in intensity until it is no longer tolerable, until something must be done, to which the rabbis alluded when they spoke of the desire to rule as a consuming crocodile – one that can digest anything in the world except for the Jews:

> Nebuchadnezzar, king of Babylonia, had a great crocodile, which swallowed everything thrown to it. Nebuchadnezzar said to Daniel: "So great is its might that it consumes everything that is thrown to it." ... Daniel took straw, hid nails within it, and fed it to the crocodile, rupturing its intestines.[2]

The Jews at first appear to be weak, digestible as straw. But it invariably transpires that these straws are nails: They do not melt away with digestion, but remain solid and sharp under pressure, and so sting ever more painfully the more one bears down upon them.

Crucial here is the way in which relative power is registered by the spirit as it seeks to grasp and control the surrounding world: That which is within the bounds of control is perceived as being small and weak ("We were in our own sight as grasshoppers, and so we were in their sight"); whereas that which is out of control is perceived to be great and powerful ("All the people that we saw in Canaan were men of great stature"). And the spirit can abide by this, remaining sated and quiet, content with what it has devoured – so long as what appears small and weak remains under control in practice, obeying the dictates of the will; whereas that which appears immense and terrifying, and which has, for this reason, been left out of control, is kept safely at a distance where it can do no harm. But the spirit will register pain, even overwhelming pain, a burning that seems as if it will never end, where what was assumed to be under one's control is found to be something other than expected: when one has been rejected by a loved one, when a precious possession has been discovered ruined, or when one is publicly proved unequal to an activity at which one is thought to excel. The hot shame, the fear and anger that come with these things, and their horror, are the contents of the crocodile-mind when the straws in its belly prove to be nails.

The Jew is the epitome of weakness, a slave, an exile, defeated, dispersed, despised. He is the first who should rightly disappear in the face of power. And this is how the ruler understands the Jews as well, too long perceiving them, with the eyes of a materialist, or of Amalek, as being strong only in accord with the arms they can muster. Yet eventually, perhaps having been stung by the arrogant disobedience of one such as Moses or Mordechai, he comes to look more closely and realizes that this is not the case. Instead of conforming to the will of the state, they are forever found to be clutching at some bit of their own agenda – "their laws are different from other people." And this Jewish insistence on a different authority other than the state is for the ruler a direct threat, as Resh Lakish asserted in depicting the Persian view of the Jews as forever arrogant, forever threatening:

> A certain people among us, which, although they are the most contemptible
> of peoples, is nonetheless exceedingly haughty. They desire our evil and are
> forever cursing the king. What is the curse that they utter against us? "The
> Lord is King forever and ever, the nations are perished out of his land"
> (Psalms 10.16).[3]

And it is this tiny, laughable resistance that is always there to be found, that never fails through eternity. No matter how badly he is burned and beaten, the Jew continues rasping out his foolishness, "cursing the king," as Resh Lakish has the Persians say, pursuing what the Czarist secret police referred to as "the protocols of the elders of Zion."[4]

But in awakening to the fact that the Jew cannot easily be brought under control, the ruler invariably makes the transition from considering him inconsequential to vastly exaggerating his power. Since the Jew cannot be ruled, the spirit begins to sense his strength, contrary to all surface indications, to be immense, as in Pharaoh's belief that his Jewish slaves are "more and mightier than we." In Esther, this same phenomenon receives eerie expression in the soothsaying of Zeresh, Haman's wife, for whom any sign of an increase in Jewish power is, as it was for Pharaoh, a sign of imminent doom: "If he be of Jewish descent, this Mordechai, before whom you have begun to fall, you will not prevail against him, but you will surely fall before him" (6.13).[5] Ironically, it is the very weakness of the Jews, their dispersion and lack of a government capable of defending their interests, that then becomes the basis for a paranoia with regard to them. That the Jews are "dispersed in all the provinces of your kingdom" implies that the degree of their subversion can be virtually infinite. Like the king's servants, the Jews are everywhere, and it is a small step from here to controlling the financial system, the press, hostile foreign powers, or the world. It is precisely this same sense of the mysterious power of the Jews that Haman uses to convince the king that there is no choice but to eradicate the menace: "There is a certain people scattered and dispersed among the people in all the provinces of your kingdom, and their laws are different from those of other peoples, and the king's laws they do not keep, so that it is of no benefit for the king to tolerate them. If it please the king, let it be written that they be destroyed" (3.8–9).

It therefore transpires that there is no such thing as a small threat to the fantasy of perfect control. The realm of the spirit's control is either subjugated or not, and the tiniest threat, if permitted to sting long enough, is therefore total. And the Jew – in his endless consultations with old and subversive documents; his perennial reservations; his ceaseless chafing against the will of the state; his conditions, refusals, and disobediences – always places the control of the ruler in doubt, necessarily offends his spirit, necessarily makes mockery of his pretensions to total power. In his tiny steadfastness, his almost pitiful solidity and indigestibility, the Jew succeeds in being the nightmare of every man of perfect rule. He is organized resistance, systematic decontrol, the smashing of the idol.

This success amid weakness of the Jew, the sting and the rage of the one who would rule, and then genocide – this is the eternal formula of anti-Semitism, the reaction of the idol whose power and whose essence the Jew denies, the idol that, upon discovering the flaws in its own power, its own falseness, must deny it at all cost. It is the lashing of the crocodile as it tries to crush the nail of which it is impotent to rid itself.

But then this means that the hatred of the anti-Semite is not without cause. And of course this is the case. We may blame Haman for succumbing to this original sin of the political world, the temptation to let his spirit dictate to him and to the world its totalist fantasy. But once he desires such power, war against the Jew becomes inevitable, as he recognizes in the Jew the desire and the ability to deprive him of what he believes is his right: the ability to attain an unflawed "rule in his own house." It was this that moved Hitler to despise the Jews, with their constant agitation against the imposition of a unified pan-German will on Austria, just as Mordechai detracts from making Persia the subject of the Haman's craving for perfect control. And Stalin, too, and the endless procession of anti-Zionists in Islam – all of whom rage for the restoration of their birthright, for their rule in their house, for the unity and singleness of purpose that can belong to a nation only so long as it is not contaminated by alien elements and alien wills, constantly speaking of something else, constantly seeking a different end to a different story.

To realize this is to comprehend the incomprehensible. It is to recognize that the torment of the Jews in history has a cause. That no matter the time or place, the one who seeks perfect rule will, through exposure to the Jews, relearn the anti-Semitism of Pharaoh and Haman. And in learning it, he will yet again set out to fight this same war, the war between the disobedient and those who can stand no disobedience; between the imposers of limits and those who can accept no limits; between the rejecters of the idols and the spirit-idol that can tolerate no rejection; between Jew and anti-Jew, as the anti-Semite is known when called by his name – a war in which every Jewish child is enlisted at birth, no matter who may wish it otherwise.

But if anti-Semitism is the inevitable false fruit of man's spirit, the figure of the Jew always appearing to the would-be ruler in whoever threatens the heart of his power, then anti-Semitism must exist even before the existence of Pharaoh's persecution of the Jews, even before Abraham, the first Jew. And, indeed, the rabbis understood this to be the case. Thus R. Levi taught:

> Cursed are the wicked, who all devise evil against Israel, each one devising according to his own idea, and then saying, "My device is better than yours."

> Esau said: Cain was a fool for killing his brother in the lifetime of his father, not knowing that his father would still have children. I will not do so, "But let the days of mourning of my father be at hand, then I will slay my brother Jacob" (Genesis 27.41).

> Pharaoh said: Esau was a fool. Did he not know that his brother would have children in the lifetime of his father? I will not make such a mistake, but I will strangle them while they are small and barely out of their mothers' wombs. And so it says: "Every son that is born you will cast into the river" (Exodus 1.22).

> Haman said: Pharaoh was a fool for saying, "Every son that is born you will cast in the river." Did he not know that the daughters would marry and have children? I will not make such a mistake, but will decree "to annihilate, to kill and to destroy" (3.13).

> So Gog and Magog in the time to come will say: Our predecessors were fools for laying their plans, they and their kings together against Israel, not knowing that they have a protector in heaven. I will not do so, but I will first attack their protector and then I will attack them. And so it says: "The kings of the earth stand up and the rulers take counsel together against Lord, and against his anointed" (Psalms 2.2).[6]

In this midrash of R. Levi, the hatred of Haman is recognized in Pharaoh before him, and in Esau, and even in Cain, before there were any Jews to hate. And it recognizes, too, that this hatred will continue to haunt the history of Israel going forward.[7]

Like anti-Semitism, the Jew existed before he was named, before he was born. That a man is thought to be small and weak but is possessed of other higher qualities, that he believes in what is right in the face of all opposition, that he disobeys rather than succumbing to the rule of the strong, that he survives when he should have perished – this is the specter of the Jew that is born in the breast of Cain, the first anti-Jew, the farmer who worked like an animal of burden to provide a suitable sacrifice to the Lord.[8] And when his brother Abel, a shepherd, labored less in the harsh sun and pondered more into the night, so that it was his sacrifice to the Lord that was preferred, he became in Cain's eyes that specter, that fear that had haunted his nightmares – that sting which can never be removed, and being unremovable, continues to impale the spirit, to infect it and inflame it, from Eden to eternity, a hatred so deep that for the sake of it he would murder his brother, that for the sake of it he would raze the world to its very foundations.

PART IV

ESTHER 4.1–4.17

W hen Mordechai learned of all that had been done, Mordechai rent his clothes, and dressed in sackcloth and ashes, and went out into the city, crying out a loud and bitter cry. ²He came as far as the king's gate, although none might enter the king's gate clothed in sackcloth. ³In every province, wherever the king's command and his law reached, there was great mourning among the Jews, and fasting and crying and wailing, many of them lying in sackcloth and ashes.

⁴Esther's maids and her chamberlains came and told her, and the queen was exceedingly distressed, and she sent garments to clothe Mordechai so that he might remove his sackcloth, but he would not accept them. ⁵Esther summoned Hatach, from among the king's chamberlains, whom he had placed in her service, and charged him to go out to Mordechai to learn what this was and why it was.

⁶Hatach went out to Mordechai, to the city square, which was in front of the king's gate. ⁷Mordechai told him of all that had happened to him, and of the money that Haman had offered to pay into the royal treasuries for the Jews, to have them destroyed. ⁸And he gave him a copy of the law that had been circulated in Susa sanctioning the annihilation of the Jews, so that he might show it to Esther and speak to her, charging her to go to the king, to plead with him and to entreat him for her people. ⁹Hatach came to Esther and told her what Mordechai had said.

¹⁰Esther said to Hatach, instructing him to tell Mordechai: ¹¹"All the king's servants and the people of the king's provinces know that there is but one law for any man or woman who comes to the king

in the inner court without having been summoned: that he be put
to death, except if the king extends to him the gold scepter that he
may live – and I have not been summoned to the king for thirty
days now."

[12]They told Mordechai what Esther had said. [13]Mordechai said
to reply to Esther: "Do not imagine in your heart that you, of all
the Jews, will escape because you are in the king's palace. [14]For if
you insist on remaining silent at this time, relief and deliverance will
come to the Jews from elsewhere, but you and your father's house
will perish. And who knows whether it was not for such a time as
this that you came into royalty?"

[15]Esther said to respond to Mordechai: [16]"Go assemble all the
Jews present in Susa and fast for me. Do not eat and do not drink
for three days, night and day, and I and my maids will fast as well.
Then I will go in to the king, though it is against the law. And if
I perish, I perish." [17]Mordechai took his leave and did everything
that Esther had instructed him to do.

10

Pressure

In the silent halls of the palace, the decree of extermination falls like the closing of the gates at sunset, and the wretched spirit of the vizier is sated. But in the streets, the people are dumbfounded, Jew and gentile alike, for if Haman will now murder an entire nation on account of the refusal of one man to bow, what might he do next?

Mordechai seeks no advice and convenes no councils to discuss the decree of extermination. Upon being confronted with it, his response is immediate: He takes to the streets. After putting on coarse cloth and smearing himself with soot, he walks through the broad places of the city screaming and wailing in grief. People rush to the windows and to the doorways. Passersby stop to take in the spectacle, to ask who is this man and what has befallen him. He makes his way through the onlookers and arrives at the palace, where the guards recognize him but prevent him from entering, for "none might enter the king's gate clothed in sackcloth" (4.2). They push him aside, threatening him, thinking he might be dangerous to the king in his anguish. Eventually, they merely push him off a distance, lest any of the king's ministers catch sight of him and blame them for allowing such a breach of decorum.

Mordechai takes a number of steps back and sits down in the street. He takes up his crying again, his presence accosting all those who enter the king's gate to pursue their duties. Some who enter the palace, seeing Mordechai there, can barely hide a smile of satisfaction, for at last the insolent Jew has been put in his place. Others, with whom Mordechai has found favor in the past, whom he has advised or whom he has assisted in various ways, gather around him. Some offer him information, others advice. He interrupts, asking them: What kind of government is this? Do you not see what has been born? Do you not see that a man of this kind will murder anyone of you who raises his head, together with all of his loved ones, even his entire people? What will become of all your interests now? And among them there are those whose hearts break to see him so, and those who understand the meaning of the thing.

Some of the rabbis emphasized Mordechai's prayers at this moment.[1] And there is no reason to doubt that supplication arises arises in the heart of one condemned to death, or that he may come to regret his faults and fear God as he never has before. But it is not for his grief, or for his repentance, that Mordechai's reaction to the decree must be considered exceptional. It is for the open, public nature of his outcry. To understand this, we need only remember that other decree, of the slaughter of the Hebrew children by Pharaoh, which, so far as we know, met with no public response on the part of any Jew whatsoever. Pharaoh ordered that the Jews be reduced to slavery and hard labor, and met with no outcry worthy of having been recorded. Then he ordered that the midwives murder the male children, and still there was no reaction such as Mordechai's. Finally, when the servants of Pharaoh begin to take up the slaughter in earnest, coming into the houses of the Jews in search of the new-born infants, tearing them away from mothers weak from birth, carrying them past fathers with teeth and fists clenched in agony. loading them onto wagons with the howling others, howling with hunger, with dirt, with fear, and finally throwing them into the Nile to drown – when all this was actually done before the eyes of the Jews, they responded with silence.

Of course, the books of Moses recount this story in order to relate not the silence, but that resistance that did take place: how the Jewish midwives refuse to collaborate in the atrocity, lying to Pharaoh in order to avoid incurring his blame; how, once the killings have started, Jocheved and her daughter hide her baby and find him a place of refuge; and how Pharaoh's daughter protects the child against her father and the state. It is by means of the bravery of these women that a leader is born to Israel through whom the Jewish people are saved.[2] And yet these, too, are stories of silence. What resistance there is takes place behind a veil of deception, concealed from the state and its officials, as well as from the Jewish public. Moreover, the resistance of the Jewish women in Egypt is in an important sense *apolitical* – its aim being to ameliorate the effects of the decree in some limited way, while making no effort to influence Pharaoh and his advisers to alter the policy of the state itself. Of course, the reason for the lack of political resistance is clear enough. The fear of the state is so great that any such effort is thought to be useless and suicidal. But the fact remains that in the absence of any evident opposition to the decree itself, the state has no reason whatsoever to move from its course.

Resistance to Ahashverosh's decree is not in principle any more safe or certain than opposition would have been in Egypt. In fact, in making public his opposition to the decree, the only thing that Mordechai can know with certainty is that he courts immediate punishment. Nevertheless, he chooses to take his anger and grief to the broad places of the capital and to the king's gate, for a reason – for a *political* reason. And that is that a claim lodged in silence, an appeal made in silence, an interest defended in silence, is one that is not lodged, not made, and not defended. The entire purpose of Ahashverosh in elevating Haman to the point where his will alone determines questions of state is to do away with politics, to silence the struggle among competing claims and truths. And if Mordechai is to prevent a repetition of the slaughter of the Jews by Pharaoh, his only hope is to find a way to break Haman's monopoly and allow another voice somehow to be heard, a voice that will speak for a different policy.

In politics, the effect of the voice that is heard by the decision maker is understood by means of a metaphor. It is known as pressure. When a trusted adviser threatens to resign if a policy is not changed; when a province is in rebellion over a measure promulgated by the central government; when a foreign government instructs its ambassador to threaten a boycott of the king's goods or war – they exert pressure. In these cases, the threat is overt, the resistance not merely evident but extortionary, suggesting to the ruler what he has not wanted to hear: that the course upon which he has embarked is not worth the cost. And while few are the individuals who can exert the pressure of a trusted adviser, a rebellious province, or the ambassador of a foreign power, this does not mean that others are without recourse. We know from experience that the public can succeed in exerting pressure on the state as well. This is the reason that flatterers and lobbyists come to court to press their claims with the king's advisers; that the public is urged to correspond with officials en masse; that public protest is conducted in the streets. These things are done so that those who may ultimately have influence can themselves be influenced, so that at the appropriate moment they may take up the cause. When this chain of pressure is understood, it becomes possible to plan a political campaign whose purpose is to muster every possible source of pressure on the ruler in favor of a change in policy, and to neutralize those forces that are propelling the state in its present direction.

Elementary though the political campaign of influence may be to politics in every society, it is astonishing that not only the skills for such work but even the awareness of its possibility do not exist among all peoples at all times. Thus the Jews in the time of Pharaoh, even those who resisted the persecution at the risk of their lives, nevertheless could not imagine responding politically. Indeed, it is the fear of confronting the ruler, the certitude that reservations voiced will result only in punishment, that is the hallmark of the thought of a slave. For this reason, the cruelties of Pharaoh's government continued for generations before any Jew thought to approach the state with the demand that they cease: before Moses, who had grown up amid the politics of the court – who had, as the rabbis suggested, grown up playing at removing the crown from Pharaoh's head and placing it on his own[3] – realized that even Pharaoh would change course if sufficient pressure were brought to bear. The story of the destruction of the Jews in Europe in our own time is likewise characterized by the utter lack of political pressure on the German regime and its allies to cease their atrocities. Even in the free countries, the activities of the Jews to bring pressure upon their governments were minimal, while the Germans themselves were ferocious in lobbying foreign governments to the ends of the earth to destroy those Jews under their control. And when one side applies pressure to attain the execution of a policy, and this policy meets with no resistance from the other side, the results are foregone.[4]

Like Moses, Mordechai is no Hebrew slave, but a man of the court, for whom the need for the political campaign against the decree is clear and pressing. And it is this that moves him to overcome the fear and self-doubt that grips every man rising to challenge the mighty, saying: "Who am I, that I should bring the people of Israel out of Egypt?" – to which the only answer can be that of the ministering angel, descending with a crown to place on the head of every man or woman setting out on a course of truth, and with the message: "I will be with you."[5] And so Mordechai, too, goes out to deliver his people.

When he first goes into the public places, Mordechai has no way of knowing who will respond, or whether they will respond to the echoes of his cries in their conscience, to the memory of past favors he had done for them, or to their own interest in checking the power of the vizier. Nor can he know for certain who may actually be able to exert the necessary influence to help. But he makes the case as well as it can be made and to as many as he can reach: He dresses in mourning, that all who see him may appreciate his terror; he cries as he makes his way through the public places of the capital, that all may recognize the crisis that has come upon them, whether they have heard the decree or not; and he takes his protest to the king's gate, that every man of influence, means, and resources may be directly confronted with what has been done, requiring each to make a conscious judgment that might otherwise have been avoided behind a pretense of "We didn't know." In doing these things, he forces them all to decide whether they are in support of the policy or against it – and if they are indeed against it, whether they are man enough to join in with pressure of their own.

11

Court Jew

Perhaps Mordechai succeeds in touching others among the courtiers in the four days he sits in sackcloth at the entrance to the palace.[1] But as is often the case, the narrative tells us only of the one instance that in the end proves to have mattered: the queen. Upon hearing of his protest, Esther is "exceedingly distressed" (4.4) and sends Mordechai a change of clothes that he may immediately strip off the dirt in which he is attired. This he refuses to do, and only then does Esther send a trusted servant to inquire into the cause of the uproar.

The sequence of events tells us much about the mindset of the queen. Esther is "exceedingly distressed," as it turns out, not by the impending slaughter of her people, of which she is ignorant, but by the appearance of her cousin before the court carrying on so and in such attire. Knowing nothing of the background, apparently not even of the confrontation that had erupted between Mordechai and the vizier days earlier, she fears only that offense will be given against the norms of court conduct, the law, and the king himself. She sees everything that Mordechai has taught her about gaining favor and influence being set to torch, and everything he has gained by years of building himself up as a loyal servant of the king about to be ruined in a single, incomprehensible act. Esther does not even need to know the subject under discussion and yet she is already aghast, refusing to go along, trying to make him stop.

When the chamberlain comes out to Mordechai, we find that the Jew is fully prepared to receive him. Any suspicion that Mordechai's act may have been ill prepared and impulsive is allayed when he explains the content of the decree, relates inside information about the vizier's effort to bribe the king, and then hands him a copy of the decree itself that he has prepared. Finally, he comes forward with a demand: that Esther go in to the king and urge him to repeal the law.

Esther quickly sends the servant back with a reply: She cannot do it. Of course, she is too polite to refuse outright, but refuse she does. And she explains herself: "All the king's servants and the people of the king's provinces know that there is but one law for any man or woman who comes to the king in the inner court without having been summoned: That he be put to death, except if the king extends to him the gold scepter that he may live – and I have not been summoned to the king for thirty days now" (4.11). Her reply thus consists of a barrage of responses, one tumbling over the next:

(i)   No, because it is against the law.
(ii) No, because I will die.
(iii) He will not forgive me because no one else behaves this way.
(iv) He will not forgive me because he does not care enough for me.
(v)   No, because my effort will change nothing.

Here, in full view, is Esther's reaction to the threat of a confrontation over the policy of the king. She cannot imagine succeeding, she is afraid to die – and there is little else. Having learned how important it is to win favor, Esther nonetheless falters when it comes time to take the next step, using this favor to exert her own influence. In her mind, the ruler cannot be approached, his mind cannot be changed, his wrath is certain and fierce. Her self-image is nothing but the corollary: She cannot possibly challenge him, she cannot change his mind, she will be destroyed if she tries.[2]

Here, too, we see the shadows of Moses' confrontation with Pharaoh. When Moses first comes to the Jews of Egypt to say he has come to liberate them, they joyously accept his leadership and his mission, for who would not agree to be quickly, easily liberated from servitude? Yet Pharaoh is not inclined to let the Jews go upon Moses' first demand, nor his second, nor his third. And his displeasure is expressed not only in words: He disapproves of the resistance instigated by the new Jewish leadership and – much as does Haman at the first sign of resistance – moves with overwhelming force to crush any deviation from submission, increasing dramatically the work demanded of the Jews and threatening punishment if they do not maintain their schedule. For this bruising confrontation the Jews are completely unprepared, and rather than responding with further steps against Pharaoh, they recoil in fear over what they have done. Turning against Moses and Aaron, they say to them: "The Lord look upon you and judge, for you have made us despised in the eyes of Pharaoh and in the eyes of his servants, putting a sword in their hands with which to slay us."[3]

The tendency to think first about the reactions of the powerful ("What will the gentiles think?") is well known in every Jewish politics. And here it is evident that this line of reasoning was already well ingrained in Egypt, at the very

founding of the Jewish people itself, when two opposing and familiar political parties formed over the looming confrontation with Pharaoh: The one,
led by Moses and Aaron, asserted that Pharaoh had slaughtered the Jews as
children, oppressed them as adults, and now sought to break them and drive
them to despair; there was nothing to be gained by appeasing him. The other,
apparently comprising most of the "official" leadership of the enslaved people, argued that only greater evil would come of angering Pharaoh, and that
this course would only bring senseless destruction: Better not to rock the boat.
Indeed, the rabbis suggested that as Moses and Aaron walked through the
street on the way to their first encounter with Pharaoh, the Jewish elders who
had at first supported them stole away one by one, so that when the actual
moment of confrontation came, there were none left to back them.[4] Returning
to their hovels, defeated in a battle that had not even taken place, they might
easily have said to one another: We were in our own sight as grasshoppers, and
so we were in Pharaoh's sight as well.[5]

Invariably, the slave is afraid to fight his master. A broken spirit also seeks
the sensation of stability and control, and this stability is supplied by the assurance of the solidity, the inevitability, of the ruler's will. The ruler's anger, on the
other hand, and fear of his punishment, are the greatest threats to this stability.
The Jew who argues for a campaign of pressure, or any other confrontation
with the power of the ruler, therefore finds that his first opponent is the leadership of the Jews themselves – those leaders who, like the elders in Moses'
time, have made their careers in accommodation. In them we have the classic
image of the "court Jew," whose success has always depended on the favor of
the ruler, and whose life security and self-esteem are built upon it as well. And
since it is ultimately the ruler's acceptance that this leader desires above all
else, the very possibility of such confrontation and the loss of such acceptance
strikes him with terror.

Yet despite her condition of subservience to the king, Esther is not a slave.
She is the most successful woman in the kingdom, accustomed to the dotage
and service of others. Does not her constant exertion of her will in royal life set
her far apart from the example of the Jewish slaves in Egypt, afraid even to lift
their heads to make a request before Pharaoh, lest he destroy them?

Closer to Esther's situation is Joseph. Highly talented and self-assured,
Joseph at no point hesitates to defy those who stand in his way. The resentment
of his brothers does not deter him from seeking to impose order on them as a
boy. And as lord over Egypt, he appears to notice no man's opposition as he
extorts the entire land into his command, buys the population into servitude,
and transfers it to the cities. Joseph is a man of immense ambition and stamina,
and nothing about him suggests the character or behavior of a slave. Here, it
seems at first glance, is a court Jew who is free.

But it is not as simple as it looks to become vizier to Pharaoh. As a Hebrew shepherd arriving in Egypt, Joseph is considered an "abomination"[6] – the slaughterer of the Egyptian god by trade, he is the very incarnation of the idol smasher: arrogant, self-absorbed, and unassimilable. With remarkable skill, he leaves all this behind, the narrative detailing a seemingly endless series of acquired traits and skills that render him ever more palatable to Egyptian tastes: He shaves, he interprets dreams, he adopts an Egyptian name, he wears Egyptian clothes, he adorns himself in gold and silver, he rides a chariot, he has men bow before him, he swears by Pharaoh, he marries the daughter of the Egyptian high priest, he has his father embalmed, he is himself embalmed.[7] He even names his first-born son Menashe, meaning, according to the narrative, "for God has made me forget ... all my father's house"[8] – and, indeed, he inexplicably declines to inform his grieving father that he is still alive. At virtually every turn, Joseph renders himself pleasing to his superiors so that he may find favor in their eyes, while his relationship with his people is attenuated.

But this surface conformity to Egypt calls our attention to something deeper. For Joseph is forever acting to please his lord, zealously harnessing his will to his father's interest, then to that of Potiphar, then to that of the keeper of Pharaoh's jails, and finally to that of Pharaoh himself. No wonder Joseph's economic proposals "were good in the eyes of Pharaoh, and in the eyes of all his servants"[9] – for Joseph never proposes anything that he does not believe to be in the best interest of his master. Even in his greatest moment of righteousness and selflessness, when he spurns the advances of Potiphar's wife, he thinks first and most naturally of the earthly master whose interest he would be betraying, and only then of the sin itself, saying: "Behold, my master does not inquire after what I do in his house, and he has placed all that he has in my hand. There is no one greater in this house than I, and he has not withheld anything from me but you, since you are his wife. How, then, can I do this great wrong, and sin against God?"[10]

No one considers himself a court Jew. Indeed, it is perhaps the defining characteristic of such an individual that, in his tireless pursuit of his master's interest, he forever believes himself to be doing what is best for his people at the same time. Even as vizier in Egypt, Joseph always speaks to his brothers of the salvation from famine that it was his role to bring the Jews:

> I am Joseph, your brother, whom you sold into Egypt. And now, do not be grieved nor angry with yourselves because you sold me here, for God did send me here before you to preserve life. For these two years has the famine been on the land, and there will be five more years in which there will be neither plowing nor harvest. God did send me here before you to preserve you upon the earth, and to save your lives through a great deliverance. So it was not you who sent me here, but God.[11]

As Joseph explains it, he has spent these years accumulating power in Egypt so that he might be able to save the lives of the Jews, and he will now do so by taking them under his protective wing and nourishing them through the coming years of privation:

> Come down to me, do not delay. And you will live in the land of Goshen, and you will be close to me, you and your children and your children's children, and your flocks and your herds and all you have. And I will nourish you there, for there are still five years of famine to come, lest you and your house and all that is yours fall into poverty.[12]

All this seems very generous at the time. But seventeen years later, with the great famine long past and the brothers now accustomed to life in Egypt, we see that Joseph is still repeating these claims: "You thought badly of me, but God meant it all for good, that I might this day preserve such a multitude of people alive. And now, have no fear, I will nourish you and your little ones."[13]

There is a certain ambiguity, to say the least, in the fact that these statements are repeated again so long after the original threat has passed. Of course, as ruler of an empire that now owns the land and directly manages its entire economy, everything that Joseph has to say is true, both during the famine and long after it. With successful management, he can truly pride himself on saving the lives of his people and many others year after year. The trouble with Joseph's theory is that it equates the will of God with the accumulation of economic and political power by the state. That is, so long as Joseph is operating the food production of Egypt, he is saving lives. And so long as the Jews depend on his providence, he is saving their lives as well – famine or no famine. Indeed, all of this had been the official government philosophy of Egypt long before Joseph's arrival, as is evident from the records the Pharaohs left of their activities. As one of them wrote of his rule:

> I was the one who produced barley and loved the grain god. The Nile [i.e., the source of water] respected me at every defile. None hungered in my years or thirsted in them. Men dwelt in peace through that which I wrought.[14]

Pharaoh's very status as god and idol was based on precisely the capacity that Joseph keeps claiming for himself: "I preserve such a multitude of people alive. I will nourish you and your little ones."

Joseph's equation of the accumulation of power with the mission of the Jew in the world is problematic in other ways as well. First, since Joseph did not know that his success in the Egyptian hierarchy would result in saving the lives of the Jews until he had already been in Pharaoh's service for nine years (and in Egypt for twenty-two), there is in his statement a retroactive justification of the accumulation of all power at all times – as though it is *always* the will of God that one pursue power. By the same token, Joseph has to make sacrifices in terms of his connection to the Jewish people and faith to be able to gain this power, and this too he seems to justify as being part of God's work, since without it he would not have been able to "save your lives through a great deliverance," and could not now continue indefinitely "nourishing you and your little ones." In other words, if saving life is the highest value, and all accumulation of power is understood to be saving life, does not God then condone any and every action taken in the service of building up political and economic power – in this case, the political and economic power of the Egyptian house of bondage?[15]

The story of Joseph is by biblical standards a massive and detailed biography, comprising almost a third of the book of Genesis. And in all this, Joseph is only once depicted as doing something that can be construed as being against the political and economic interests of his master. The event in question concerns the burial of Jacob, who calls Joseph to his deathbed after seventeen years in Egypt and makes him swear he will see to burying him in Israel: "He called Joseph, his son, and said to him: 'Do not bury me, I pray you, in Egypt. But I will lie with my fathers, and you will carry me out of Egypt, and bury me in their burying place,' and he said: 'I will do as you say.' And he said: 'Swear to me,' and he swore to him."[16]

Of all biblical figures, Jacob is the most tried in deception, and so he takes little for granted. It is clear that he suspects his son, the servant of Pharaoh, and not without reason. Pharaoh and his ministers are depicted as being enthusiastic over only two ideas during the eighty years that Joseph rules in Egypt: Joseph's proposal for meeting the emergency of the famine, and Joseph's invitation to his father and brothers to come weather the last five years of famine under his protection in Egypt. Upon hearing of it, Pharaoh reissues the invitation to the brothers, although in slightly stronger terms: "Now you are commanded: Do this."[17] And they obey, bringing Jacob and his dependents to be resettled in Egypt. Moreover, Pharaoh orders them to leave their possessions behind, promising to replace them. His intention is to increase their dependence on the Egyptian state, but Jacob, already suspicious, ignores him and brings their possessions anyway.[18] The motive behind Pharaoh's interest in Jacob and his clan is plain. He fears that his great adviser may decide to return to his home in Canaan, and perhaps even stir up trouble on the border, and he moves to neutralize the threat by transplanting the Hebrews within easy reach. And his political calculations are apparently sufficient to justify what otherwise might have been a rather unseemly decision to import a tribe of shepherds into the land.

For twelve years after the famine abates, Pharaoh succeeds in keeping the Hebrews in Egypt. The silence of the text on this point suggests that no one dared to raise the subject, since Pharaoh was in any case not about to let anyone leave, and it would have been worse than pointless for this to be explained explicitly. The issue finally comes to a head when Jacob lies dying, the wily patriarch using his last breath to challenge the will of Pharaoh by making Joseph – the only son with the influence to press Pharaoh to do anything[19] – swear to bury him in Hebron with his fathers. For the first time in his life, Joseph finds himself bound to act against the king's interest: Jacob has demanded that the brothers all be allowed to return to Canaan, albeit only for a burial. But what if they make use of the opportunity to refuse to return? Indeed, might not Joseph, seeing his brothers go, succumb to the temptation and defect himself?

Trapped into a solemn commitment to his father that he cannot break, the reaction of Joseph, ruler of Egypt, is astonishing:

> When the days of mourning were past, Joseph spoke to the house of Egypt, saying: "If now I have found favor in your eyes, speak, I pray you, in the ears of Pharaoh, saying: My father made me swear, saying, 'Behold I die, and in my grave that you have dug for me in the land of Canaan will you bury me.' Let me go up and bury my father, I pray you, and I will come back."[20]

Pharaoh does indeed consent to allow Joseph and his brothers to go up – with a military escort, while their children and herds are held hostage in Goshen.[21] But what kind of behavior is this on Joseph's part, going to Pharaoh's other servants and begging them to try to influence him, and this only if Joseph has managed to "find favor in your eyes"? The incongruity of it brought the rabbis to jest at Joseph's expense, saying: "To whom did he speak? To the queen's nurse, asking her to persuade the queen, who in turn should persuade the king."[22] And why does he blame it all on Jacob, who "made me swear," as though he, Joseph, would never have dreamed of such a thing? Is Joseph, after twenty-six years of rule over Egypt, after having saved the nation from starvation, after having concentrated all its wealth and might in Pharaoh's hands – is he *afraid* to go in and ask the king for leave to go and bury his father?

The answer is that he is. For mighty though Joseph may be, he is not free. No longer a shepherd like his fathers, he is instead a servant to Pharaoh in the house of bondage. There is no question, of course, but that this house of bondage remains one of the great political and economic powers on earth, with the ability to give life and take it away. And there is likewise no question but that a man such as Joseph necessarily feels himself to be free, as he gives orders to others morning and night and disposes of their lives, loved ones, and property as he deems fit. But compelling as this experience may be, it is an illusion. For the first among slaves may be powerful, but a slave he remains, subject to annihilation by his master at a moment's notice, in Pharaoh's house no less than in that of Potiphar. And when, once, Joseph realizes that he must act contrary to the will of Pharaoh, when once he is faced with a possible *loss* of favor, and the wrath that comes to Pharaoh when he senses betrayal, Joseph is struck with the self-same terror of the Hebrew slaves facing that other Pharaoh generations later. Before this terror, Joseph gives in, dooming his people to slavery and atrocity at the hands of a Pharaoh that he – unlike his father Jacob – could not bring himself to challenge. For this reason, the rabbis observed that "as soon as Jacob our father died, the enslavement of Egypt began for Israel."[23]

In the end, it seems that Joseph, too, knew that he had been defeated, for as he lay near death, looking back at the results of his life's efforts, he felt compelled to say to his brothers: "I am dying, but God will surely remember you and bring you up out of this land ... and you will carry my bones out from here."[24] Joseph had succeeded in fulfilling his dreams, but he had ultimately delivered no one, not even himself. The work of redeeming his people he left to someone else, to someone who would succeed where he had failed.[25]

The sense of loss that permeates this ending to the story of Joseph, the most gifted leader the Jews had ever had, is captured in a parable of R. Levi:

> It can be compared to a man who brought his wine into the cellar, and thieves came and took away the barrels and drank their contents. When the owner of the wine found those who had stolen the barrels of wine, he said to them: "You have drunk the wine. At least return the casks to their place."[26]

And what of Esther? Was she not also as wine, stolen unfinished in youth, to be drunk by strangers? And might her end not be such as this, as well – her gifts and her beauty spent in futility, drained to the dregs in the service of one not her maker?

Rarely is anyone privileged to grasp the iron relationship between his decision of the moment and the greater effects that this decision stands to bring upon the rest of his life. And Esther too, in the rush of the moment, at first fails to see and falters, thinking of the favor of her ruler, fearing its loss: "All the king's servants and the people of the king's provinces know that there is but one law for any man or woman who comes to the king in the inner court without having been summoned: That he be put to death" (4.11). Yet her character is, in the final analysis, of a different sort than Joseph's, and Mordechai has been able to offer her lessons in politics that Jacob, separated from his son too early, was never able to provide.

I2

The Decision

The Persian political books of the Bible were written in the wake of the destruction of Jerusalem, for a Jewish people once again confronted with the terrifying dilemmas of Joseph in Egypt: whether to attempt to use the worldly power of the state-idols for the sake of Jewish survival – despite the fact that it is precisely such supposedly "productive" use of idolatry that the Jews had set out to abolish. And while all of them, Daniel, Nehemia, and Esther, accepted Joseph's premise that if the Jews were to make it through the exile, they would have to collaborate with the state in order to gain power for Jewish ends, they rejected the ending to the Joseph story as the only possible outcome. Surely, they argued, one should have been able to achieve favor and wield power in Egypt – and yet have been strong enough, when the moment of terror came, to defy the idol and deliver one's people.

In the book of Daniel, in fact, facing up to Joseph's dilemma is made to look easy. The leaders of the Jewish exile in Babylonia, Hanania, Mishael, and Azaria, are brought before Nebuchadnezzar, the emperor who had destroyed the Jewish kingdom, and ordered to bow before the gold idol he has erected. The king's law decrees that they should obey or die. In the critical moment of decision, they muster a defiant and disobedient response almost without concern or hesitation, so powerful is their faith that God will assist them if they do the right thing:

> O Nebuchadnezzar, we have no need to answer you in this matter. For our God whom we serve is able to deliver us .... But even if he does not, let it be understood, O king, that we will not serve your gods, nor worship the gold image that you have erected.[1]

Once the Persians are in control of the city, Darius becomes emperor and he promotes Daniel to high office. But eventually, Daniel too finds himself being ordered, this time under Persian law, to desist from saying prayers to God, and to pray only to Darius himself. Learning of this law, he also refuses obedience, although he knows that he will be thrown to the lions.[2] In both cases, the appropriate Jewish response to the demands of the idolaters is obvious, and a miracle takes place so that all ends well.

In Nehemia, on the other hand, there are no miracles to be had, and the question of whether to risk the ruler's wrath for what is right appears difficult and frightening. Nehemia is serving as cupbearer to the Persian king Artahshasta,[3] a sensitive position requiring a substantial measure of confidence on the part of the king, since it entails ensuring that his cup has not been poisoned. But as in Esther, Nehemia's special relationship with the king turns into a crisis of conscience when his brother comes to Susa, bringing him news of the misery of the Jewish remnant in Jerusalem: "The survivors who were not taken into captivity are suffering terrible hardship and degradation, and Jerusalem's walls are broken and its gates burned with fire."[4]

Jerusalem had been destroyed for being rebellious, and the narrative makes it abundantly clear that the effort to rebuild the ruined city – which would in practice amount to the resurrection of Jewish military power – could easily be construed as a threat to the empire and rebellion against the king.[5] Indeed, numerous diplomatic efforts had been made by the enemies of the Jews to persuade the Persian kings that it was a security risk to allow such work to proceed.[6] Nehemia, whom the subsequent account reveals to be a gifted statesman, is thus rightfully terrified to make an approach to the king on Jerusalem's behalf, realizing that he could easily be taken for a traitor and lose everything. Yet if he, whom the king trusts with his life, will not go in to intercede for Jerusalem, then who will?

Upon hearing his brother out, Nehemia decides to try to use his influence with the Persian king, although it may mean forfeiting his position or his life:

> It came to pass, when I heard these words, that I sat down and wept, and
> I mourned for days, and I fasted and prayed before God in heaven: ...
> Prosper your servant this day, and grant him mercy before this man. For
> I was the king's cupbearer.[7]

Only after these trials does he go in to the king and make precisely the request that Joseph was never able to utter in all his years in Egypt: that the king permit him to leave his service and go up to the land of Israel to be governor there for the sake of his people. The king responds by asking Nehemia how long he will be gone.[8]

In Esther's case, the stakes are even higher. She faces a king who has already made a decision, a vizier who has staked his career on ensuring that the plan is executed, and a prescribed penalty of death for herself if she makes the wrong move. Moreover, the decision to approach the king will open a political war within the palace, something with which she has little experience, and upon which the very lives of the Jews of the empire depend. Nevertheless, Esther's story rejects Joseph's course as well, not only because of his failure of nerve in not confronting Pharaoh, but also because of the problematic philosophy that seems to render his failure inevitable: Joseph is unable to act where his deeds are likely to displease his master because of his tacit assumption that the good of the Jews (and of the world) depends on the preservation of his power. That is, since, as he repeatedly claims, it is God's will that the Jews be saved through him, it is always his duty to do whatever it is that will preserve his power intact.[9] Ironically, it is just this faith in his own divine mission that paralyzes Joseph, preventing him from using his power lest he lose it – and as becomes evident, power that one is afraid to use is not power at all.

It is this theory, of the divine will singling out a single person as the sole possible savior, that Mordechai categorically rejects – in a passage dramatically emphasized by virtue of its being the only place that he is quoted verbatim in the entire narrative. In contrast to Joseph's self-assurance that the divine plan is manifest and that he is it ("God did send me here before you to save your lives through a great deliverance"), Mordechai argues that while one may have a critical role to play in some divine plan, this cannot be known for certain ("Who knows whether it was not for such a time as this that you came into royalty?"[10]), and that if one proves unwilling or unable to fulfill such a role, it will be played by someone else ("For if you insist on remaining silent at this time, relief and deliverance will come to the Jews from elsewhere") (4.14).

Had Mordechai sought to advise Esther on the basis of Joseph's understanding, he would have argued as follows: Since, as queen of Persia, Esther is in a unique position to assist the Jews and others, there is virtually nothing as important as the maintenance and advancement of her position. Any action that could jeopardize her favor with the king would be a reckless dissipation of the only hope of the Jews being saved. Esther should therefore refrain from challenging the king, and await an opportunity when her influence might be of use.

But the consequences of such a position are far-reaching. If the influential Jew, considering himself to be indispensable, begins weighing his every action exclusively on the basis of how it affects his own power and the favor of those on whom his power depends, the result will be the helplessness amid the illusion of freedom that is the bottom line in the Joseph narrative. It is simply absurd to imagine that the needs of the Jews as a people will at every crucial moment coincide with the interests and inclinations of Pharaoh, of Ahashverosh, or of any other foreign ruler or state upon which the Jews depend. A Jew whose only understanding of his service to his people is to build ever greater monuments of favor and authority within the power structure of a foreign state must inevitably find himself facing situations in which the vital needs of the Jews are ignored, while he himself remains silent for fear of offending those who could deprive him of his position.

In disavowing this theory, Mordechai's first line of attack is a counterintuitive one. He seeks to deflate the importance that the individual in a position of power naturally tends to assign himself. By emphasizing the traditional belief that the Jewish people are in any case eternal,[11] and the survival of the Jews therefore foregone with or without Esther's help, he ironically renders her free to act. Only if it is clear to her that the Jewish people do not need her to retain her position at all cost is it possible for her to take risks that might very well end in the weakening or even elimination of her influence.

But the belief in the eternity of Israel has its problematic aspect as well. For if relief and deliverance will surely come from elsewhere, then what possible reason can there be for Esther to act at all? It is from just such views that religious quietism arises: the belief that God will take care of everything, that man is in any case too small to alter the course of events, that God's will is done with or without one's involvement. Here, too, the tendency is toward paralysis. It seems that boldness is so difficult that in any case a reason will be found to avoid it.

Against this tendency, Mordechai makes a second argument in the same passage. His entire speech is as follows:

> Do not imagine in your heart that you, of all the Jews, will escape because you are in the king's palace. For if you insist on remaining silent at this time, relief and deliverance will come to the Jews from elsewhere, but you and your father's house will perish. And who knows whether it was not for such a time as this that you came into royalty?" (4.13–14).

The argument he makes with regard to Esther's destiny as the savior of the Jews, then, is twofold:

(i) *Perhaps* it is in order to save that Jews that you have risen to power, but –
(ii) if you are silent, you and yours will *certainly* be lost.

At first glance, Mordechai's insistence that inaction will lead to Esther's destruction seems contrived. Of all the Jews in the empire, Esther stands the best chance of being spared. The king adores her and is unlikely to let a second wife go the way of the first.[12] Moreover, no one in the court is aware that she is a Jew. If anything, Esther's position seems itself to be the best guarantee of the persistence of the Jewish line. In asserting, again against all intuition, that while others may be saved, it is Esther's doom that will be sealed by her inaction, is he merely engaging in a bit of tough rhetoric to try and prod her into motion?

Mordechai is not just engaging in tough rhetoric. He is in deadly earnest. For although the fate of the Jewish people as a whole cannot and should not be understood to be in Esther's hands alone, there is nevertheless a portion of her people whose fate may very well depend on her. After all, had not Joseph's silence permitted Pharaoh to massacre the Jews in their thousands and to maintain them in bitter slavery for centuries – this despite the fact that relief and deliverance did eventually come from elsewhere, from Moses? That the Jews as a people will in some way be saved in no way ensures that Esther and her father's house – and even six million of her father's house – will not be lost through the inaction of those who could have acted but did not. No one can know what will come of his efforts. And yet with hindsight, Esther may find that her deeds saved, not the Jewish people, but her "father's house" in a large sense, that portion of the Jews that she loves and knows, and that constitutes her people in her time and place. When one recognizes that such power nevertheless does reside in the individual, one has no choice but to consider and reconsider: "Who knows whether it was not for such a time as this that I have been placed here?"

It is precisely the retention of one's shepherd freedom, the ability to act *against* the interest of worldly power in the service of something higher, that is the source of man's greatness. It is not Joseph's building of Egypt that is unique in history; for there is virtually no man who does not work to build up the place in which he lives. What is unique is Moses' rejection of Pharaoh's court, with all the power that it offered him, in order to protect a slave who was being treated unjustly, and in order to lead his people into the wastes of Sinai. Without Moses, Joseph's empire-building would not even have made a scratch on the collective memory of mankind.

But there is more to it than this. For Mordechai's words are carefully chosen: If Esther is silent at such a time, then, who knows, perhaps she will have missed the opportunity to save thousands. But one thing is certain: that she herself will be "lost," and with her, the house of her father Avihail in the literal sense, of which she is the only surviving member. How does Mordechai know this?

Mordechai's certainty comes from an understanding that the battle of the court Jew is ultimately the struggle to save, not the Jewish people, but himself. Exposing himself to the relentless encroachment of foreign values, allowing himself to become preoccupied with the pursuit of favor, in effect transforming himself into the tool of an alien master rather than of his own conscience, he balances himself on a precipice in the hope that there he will be able to do good. Perhaps, as Joseph claims, he will sometimes be able to achieve that good in the course of executing his assigned duties. But the proof that he lives as a Jew comes not when he executes his assigned tasks on the path to worldly power. It comes when he *cannot* pursue these tasks as expected – when the demands of power, expedience and the interest of the state are opposed to what is Jewish and what is right, when he stands to lose everything as Abraham lost everything in rejecting Mesopotamia. Only then does it become clear whether he is still fighting the battle of the Jew, or whether this cause has been sacrificed to the enslaving idol. In the rejection of the idol, *only* in the rejection of the idol, does the Jewish soul persist.

This is why, while Esther may or may not succeed in saving numbers of Jews by interceding with the king, the only one who will be lost for certain through her silence is herself. Remaining unmoved when tens of thousands of innocent people, her own people, stand to die, she will have finally and completely returned to that condition of powerless, spiritless bondage, which as a Jew she should have left behind in Egypt. Remaining unmoved before the cries of the persecuted, her heart like a stone, her face like a carving of wood, she will serve a lie that, by her own subservience, she makes as a god. And this is the meaning of the biblical teaching with regard to the idols: "Mouths have they but they cannot speak. Eyes have they but they cannot see. Ears have they but they cannot hear .... Like them will be those who make them."[13]

It is when she understands that such is the choice before her that the greatness of the queen is revealed. Esther, who has ever sought the favor of others, who always did as she was told, who would never ask anything for herself, faces the moment of truth. She must choose between building up the horror that has reared itself up before her, the fear of it, the numbing paralysis and amnesia of it; and picking up a stick to swing with all her might, with anything and everything she has ever had in her, to smash it. Recognizing what she must do, she breaks with her past, and for the first time in her life issues the order that Mordechai immediately obeys:

> Go assemble all the Jews present in Susa and fast for me. Do not eat and do not drink for three days, night and day, and I and my maids will fast as well. Then I will go in to the king, though it is against the law. And if I perish, I perish (4.16–17).

PART V

ESTHER 5.1–5.14

I t came to pass on the third day that Esther dressed in royalty and stood in the inner court of the king's house, facing the throne room, while the king was sitting on his royal seat in the throne room, facing the entrance to the chamber. ²And it came to pass that when the king saw Esther the queen standing in the court, she won favor in his eyes, and the king extended to Esther the gold scepter in his hand, and Esther approached and touched the tip of the scepter.

³The king said to her: Queen Esther, what is your request? Even if it be half the kingdom, it will be given you."

⁴Esther said: "If it please the king, let the king and Haman come today to the banquet that I have prepared for him."

⁵The king said: "Hasten Haman to do as Esther has spoken." And the king and Haman came to banquet that Esther had prepared.

⁶The king said to Esther during the banquet of wine: "Whatever your wish, it will be given you. Whatever your request, up to half the kingdom, it will be done."

⁷Esther responded and said: "My wish and my request – ⁸If I have won favor in the king's eyes, and if it pleases the king to grant my wish and to fulfill my request – then let the king and Haman come to the banquet that I will prepare for them, and tomorrow I will do as the king has said."

⁹Haman went out that day happy and in high spirits, but when Haman saw Mordechai in the king's gate, how he neither stood nor stirred before him, Haman was filled with rage against Mordechai.

¹⁰Haman restrained himself and returned to his house, and he sent for his friends and for Zeresh his wife. ¹¹Haman recounted to

them the glory of his riches, and the great number of his sons, and everything in which the king had promoted him and elevated him above the princes and servants of the king. [12]Haman said: "Even Esther the queen brought no one with the king to the banquet she had prepared other than myself, and tomorrow, too, I am invited to her along with the king. [13]Yet all this is worthless to me, so long as I see Mordechai the Jew sitting at the king's gate."

[14]Then Zeresh his wife and all his friends said to him: "Let a tall gallows be made, fifty cubits high, and in the morning tell the king to have Mordechai hanged on it. Then go with the king to the banquet in good spirits." The idea seemed good to Haman, and he had the gallows erected.

13

The Plan

There follow two terrible days in which Esther prepares herself to go in to the king. We know that Esther was fasting, and we may surmise that she prayed a good deal as well.[1] But the better part of her seclusion is devoted to long hours poring over what she knows of the king, searching for a way to counterbalance the interest he believes he has in harming the Jews. From the information she has, it is apparent that the scheme is the vizier's, and that Ahashverosh's acquiescence comes of his desire to promote Haman and permit him to consolidate his control over the empire. And if the king considers it crucial at this stage to rely on Haman's judgment, then there will be no point in arguing with him about a policy whose actual content probably matters little to him. What is needed is to damage Haman's favor with the king, so that Ahashverosh feels he has something to lose in so quickly accepting Haman's goals as his own. Only then will it be possible for another voice to be heard.

It is through this trail of reasoning, followed doggedly through the mists of fear and exhaustion, that Esther's plan begins to emerge.

When the queen enters the inner court of the palace less than three days after the promulgation of the decree, there is little to be seen of the beauty for which she is known throughout the empire. Pale, haggard, weak, she has been without food or water for days.

The king gazes in her direction and points to her with his scepter, lifting the decree of death. He loves her "more than all the other women" in the kingdom (2.17), and having already suffered the loss of his first wife because of an impulsive application of law, he is in no rush to go through this again. Moreover, as when Nehemia comes before Artahshasta, Esther has made sure that her appearance is irregular and pitiable, so that the king can clearly see something is wrong.[2] Since the king always delights in a display of magnanimity where he has nothing to lose and everything to gain, it is hardly a great surprise that Esther "finds favor in his eyes" (5.2). Now the drama truly begins.

The king understands that Esther would not risk her life without having some terribly important matter to take up with him, and so he asks her: "What is your request," and then adds his standard, hyperbolic form of pretended largesse: "Even if it be half the kingdom, it will be given you."

The queen responds according to her plan: "If it please the king, let the king and Haman come today to the banquet I have prepared for him" (5.3–4).

The king is pleased to comply, ordering that Haman be "hastened" to appear. But Esther did not transgress the king's law only to have such a gathering. Or did she? Ahashverosh is ready to get to the bottom of the matter, and upon taking part in the banquet of wine hours later, he repeats his question, again asking Esther what her request might be.

Esther reaches for the next line in her script, but instead comes forth with only a terrible stammer, rifling through a series of meaningless hesitations before coming to an answer, evidently not the one which she had prepared:

> "My wish and my request –.[3]
> If I have won favor in the king's eyes,
> And if it pleases the king to grant my wish
> And to fulfill my request –
> Then let the king and Haman come to the banquet that I will prepare
>   for them,
> And tomorrow I will do as the king has said."

At the end of all this, she arrives at the same point where she had been in the throne room that morning: "Let the king and Haman come tomorrow to the banquet that I will prepare for them." Lest the king think that she is playing with him, she adds: "And tomorrow I will do as the king has said" – that is, she will reveal the concealed request that is behind her initiative (5.8).

Why does Esther invite the king to come to a pair of wine-sodden dinners with her, in the company of his vizier, instead of coming out and demanding that the decree be repealed and the Jews saved?

The reason is that she does not believe he will grant the request. Esther is well liked by the king, and he may be willing to hear her out. But a direct assault on the decree means pitting her own untried credibility in matters of policy against the settled opinion of the vizier, whom the king has appointed, after all, to conduct policy. Moreover, such an attack would force Ahashverosh to choose between Haman's policy and a different one proposed by Esther – precisely the kind of politics of conflicting interests he has sought to avoid. Having staked his kingdom on the belief that Haman's advice is preferable to hearing out such competing claims, the chances are excellent that the criticism of a young queen whom he calls to visit him only sporadically will just anger the king and result in her being discredited in his eyes.

What is needed is to drive a wedge between the king and the vizier, something that will give Esther the leverage she needs to pry Ahashverosh away from him. To do this, she must avoid the trap of arguing policy directly, and find a way of challenging Haman's trusted status on other grounds, causing the vizier to appear flawed in judgment or even suspect in the eyes of the king.[4]

It is to achieve this that Esther proposes that Ahashverosh come to her dinner, telling the king that she wishes to invite "the king and Haman to the banquet I have prepared for him." Behind a superficial innocence, Esther's intention is to make a highly unusual, even disturbing request: For why should the queen, who has not had the benefit of seeing her husband for a month, wish to organize an intimate, romantic dinner for three? Moreover, she invites "the king and Haman to the banquet she has prepared for him." Which of her guests is the "him"? Him *whom*?

The trouble is that the invitation and its acceptance occur too quickly, and within hours the three of them are together, the king again inquiring as to Esther's request. Has Ahashverosh understood any of the implications of what the queen has said to him, of the event taking place before his eyes? She cannot tell, and she has no reason to think so. He shows no signs of having understood anything. He just sits there drinking, laughing, opining, as though all is well. When the moment comes, and the fate of her stratagem and her people hangs in the balance, Esther feels she cannot risk taking the next step. The vizier's favor with the king is still as it was, far too great for her to move against him, and she determines to try again. She will request another banquet, bearing the same disturbing message, but this time with one measure less of subtlety: "Let the king and Haman come to the banquet I will prepare for them."

If he does not understand this time, she will no longer be able to wait. By the next afternoon, she will already be in danger of trying the king's patience, of causing him to feel she is toying with him.

For them, for *them*.

This bizarre locution of the queen's is not lost on Haman, who immediately feels the power of the wine, the power of the queen's words. Drunk on what she has said, he immediately runs to his friends and preens: "Even Esther the queen brought no one with the king to the banquet she had prepared other than myself, and tomorrow, too, I am invited to her, along with the king" (5.12). But will the king be quick enough to perceive the threat?

Esther has made her move, the die is cast. Either the night will do its work, or she will have to confront Haman as he is, standing against her with the full backing of the king and all the might of the empire still tightly in his hands.

14

Reaction

The vizier now has an enemy whose moves he can only follow in part. As we would say today, Mordechai is engaged in creating public pressure against him, while Esther works to undermine his position through quiet diplomacy. And although Haman misses the connection between the queen's flattery and the decree against the Jews, he is fully aware of something else: As he leaves the banquet, he passes Mordechai in the king's gate. And the Jew, who has until now refused to bow down to him, "neither stood nor stirred before him" (5.9). This failure even to acknowledge Haman's presence is a further insult, from which it becomes perfectly clear that the decree has failed to stem Mordechai's public campaign against him. A decree to destroy Mordechai's entire people, which would have induced another man to come to the vizier begging for mercy, or at least caused him to disappear in degradation, has done nothing to alter the Jew's posture of public contempt. Indeed, it has caused him to escalate, and small though this gesture of contempt may be, it is a sure sign of deeper trouble brewing, unseen and yet felt beneath the surface.[1] The decree is scheduled to be implemented only in eleven months' time, and in politics eleven months is an eternity, during which a concerted resistance can generate sympathizers at all levels. It is this feeling, the intensifying sensation of uncontrol before a menace not understood, which appears in Haman's soul as the thrashing of his crocodile spirit, a nail stuck in its innards, unable to reassert rule despite the application of the most violent pressure.

Distressed, Haman summons his friends and advisers to discuss what should be done. He recounts to them his recent successes in consolidating ultimate power in the empire, but concludes with a fit of inspired hatred: "Yet all this is worthless to me, so long as I see Mordechai the Jew sitting at the king's gate" (5.13).

Recognizing the threat to the vizier's position, Haman's advisers propose a surgical strike to neutralize Mordechai's opposition: "Let a tall gallows be made, fifty cubits high, and in the morning tell the king to have Mordechai hung on it" (5.14).[2] Their intention is twofold. First, the threat from Mordechai must be eliminated as rapidly as possible. So long as the Jew continues to be a player in the court, he will work to discredit Haman and incite dissension. Even courtiers unfriendly toward the Jews will be encouraged by the vizier's failure to impose his order, and will begin generating their own excuses for weakening his rule and bringing him down. Unless Mordechai is quickly eliminated, there is no way of ensuring that the decree, and even Haman's position itself, will be safe.[3] Second, the height of the gallows, which will tower over most of the buildings of the city, is intended to produce public pressure against that which Mordechai has been broadcasting. Where Mordechai's campaign has been aimed to show that there can be resistance, Haman's gallows is aimed to demonstrate that such resistance is chimerical. It stands out, in other words, as a warning: Disobedience no sooner stirs than it is doomed.

The move proposed by Haman's advisers is not, however, without risk. The vizier, although in full favor with the king, must also make sure that his requests are couched in terms of the king's interest and not his own. While Ahashverosh is determined to secure Haman's absolute authority over others, he is himself hardly in awe of Haman, whom he is careful to abuse in little ways – having him "hastened" here and there by the chamberlains, for example – in order to remind him whence his authority derives (5.5, 6.10, 6.14).[4] In hoping to have Mordechai eliminated, Haman is, ironically, in a position similar to that of Joseph requesting to go up to Canaan to bury his father. The request is obviously not a demand designed to strengthen the king, but a confession of personal need and insecurity – this, in fact, had been the reason that "it was disdainful in his eyes to lay hands on Mordechai alone" to begin with (3.6). Whereas the Jews as a people can be supposed a security threat to the entire empire, the vizier's desire to rid himself of an opponent who, after all, is known to object principally to Haman himself, is difficult to interpret as anything other than the political assassination of a rival member of the court.

That Ahashverosh, who generally concerns himself with appearing magnanimous and disbursing gifts, may not appreciate the merits of this proposal to do away with Mordechai, is an open possibility. But against the need to eliminate the leader of his opposition before he can rally allies and pose a genuine threat, this concern pales and is passed over. The meeting of the vizier's camp ends with a resolution of consensus: against the opposition, a swift, brutal reaction, from which the Jews will be unable to recover. In the morning, Haman will go in to request Mordechai's execution.

PART VI

ESTHER 6.1–8.2

T hat night, the king could not sleep, so he ordered that the book of records, the chronicles, be brought out and read before the king. ²There it was found how Mordechai had denounced Bigtana and Teresh, two of the king's chamberlains of the guardians of the threshold, who had plotted to lay their hands on Ahashverosh the king.

³The king said: "What honor or promotion has been conferred upon Mordechai for this?"

And the king's youths, who attended him, replied: "Not a thing has been done for him."

⁴The king said: "Who is in the court?" And Haman had come into the outer court of the king's house to ask the king to hang Mordechai on the gallows he had prepared for him.

⁵The king's youths said to him: "It is Haman standing in the court."

And the king said: "Let him in."

⁶Haman came in and the king said to him: "What should be done for the man whom the king desires to honor?"

And Haman said in his heart: Whom should the king desire to honor more than me?

⁷Haman said to the king: "The man whom the king desires to honor – ⁸Let a royal robe be brought that the king has worn, and a horse upon which the king has ridden, and with the royal head-piece on its head. ⁹And let the robe and the horse be entrusted to one from among the king's most noble princes, and let him attire the man whom the king desires to honor, and lead him on the horse

around the city square proclaiming before him: Thus will be done for the man whom the king desires to honor."

¹⁰The king said to Haman: "Hurry, and take the robe and the horse as you have said, and do so for Mordechai the Jew, who sits in the king's gate. Omit nothing from all you have said."

¹¹Haman took the robe and the horse, and he dressed Mordechai and led him around the city square, proclaiming before him: "Thus will be done for the man whom the king desires to honor."

¹²Mordechai returned to the king's gate, and Haman returned to his house, aggrieved and with his head covered. ¹³ Haman told Zeresh his wife and all his friends everything that had happened to him, and his advisers and Zeresh his wife said to him: "If he be of Jewish descent, this Mordechai, before whom you have begun to fall, you will not prevail against him, but you will surely fall before him."

¹⁴While they were yet talking with him, the king's chamberlains arrived, hurrying to bring Haman to the banquet that Esther had prepared.

¹So the king and Haman came to drink with Esther the queen.

²The king again said to Esther, on the second day of the banquet of wine: "Whatever your wish, Queen Esther, it will be given you. Whatever your request, up to half the kingdom, it will be done."

³Esther the queen replied and said: "If I have found favor in your eyes, my king, and if it please the king, let my life be given to me as my wish, and my people as my request. ⁴For we have been sold, I and my people, to be annihilated, to be killed, and to be destroyed. Had we been sold as slaves and serving women, I would have remained silent, for this suffering would not have been worth the injury to the king."

⁵Ahashverosh the king spoke, saying to Esther the queen: "Who is it, and which is he, who has inclined his heart to do so?"

⁶Esther said: "A tormentor and an enemy – this evil Haman." And Haman was struck with fear before the king and the queen.

⁷The king rose in his rage from the banquet of wine and went out into the palace garden, while Haman stayed to plead for his life with Esther the queen, for he saw that the king had determined ill against him.

⁸The king returned from the palace garden to the pavilion of the banquet of wine, and found Haman fallen upon the divan on which Esther lay. And the king said: "And would he even conquer the queen with me in the house?"

The words left the king's mouth, and Haman's face fell.

⁹Harvona, one of the chamberlains before the king, said: "And there stands the gallows that Haman made for Mordechai, who spoke well for the king – in Haman's house, fifty cubits high."

And the king said: "Hang him on it."

¹⁰They hanged Haman on the gallows prepared for Mordechai, and the rage of the king subsided.

¹On that day, Ahashverosh the king gave the house of Haman, the persecutor of the Jews, to Esther the queen.

And Mordechai came before the king, for Esther had told what he was to her. ²The king slipped off his ring, which he had retrieved from Haman, and gave it to Mordechai. And Esther placed Mordechai over Haman's house.

15

Power Shift

With the close of the meeting of Haman's faction, the struggle over the future of the decree and the future of the Jews has reached its height. On the morrow, both parties plan to launch their decisive moves: Haman will go to the king in the morning to demand the immediate execution of the leader of the opposition; in the afternoon Esther plans to attempt to dislodge the king from his unconditional support of the vizier and his decree. It is the disposition of the king that will be decisive, and in the effort to sway it the Jews have managed to land their blow first.

"That night the king could not sleep" (6.1) – for as he lies in bed, turning the day's events over in his mind, the queen's provocation finally finds its mark. What was the purpose of the banquet? Why had she so desired the presence of the vizier? Had she indeed said, as he remembered, that the banquet was intended to honor both of them? If she so much wanted to see the vizier, perhaps she had an interest in him – or he in her.[1] And if this was the case, perhaps here was another conspiracy on his life?[2] Could this be the purpose of the banquet? But Haman would never dream of taking the place of his king, who had raised him to such prominence. Or would he? As the hours wear on, the king is tossed and torn between the two great fears that have haunted his reign: the loss of his queen and the loss of his life, both threatened once again at the hands of those closest to him. And had he not taken Haman, the wretch, to protect him from precisely these terrors, to make his world stable for him? To whom could he possibly turn?

With this, the king for the first time comes to recognize the weakness of the political position in which he has cornered himself. For it is by means of his authority to decide among the competing views presented by his advisers that the king maintains his power: Each adviser depends on the king to secure his view against those of the others. Once the king has granted one of his men the right to eliminate all opposition, he has granted him complete freedom of action – freedom that, sooner or later, becomes the power to do without the king. Panic-stricken over this revelation, the king comes clean awake and calls for his youths. Would it not be better to have another minister on hand who could keep an eye on the vizier?

He orders that his servants bring the chronicles to be read in the hope of finding some hint of Haman's treachery against him, some hint of someone who can protect him. They begin to read, and in this way he returns to the attempt on his life that triggered Haman's installation: "There it was found how Mordechai had denounced Bigtana and Teresh, two of the king's chamberlains of the guardians of the threshold, who had plotted to lay their hands on Ahashverosh the king. The king said: 'What honor or promotion has been conferred upon Mordechai for this?' And the king's youths, who attended him, replied: 'Not a thing has been done for him' " (6.2–3).[3]

In reviewing the events leading to Haman's rise, the king begins to piece together the case against the vizier. Was it not Haman who had informed him that it was "of no benefit for the king to keep the Jews," when here it was written that the Jew had in fact been responsible for saving his life? Perhaps Haman had even been involved in the plot that the Jews had succeeded in foiling? And then there is Haman's suspicious mania for control, which had led the king to elevate him in the first place – but which has now succeeded in laying a hand on his signet, and on his banquets with his wife, and on who knows what else.

Moreover, in mulling over the attempt on his life, the king finds evidence of something else: the presence of others in the court who are willing to side with him in adversity, others who are perhaps more loyal than the vizier. Troubled and frightened, Ahashverosh weighs advancing them, taking them in.

It is in this moment of doubt, as Ahashverosh struggles to grasp his world by judging competing theories and claims, that the politics of the empire begins to return. In the answer of the king's youths, that "Not a thing has been done for him," is the first voice of any adviser reported in the narrative since Haman's elevation. Faceless, nameless, they are at least opinions other than that of the vizier – opinions that intrude on the king's apolitical honeymoon, as Rava suggests, not out of any special sympathy for Mordechai, but because they detest the monopoly of power that has been granted Haman.[4] With this intrusion, the king begins the laborious effort of listening to others again.

By the time Haman arrives with the dawn to make his move and try to recoup control, the king has already shifted into a contrary state of mind. Haman seeks to elevate himself yet further, but the king is weighing whether the vizier would not benefit from being taken down a notch or two. Perhaps by being forced to make room for another, Haman will understand who rules and who is the servant. The vizier enters to speak to Ahashverosh, but the king's agenda is not Haman's. The exchange that follows is a verbal elaboration of the shift in political favor that has taken place during the night.

"What should be done for the man whom the king desires to honor?" the king asks, as if to seek advice, when in fact his eye is already set on humiliation. The sport is in learning what kind of humiliation it will be, turning Haman's own desire to rule against him, letting it devour itself.

Haman's conception of the ordering of the Persian state allows for only one interpretation of the king's question: truly an idolater to the core, he continues to identify the good of the realm with his own perfect control. For him, there is only one appropriate address for all honor. To honor someone else is to create rivalry and danger, allowing another to vie for the favor of the king, to him an impossibility. So "Haman said in his heart: Whom should the king desire to honor more than me?" (6.6). And he responds with that infamous fantasy of self-indulgence and usurpation: "The man whom the king desires to honor –. Let a royal robe be brought that the king has worn, and a horse upon which the king has ridden, and with the royal headpiece on its head. And let the robe and the horse be entrusted to one from among the king's most noble princes, and let him attire the man whom the king desires to honor, and lead him on the horse around the city square, proclaiming before him: Thus will be done for the man whom the king desires to honor" (6.7–9).

With each word, the king, now looking upon Haman for the first time as a possible threat, becomes more convinced that his suspicions are well placed. It is with evident satisfaction that he carefully pronounces the doom that demotes Haman once more to the position of a courtier among others, one voice among the many interests of Persia: "Hurry, take the robe and the horse as you have said, and do so for Mordechai the Jew, who sits in the king's gate. Omit nothing from all you have said" (6.10).

And so it is done. The vizier, the paradigm of total power, seeks out the dissident Jew and publicly carries out the doom of submission to him – just as the other men of power in the court had humbled themselves before Haman in the preceding weeks.

But there is more here, as well. For Haman's humiliation is also an admission, before a city that had stared in awe at the height of his gallows only that morning, that all for which Haman had hoped is in fact vanity. No man may claim for himself the authority to dictate truth, to elevate his own perspective into the absolute. The parade through the streets in which the idolater concedes the potency of the truth beyond himself, outside himself, is none other than the retelling of the dream of the Jewish faith: that the idol be brought down to its proper size, that the figurine of gold be recognized as a lump of metal in the hand of man. That each idol, as the rabbis had it, should bow down in recognition of the truth, in so doing bringing oblivion upon itself.[5]

In Haman's camp, his advisers respond to the vizier's humiliation with the wildly pessimistic pronouncement that "If he be of Jewish descent, this Mordechai before whom you have begun to fall, you will not prevail against him, but you will surely fall before him" (6.13). With Haman still vizier and the Jews still condemned to death, including Mordechai himself, there is no reason to think that this assessment is literally correct, any more than was Pharaoh's assessment of the Israelite slaves under his whip as "more and mightier than we."[6] Nevertheless, there is some truth in what Haman's counselors have to say. Haman's effort to kill off the Jew for standing against him, and so consolidate complete control over the state, came too late. And now that Mordechai has been publicly recognized for his services to the king, the opportunity be rid of him has slipped from between Haman's fingers, perhaps never to come again. The configuration of power in the state has now shifted, with another faction moving ahead of the vizier's, pressing its advantage. Events are no longer in Haman's control.

16

Downfall

Not only among Haman's advisers, but in the camp of the Jews as well, the humbling of Haman is understood to signal a shift in power and the moment to act – before Haman should have the chance to revive, defend himself, and recover his losses.

Haman is brought to the queen's banquet, and there the king repeats his query for the third time: "Whatever your wish, Queen Esther, it will be given you. Whatever your request, up to half the kingdom, it will be done" (7.2).

This time, the narrative records no hesitation in the queen's voice. The king will give her a fair hearing now or he never will. She makes her appeal in words she has rehearsed a hundred times:

> If I have found favor in your eyes, my king, and if it please the king, let my life be given to me as my wish, and my people as my request. For we have been sold, I and my people, to be annihilated, to be killed and to be destroyed. Had we been sold as slaves and serving women, I would have remained silent, for this suffering would not have been worth the injury to the king (7.3-4).[1]

A terrific silence reigns as the king struggles to grasp what she has asked of him. Could someone wish to murder the queen? Should he be forced to go through such torment again? He asks so that he should be able to understand:

"Who is it, and which is he, who has inclined his heart to do so?"

"A tormentor and an enemy – this evil Haman" (7.5–6).

Ahashverosh seethes, the temperature rises. Livid, shaking with rage, he storms out into the garden. The vizier is struck with terror, the very same terror of standing alone before the wrath of the king with which Esther has lived every day, every hour, since learning of the decree.

But why does the king leave the room? What does such behavior really mean? Storming out if insulted or embarrassed, slamming a door behind, or similarly, not speaking with someone for years, abandoning a flagging marriage without a word, resigning from high office, and in the extreme, suicide – all these are familiar, and they are the same. It hardly ever makes sense to act in this way if one is strictly calculating benefits against costs, but these are not actions of reason and interest. They are actions of the spirit, which, finding no possible recourse for the reestablishment of control, establishes mastery at the expense of self-interest through the demolition of the situation itself. In departure, that which cannot be controlled is nonetheless brought to bow to one's will. Even in suicide, the action of the spirit is the same, its need to control winning over the needs of the body, control being firmly and finally regained in the purposive destruction of all that has heretofore resisted control. Such an action is therefore not only one of self-destruction, but also of powerlessness, since it proves that control cannot have been imposed in any other way.

Ahashverosh leaves because he has lost all control of the situation, of his world. His wife, it transpires, is a Jewess. And Haman – did he know this? – has tried to murder her. All his efforts to gain security have come to nothing, and he is once again alone. But how can he rule now? Who is he to rely on? Surely the vizier is dangerous, is insane. In his lust to rule, he would murder the queen.

The king, obsessed from the outset with the need to "rule in his own house" lest he find that he rules nowhere, has discovered that he has again lost control of his wife, this time to his own vizier.[2] Esther's stratagem, her arousal of the king's jealousy and suspicions, has therefore brought appearances into line with the truth: Haman has in fact sought to take his queen from him. True, the vizier's assault on the queen was not sexual in nature. But it was close enough, precisely because of Haman's inability to distinguish what is his to lay his hands on from what is not.[3]

And now the king understands this as well, and as he returns from the garden, he speaks aloud the thought that Esther had put in his mind the day before: "The king returned ... and found Haman fallen upon the divan on which Esther lay. And the king said: 'And would he even conquer the queen with me in the house?' " (7.8).[4]

17

Allies

Ahashverosh prefers to consult before he makes a move, and the crisis that brings about Haman's ruin is pointedly no exception. Even at the height of his wrath, when the king determines that the vizier has arrogated to himself the authority to murder the queen and destroy his life, Ahashverosh accepts the advice of one of his chamberlains, Harvona, who suddenly materializes from nowhere in order to help guide the course of events:

> Harvona, one of the chamberlains before the king, said: "And there stands the gallows that Haman made for Mordechai, who spoke well for the king – in Haman's house, fifty cubits high."
> And the king said: "Hang him on it" (7.9).

Who is this Harvona and what does he want? He is mentioned once before as one of the king's inner circle of attendants (1.10). But like all the king's other loyal servants, he disappears from the tale with Haman's elevation. Like the others who have been pushed aside by Haman, Harvona keeps close track of the politics of the court. Here we see that, like Mordechai, he knows the finest details of what has been taking place: what Mordechai did for the king, the grudge that Haman held against the Jew, and even the precise height of the gallows that looms over the city. Yet his name does not appear until now because he has remained silent throughout the development of the conflict. When Haman is appointed, he acquiesces in the new reality, paying whatever shameful homage is required, swallowing the insult and nursing his resentment out of sight. When Mordechai resists, he does not join him, remaining silent as the king's servants press this last recalcitrant courtier to bow before Haman. And when the Jew appeals for help against the liquidation that Haman has ordered, Harvona does nothing to deploy himself in the Jews' camp. Throughout the ordeal, in fact, Harvona has been useless. But when the king's wrath is kindled

against the vizier, and the question that hangs in the balance is how this anger
will expend itself, Harvona directs it and transforms it into a decision, a policy,
playing a part similar to that of Memuchan in the Vashti affair. It is Harvona,
in fact, who hands Haman the final blow that ensures that he is executed,
where he might otherwise have somehow escaped with his life.

The reason for Harvona's actions is not hard to identify. Regardless of where
his personal sympathies lie, Harvona understands himself to have no interest in
risking his own position in the struggle against Haman while the opposition to
him is weak. Certainly, the vizier's authoritarianism means a deterioration in
his own personal station, and as such is unlikely to have made Harvona much
disposed to sympathize with him. But as the public displays of obeisance to
Haman are meant to indicate, it is in Haman's hands that power lies, and those
who seek favor in the court do well to seek it with him. So long as the vizier's
influence is over the king, Harvona sees little choice but to ingratiate himself
with him to whatever degree possible, and certainly to avoid any friction.

Harvona's move to come to the assistance of the Jews – both emphasizing
the good that Mordechai has done for the king, and serving the death blow
to their mortal enemy – is therefore a defection from the camp of Haman's
supporters to that of the Jews. He recognizes the shift in power that has taken
place, and determines to place his bet on the ascendant party, the party he
believes will soon enough be in control: Mordechai and Esther.

A similar approach is taken by Pharaoh's cupbearer in the Joseph narrative.
Joseph, having been unjustly condemned to the dungeon for his purported
misdeeds in Potiphar's house, makes every effort to be of service to the king's
adviser when the chief steward likewise provokes the anger of his master and
is incarcerated. Having done the king's cupbearer a good turn in relieving him
of the fear that had resulted from his uninterpreted dream, Joseph tries to turn
this favor into support for his own efforts to win release from prison:

> But remember me when it is well with you, and show me kindness, I pray
> you, and mention me to Pharaoh, and bring me out of this house. For I was
> stolen out of the land of the Hebrews, and here too have I done nothing
> that I should be cast in the dungeon.[1]

Yet the cupbearer turns a deaf ear to Joseph's pleas for assistance. Neither the
favor Joseph has done him, nor his appeal to "kindness," nor his appeal to justice succeed in moving the king's adviser, who sees fit to forget the Hebrew and
his troubles for two full years while Joseph continues to languish. In this case,
too, it is the strict political interest of the chief steward that determines the
degree of his allegiance to Joseph. Having narrowly avoided death for incurring the disfavor of the king, he is hardly interested in exposing himself by
interceding on behalf of others. He feels his position and his life still to be in the

balance – although this may not be any more true of him than it is of the king's other servants – and his every effort is in the direction of pleasing Pharaoh, not in making demands of him. It is only after the king has reached a peak of frustration over his uninterpretable dreams, having failed to obtain a useful interpretation from his advisers, that the steward decides he has something to gain, and probably nothing to lose, by returning the favor that Joseph did for him: If the king is pleased with Joseph, it will only increase his estimation of the steward, whereas if he is not, it was only out of desperation that the steward suggested "the young man, the Hebrew slave."[2]

The critical moves, both in bringing about Haman's downfall and in Joseph's rise to power, are therefore supplied by interested parties whose concern for the well-being of the Jews is questionable or nonexistent, and whose assistance is provided out of strict concern for what will be of benefit to them. That politics makes for strange bedfellows is well known. But an important implication of this maxim, emphasized in the biblical texts, is this: In order to secure the success of any political campaign or effort, regardless of the loftiness of the goal, one must cultivate and make use of such allies – the great majority of men who will side with power, and who will never lift a finger to help the Jews, or anyone else, unless it is made evident that such support is in their own interest. This is the case so universally that it amounts to a natural law of politics: *that strength attracts strength, and power attracts power.* And this is a law to which we will have reason to return.

Harvona's intervention on the side of the Jews allows for an outcome that Esther would not likely have suggested herself. The king immediately orders that Haman be taken out and hanged. But Esther, having scored a decisive gain with the king, does take advantage of his confusion to push through a second, fateful decision without which the story might still have ended in tragedy: the elevation of Mordechai to the position of vizier. "On that day, Ahashverosh the king gave the house of Haman, the persecutor of the Jews, to Esther the queen. And Mordechai came before the king, for Esther had told what he was to her. The king slipped off his ring, which he had retrieved from Haman, and gave it to Mordechai. And Esther placed Mordechai over Haman's house" (8.1–2).

It suits the king to place Esther and Mordechai over all that had been Haman's at this moment, making use of the Jews, the vizier's enemies, to degrade his memory. Ahashverosh thus gives Haman's position and his property, even the signet ring that should rightly have gone back to the king's hand, to those the vizier despised, with the aim of emphasizing how completely Haman's will has been erased. Yet all this is to a large degree show, containing far more hatred of Haman than respect for the Jews. Ahashverosh has no intention of granting Mordechai the extraordinary position of authority he had sought for Haman. There are no proclamations that place the Jew "above all the princes" or require "all the king's servants who were in the king's gate to bow and prostrate themselves" (3.1–2). Instead, Mordechai's promotion to a more conventional position signals the rebirth of history, the restoration of the politics of the empire as it had been before Haman's elevation. Mordechai had saved the life of the king from those who were disloyal to him, and now, belatedly, he is rewarded with a position of trust and responsibility, as one important voice among many.

With Haman out of the way, the queen having demonstrated her influence, Mordechai positioned in the highest political post in the kingdom, and Harvona and others turning to side with the Jews, there can be no question that the constellation of power has improved decisively. Haman's rule has not lasted even a month, his ruin the product of his own idolatrous aspirations. And yet the machinery of extermination that he has set in motion has not been turned aside. His many allies and sympathizers remain to do the work he began.

PART VII

ESTHER 8.3–8.17

A nd Esther spoke before the king yet again, and fell at his feet and cried, and pleaded with him to avert the evil of Haman the Agagite, and the scheme that he had devised against the Jews. ⁴The king extended to Esther the gold scepter, and Esther rose and stood before the king.

⁵She said: "If it please the king, and if I have found favor before him, and if the thing seems right to the king, and if I am worthy in his eyes, let it be written to revoke the letters devised by Haman, son of Hamedata the Agagite, which he wrote to destroy the Jews who are in all the king's provinces. ⁶For how can I bear to see the evil that will befall my people? And how can I bear to witness the destruction of my kindred?"

⁷Ahashverosh the king said to Esther the queen and Mordechai the Jew: "Behold, I have given Haman's house to Esther, and he himself has been hanged on the gallows because he would lift a hand against the Jews. ⁸And you, write concerning the Jews as seems good in your eyes, in the king's name, and seal it with the king's ring. But an edict written in the king's name and sealed with the king's ring cannot be revoked."

⁹The king's scribes were summoned there and then, on the 23rd day of the 3rd month, the month of Sivan, and it was written exactly as Mordechai instructed, to the Jews and to the satraps, and to the governors and the princes of the provinces from India to Ethiopia, 127 provinces, to each province in its own script and to each people in its own tongue, and to the Jews in their own script and their own tongue. ¹⁰He wrote in the name

of Ahashverosh the king and sealed it with the king's ring, sending letters by couriers on horseback, riding the swift thoroughbred
steeds of the king's service: ¹¹that the king had permitted the Jews
in every city to gather and to defend themselves – to annihilate,
to kill and to destroy the forces of every people and province that
threaten them, children and women, and to take their property for
plunder – ¹²in a single day in all the provinces of Ahashverosh the
king, on the 13th day of the 12th month, that is the month of Adar.
¹³The contents of the letter were to be circulated as law in every
province, and were to be published among all peoples, that the Jews
should be ready on that day to avenge themselves upon their enemies. ¹⁴The couriers, riders of the swift steeds of the king's service,
went out with great haste by order of the king, and the law was
distributed in Susa the capital.

¹⁵Mordechai went out from before the king dressed in royal garments of blue and white, with a great crown of gold, and a robe of
fine linen and purple, and the town of Susa rejoiced and was glad.
¹⁶The Jews had light and gladness, and joy and honor. ¹⁷And in
every province, and in every city, wherever the king's command and
his law reached, the Jews had gladness and joy, a feast and a holiday, and many from among the people of the land became Jews, for
fear of the Jews had fallen upon them.

18

The Last Appeal

Esther's coup succeeds in deposing the vizier and placing her cousin at the top of the Persian government. But it does not save the Jews. Indeed, in her principal mission, convincing the king to allow the Jews to escape his decree with their lives, she has failed completely.

It is true that Esther does approach Ahashverosh at her second banquet with the demand that she and her people be saved from Haman. But the king's reaction has nothing to do with the Jews – for whom, to judge by his original complicity in having them all murdered, he would appear to care very little. When he responds to Esther's plea by asking, "Who would presume to do so?" he is referring not to the annihilation of the Jews, but to the threat to the queen. It is the protection of the queen that is, after all, an issue of immediate, burning interest to Ahashverosh. The rest of the Jews, and even the fact of Esther's being a Jewess, appear hardly to scrape his consciousness.

And so things stand for quite a long while. After Haman is hanged and his duties as vizier have been transferred to Mordechai, the king goes back to ignoring the impending destruction of the Jews, just as if Esther had never broached the issue with him. The king's anger over the threat to himself and his household has been appeased by Haman's death, and with this the case is closed. It is not even clear that he heard the second part of Esther's plea: that her people be delivered.

A month goes by, and then a second. Yet the decree of destruction against the Jews remains in force, unchanged.[1] The king is immersed in the business of making order in a politics that has been convulsed by two swift changes in government, and Mordechai finds himself with the pressing and ponderous concern of making a responsible impression in his new post. The narrative stresses that Ahashverosh is generally far more concerned with his honor than with the status of the royal treasuries – giving out "royal wine aplenty from the hand of the king" for half a year (1.7), granting a remission in taxes and giving out gifts "from the king's hand" in honor of his wedding (2.18), waiving away Haman's offer of a vast contribution to the state budget as though it were nothing (3.11), and preferring to respond to petitions with offers of "even if it be half the kingdom it will be given you" (5.3). Indeed, the only time Persia is portrayed as securing sources of financing for all the king's gestures is under Mordechai's tenure as vizier when, like Joseph, he raises taxes and sets the state on the path to solvency and power: "Ahashverosh the king levied taxes on the land, and on the islands of the sea" (10.1). But this new policy must not have been an easy sell with the king and the court, and Mordechai does not dare raise subjects other than those needed to obtain the contradictory aims of pleasing the king and responsibly operating the state.

Only after weeks of frustration and worry does it become apparent to Mordechai and Esther that there is to be no response. Ahashverosh is simply not concerned to alter this policy. Having returned with his tail between his legs from his experiment in totalitarianism, Ahashverosh clings to the old rule of the laws, under which even the king does not alter a law once it has been decreed. Moreover, he has little interest in humiliating himself by rescinding the edict even if a way out can be found, an act that would amount to a public admission of his own confusion and weakness. What is more, he may not have been convinced that Haman was all wrong about the Jews, who after all have proven to be a deadly opponent. Perhaps it is still "of no benefit for the king to tolerate them"? (3.8).

Whatever the explanation, it becomes clear that without a further effort from Esther and Mordechai, the decree will remain in force and the enemies of the Jews will have their way in spite of everything. It is difficult to imagine a more miserable realization. For all that Esther had done, her people were not to be saved. For all her belief that time was of the essence, that she should immediately risk her life rather than let a day go by with the terrible decree in place, here time was dragging on, the awful date approaching, and nothing was being done.

Mordechai has used the intervening time to do everything in his power to gain the confidence of the king. But it is nevertheless obvious that if another appeal is to be made on behalf of the Jews, it is Esther who stands the better chance of influencing Ahashverosh: It was her word that had brought down the vizier, and the king's professed concern for her appears to be deep and genuine. These things cannot be said of Mordechai. Yet Esther's position with the king may not have been as clear as all that either. After all, if she had been able to approach the king without once more entering the throne room unsummoned, she certainly would have, which suggests that the king may have been avoiding her for some time – perhaps even since Haman's downfall. We can only guess whether this was from embarrassment, or from a desire to restore his illusion of control over events, or because he was still nursing a grudge over what had happened, or because he did not wish to discuss the fate of the Jews with his politically partisan wife – or for all of these reasons. And if, when she first approached the king, it had seemed highly likely that he would not want to do away with her, the brooding silence now had put everything in question.

Spring has given way to the deep Persian summer, and sixty-six precious days have gone by before Esther and Mordechai finally reach the conclusion that there is no choice but for Esther once more to gamble with her life.[2] Realizing that this is the last chance for her and her people, Esther again decides to act. She enters the throne room and collapses in tears at the king's feet, pleading the cause of the Jews in public for the first time, even before the king is able to react to her presence.

This time, there is no feint on Esther's part. She leaves no doubt in the king's mind as to what she wants: He can choose to spare her life and confront her face to face on the issue of her people – or he can avoid the subject for good at the cost of having her executed.

Although Ahashverosh still has no interest in discussing the Jews, his hand is forced. The humiliation of losing his queen would be too great, and he extends the scepter to her a second time. But this time he says nothing, grudgingly refusing to solicit her request according to the accepted formula. Passive, morose, he just lets her talk.

Esther's second appearance in the throne room barely resembles the first. Gone are her hesitation and stammering, her lack of confidence. Gone are Ahashverosh's pompous displays of his power to grant her things. They both now recognize the power that she has in the court. Politely, but forcefully, she presents a demand that she believes he has to accept: "If it please the king, and if I have found favor before him, and if the thing seems right to the king, and if I am worthy in his eyes, let it be written to revoke the letters devised by Haman, son of Hamedata the Agagite, which he wrote to destroy the Jews who are in all the king's provinces. For how can I bear to see the evil that will befall my people? And how can I bear to witness the destruction of my kindred?" (8.6–7).

Esther's carefully rehearsed address has three parts, each corresponding to a different instrument of political pressure to which the queen appeals: the king's interest in those things that he desires; his presumed interest in the cause of justice; and his fear of losing her:

Interest:

(i) If it please the king;
(ii) If I have found favor with the king;

Justice:

(iii) If it seems right;
(iv) If I am worthy;

Fear of Esther herself:

(v) I cannot bear to see this evil;
(vi) I cannot bear to witness this destruction.

Some of these expressions have appeared in Esther's earlier approaches to make requests of the king – the invitation to her first banquet (5.4), the invitation to her second banquet (5.8), and her first plea for the deliverance of her people (7.3) – but there is also much here that she has never been willing to say to Ahashverosh before.

The first part, appealing to the king's interest, consists of standard formulations for making a request from a king, which Esther has always used before in her dealings with Ahashverosh. (i) "If it please the king" constitutes an appeal to whatever the king wants and considers desirable, and serves to present her proposed course as one that should be pleasing to him because it is in his interest. Esther herself has used this formulation each time she has made a request of the king, beginning with her first approach, in which she invites the king and his vizier to her banquet. It is also used in every other political appeal in the narrative, whether by Memuchan, Haman, Esther, or the king's youths.[3]

The second appeal to interest, (ii) "if I have found favor with the king," is more personal and less direct, drawing the king's attention to the fact that it is in his interest to act for the sake of someone whom he desires to please, even if the requested action is in itself of no interest to him. This is the kind of vicarious interest of which "boss" politics is made, with favors constantly being disbursed to keep various clients and vassals feeling taken care of and, consequently, in line. Even this mild effort indirectly to focus on someone other than the king seems to have been a bit presumptuous, however, since no one dares make use of it other than the queen, and she herself musters the courage to do so only upon making her second and third requests of the king.

The other components of Esther's speech are unique to her history, as well as being unique in the entire narrative, demonstrating how far she has come both in her political wisdom and in her willingness to confront the king. Esther makes two appeals to justice, which mimic the pattern of her appeals to interest: (iii) "if it seems right" and (iv) "if I am worthy" – turning first to the objective question of the justice of sparing the Jews (even if the king has no political interest in doing so), and then to the question of whether she herself is deserving of having this done for her (even the king has no interest of his own in granting her such a favor).

Issues of justice are a critical factor in political pressure because they appeal to considerations that are capable of inducing the listener to rise above the constraints of his own petty self-interest, and more than a few men can be induced to take at least some action on these grounds. Yet appeals to justice are also important in the case of a rascal such as Ahashverosh, even though his actual concern for justice is demonstrably trivial, because they play to the interest of every ruler in *appearing* just to maintain the respect of his subjects.[4] Ahashverosh in particular is known for his cultivation of the appearance of justice, consulting with the learned whenever such are present "for such was the king's habit before all who knew law and judgment" (1.13).

But there is more to this part of the confrontation than an effort to embarrass the king into doing the right thing. With these formulations referring to the moral judgment of the king ("if it seems right to the king," "if I am worthy in his eyes"), Esther honors him, but in a manner that steers his attention to things that exist outside of his juvenile desires. No matter how politely the point may be phrased, questions of justice deal not with personal perceptions, but with objective issues of what is right and wrong, good and evil in the world: If saving the Jews is right, then any other determination on the part of the king is wrong. If Esther, after years of devoted service, including saving the life of the king, is not to be considered worthy of having her request granted, then Ahashverosh is obtuse in his ability to judge those around him. And it is important that he sense that such are her opinions.

To broach questions of objective truth before Ahashverosh is in itself to challenge the feeling of omnipotence with which the king likes to pamper himself – just as it had been a challenge to Haman before him. But it also reflects an accurate reading of the strength of the man. Ahashverosh, for all his rages, is afraid to rely on his own judgment in making decisions, afraid of exposing himself, afraid of embarrassing himself, and afraid of losing control. Esther correctly guesses that the more strongly he is aware of the steadfastness of her position, the more likely he is to take it as a given and respond favorably. That is, she must appeal to justice in order to make it clear to Ahashverosh that a decision based solely on what he believes to be in his own personal interest is unacceptable. The policy of the state must square with reality – which is to say, with Esther's reality.

Among other things, Ahashverosh's personal weakness suggests a fear of rejection as well, and it is to this fear that Esther appeals in the third, climactic part of her speech, when she asks: (v, vi) "How can I bear to see the evil that will befall my people? How can I bear to witness the destruction of my kindred?"

By this point, all pretense of playing to the king's interest is, incredibly, dropped, and Esther, perhaps alone among the petitioners whom Ahashverosh can remember, steps forward as an independent player with an independent interest to which she demands that he attend: The queen wants the Jews saved because she herself cannot stand to have it otherwise. Ahashverosh can save the Jews because it suits him, or he can save them because it is right. But if he does not, the queen will not be able to "bear" it – whatever this may mean – and it is he who will have to cope with the consequences.

The full force of the queen's threat cannot be appraised without remembering Vashti, who would not show off her beauty before the drunken crowd at the king's summons. She, too, had publicly pitted her independent interest against his command. The throng, the advice, the drink, the humiliation, all had braced him to fight, to eliminate her independent will and restore his own rule. But in securing victory for his spirit, Ahashverosh had lost, paying for his refusal to accommodate with years of painful second thoughts. This time, there is no throng, no advice, no drink: only the humiliation of backing down and rescinding his foolish law, standing against the power of the queen – understated, hidden, mysterious, but there to be felt – the eternal, imponderable power of the weak over the mighty.

Ahashverosh has only two choices as he sits before the watching eyes of the courtiers: He may try to discredit Esther and distance himself from her position, as he did with Vashti. Or he can seek conciliation with Esther and the Jews by distancing himself from Haman's law.

As he looks down from his throne at Mordechai and the others, he recognizes that there is no way of avoiding the issue. Refusing to respond to Esther would amount to a negative response, and he is not strong enough to open up such a fight. His hand forced, the king fumbles for a defense that will allow him to accept the queen's position while minimizing the damage done by an about-face. He professes to have done everything within his power to protect the Jews: "I have given Haman's house to Esther," he announces to the court, "and he himself has been hanged on the gallows because he would lift a hand against the Jews" (8.7).

Upon hearing these words, anyone present in the court would have instantly recognized the victory Esther had won. For two months, loyal servants of the king have maintained the face-saving fiction that Haman's death was brought about by his treachery against the king and queen, a story that Ahashverosh himself had concocted upon discovering Haman begging for mercy on the queen's divan (7.8). The rivalry between the deceased vizier and the Jews, as well as Haman's plan to have the Jews massacred, had been oddly left out of the story, for the simple reason that it would have embarrassed the king, whose intention to have all the Jews of the empire exterminated had been well known.[5]

Yet to hear the king now, he never was the scourge of the Jews, having actually championed their cause. According to this new version, Ahashverosh had brought Haman down "because he would lift a hand against the Jews." In so saying, Ahashverosh officially accepts the premise that the persecution of the Jews is unjust and undesirable. The extermination order itself is still on the books, he implies, not through any fault of his own, but only because "an edict written in the king's name and sealed with the king's ring cannot be revoked." Had it been up to Ahashverosh, the kingdom is now to believe, it would all have been different. Indeed, as far as the king is concerned, Mordechai, the new vizier, can "write concerning the Jews as seems good in your eyes, in the king's name" (8.8). It is not he, but the law of the land that stands in the way of saving the Jews.

This is political legerdemain at its finest, but there is no one in the court who has the will and the authority to challenge the revolution that has just occurred in imperial policy. Like Harvona, the king himself has now recognized which way the winds are blowing and switched sides – marking the actual political watershed from which point a favorable conclusion of the story becomes a real possibility, the odds actually shifting in favor of the camp of the Jews for the first time.

19

Political Power

By the time of the king's "conversion" to the cause of the Jews, only eight
months remain before the day that Haman's followers believe will see their
vengeance and ultimate triumph.[1] With the king's at least nominal support for
the Jewish cause, it now becomes possible for Mordechai to work openly to
undermine the forces that continue organizing in preparation for the massacre.

As vizier Mordechai has at his disposal the influence of the central government of the empire. Nevertheless, it is easy to underestimate the task before
him. For while the belief that Ahashverosh wants all the Jews murdered has
been abroad for only about ten weeks, the machine now set in motion has
been much longer in the making. It is evident from the narrative that fear of
the Jews and hostility toward them are not something new to Haman's followers, nor to others in the kingdom.[2] The king's decree was not, therefore,
meant to move the empire to do something to which none would otherwise
have been inclined. In the manner of state-sponsored pogroms elsewhere, it
was rather an official assurance that the state would stand aside if individuals and local governments did as they had wanted to do for years. With an
imperial decree in force to the effect that the Jews were to be massacred, there
had been no shortage of enthusiasts setting to work to prepare for the great
day. Nor did they have any difficulty in persuading the fence-sitters to join in
with Haman in a position of unquestioned predominance. For all of these,
Haman's death had been a blow, but it had also made him a martyr of the
anti-Jewish cause, exciting calls for revenge across the empire. The fact is that
the machine Haman had set in motion would not be so easily turned aside
under any circumstance.

Moreover, Mordechai's political aims at this point are not as simple as might
be supposed at first glance. While a military triumph for the Jews might seem

a fine thing, Mordechai cannot satisfy himself with this. He must somehow secure the life of every individual Jew, everywhere in the empire. From this perspective, it is clear that any scenario in which an overwhelming victory for the Jews and their allies is not a foregone conclusion will end in disaster. The date designated by Haman will trigger warfare against the Jews throughout the empire, in which the casualties on both sides will be massive, and the weaker among the Jewish communities will have been destroyed before the fighting has ended.

Without the ability to alter Haman's decree, Mordechai has before him only one way to prevent such a catastrophe. There can be no hope of preventing massacres without bringing the might of the empire to bear against the anti-Semites – as would have been the case if they had tried to organize the murder of innocents without the encouragement of an official decree. He therefore has to build an alliance of supportive forces great enough so that the anti-Semites will find themselves abandoned by their following and without the capacity to mount a serious assault against the Jews in any province. But how can this be done?

Herein lies the fundamental question that is the subject of politics: How can the individual, weak as he is, move the group of the many to act in accordance with his will?

In politics, weakness does not attract the interest of strength, does not bring strength around to its cause, does not move strength to action. But strength attracts strength, and power attracts power. The strong have every reason to be attracted to those they believe to be strong, and to assist them in attaining their aims. This is (i) so that they may win favor with them and later receive assistance from them in return; (ii) so that they may avoid arousing the ire and ill will of the strong; (iii) so that they may be perceived as being influential with the strong, and thus powerful themselves; and (iv) so that they take part in winning combinations in which they may claim a share of the spoils. None of these reasons for joining in with the strong can be said to apply to the weak. The weak can rarely return favors of value; they can rarely do damage worth fearing; there is little value in being perceived as having influence with them; and there are no spoils to be gained in joining in their moves, since it is ever apparent that they will lose.

And thus to the fundamental question of all politics, there is only one possible answer: The weak, to the degree they can make themselves seem strong, can attract the support of the strong, thereby becoming strong in reality; and to the degree that they fail in this, they can expect no help from men.

It is in a sense to the credit of contemporary readers that this most basic political truth often strikes them as so alien, that it at first appears unintelligible. If one is unschooled in politics, it seems precisely the opposite should be the case: that weakness should attract strength – that one should strive to defend the weak and assist the poor and the oppressed, as the prophets of Israel call upon us to do. But such biblical moral principles are advanced to remedy nature as we find it, "natural law" coming as it does to repair what we find intolerable in the way the world works – and in the ways of politics especially.[3]

The Bible emphasizes that the righteous, both Jews and gentiles, have always made it their business to use their strength to protect the weak. But as is clear from the biblical narrative, these righteous women and men are the exceptions. The reality is as Machiavelli became notorious for insisting: The world does not much run according to these precedents.[4] The book of Esther sticks close to the gritty functioning of the common political world – in which no one stood to defend Vashti when the king was poised to destroy her, in which no one stood to defend Esther or the other women when they were to be forced into the harem, in which no one joined Mordechai in refusing to bow to Haman, in which no man stood with Mordechai to openly oppose the extermination of the Jews at the word of the king. Indeed, not one among the mighty and the many of the empire dares to stand up against Haman in anything so long as he is strong, and Harvona, the first to break ranks and openly turn against him, does so only after "the king had determined ill against him" (7.7) – that is, not until after it is clear that Haman is already doomed.

It is the grim consistency with which considerations of political interest prevail over every other motive, even more than the absence of explicit mentions of God, that imparts to the narrative of Esther the dark sense that its action takes place at the edge of the abyss. Men live in such a world unless they make it otherwise, and it is according to the world's rules that Mordechai must play if he is to win.

The narrative describes six ways in which Mordechai acts to fight and win the political war, rallying the strength of the empire to his side and causing the anti-Semites to despair and give up on implementing the original edict. The first three acts of Mordechai are described in the account that follows Esther's second appeal for the lives of the Jews: (i) Mordechai's decree permitting the Jews to assemble and defend themselves (8.9–14), (ii) Mordechai's public appearances in Susa (8.15–16), and (iii) the public celebrations among the Jews (8.17).

The next chapter, which treats the course of the war itself, makes it clear that these are only the first successes in a concerted political campaign that Mordechai wages over the next months in order to make the military victory possible:

> The Jews gathered themselves in their cities in all the provinces of Ahashverosh the king, to lay their hands on those who sought to harm

them, and no man could stand before them, for fear of them had fallen on all the peoples. And all the princes of the provinces, and the satraps, and the governors and those that conduct the king's affairs supported the Jews, because the fear of Mordechai had fallen upon them. For great was Mordechai in the king's house, and his reputation had gone out to all the provinces, for the man Mordechai grew greater and greater (9.2–4).

Thus in addition to actions taken immediately upon the appearance of his decree, Mordechai's political offensive to save the Jews includes three more aspects: (iv) organizing Jewish military power (9.2), (v) rallying the support of provincial and local governments (9.3), and (vi) building up his own reputation (9.4).

It is worth looking at the way these elements are assembled to form a comprehensive political campaign. The first efforts of any political offensive must be aimed at the morale of one's own camp, for if they are not psychologically prepared for the coming fight, it will be impossible to project whatever strength they may have in potential. This means that to have a real chance of coming out of this ordeal victorious, the Jews must believe that they can win; and only if they believe that they can win can they impress upon their enemies that they may lose.

No one understands this as well as Haman, whose original decree was crafted to fight just this psychological war, robbing the Jews of their self-confidence by demonstrating that their independence and power amounts to a nullity, instructing: "To annihilate, to kill and to destroy all the Jews, the young and the elderly, children and women, in one day – on the 13th day of the 12th month, the month of Adar – and to take their property for plunder" (3.13).

This first decree had consisted of three parts, each forged in the image of the obsessed anti-Semite's lust for the complete degradation and disempowering of his opponents: (i) to annihilate, to kill and to destroy the Jews, (ii) to kill their children and women, and (iii) to take their property for plunder.

Thus the almost comical emphasis on how the Jews, every one, were not only to be "annihilated," but also "killed" and "destroyed," was intended by Haman to connote perfect rule, without exception, without hope of escape. The emphasis on "children and women" was a further step in the terror, demonstrating that nothing would be left of anything that the annihilated Jews had valued and hoped for during their lives. And the almost anticlimactic insistence on taking "their property for plunder" – which one might have thought to be an issue of little interest to people who were being informed of their own deaths and those of all their loved ones – was intended to deepen their anguish. Rather than ordering that the properties be handed over to the king's treasuries, Haman chose to leave the possessions of the Jews in the hands of those who had murdered them. The Jews were to understand that not only were they to be murdered, but that others, their murderers, would reap the benefits of all they had hoped for and labored toward in their lives.

The contempt for issues of property comes from a perspective in which things are measured in terms of their supposed objective worth: How can one compare property ("things") to the value of the life of a human being? But the narratives of the Bible are more sensitive than we tend to be to the way in which things come to be of value to the individual. People spend their entire lives building up a home or a business or a farm in order to create things that are the fruit of their lives, and that they will pass on to those people who are most precious to them. For the individual, the property in question is not a material object at all, just as the children in question are not merely individual lives. The property, like the children, is an achievement of a person's spirit. It has come to be what it is through his own rule – not merely his labor, but his labor as the process through which his control and rule, his decisions and creativity, his power, is exerted upon the world. Because both the children and the property continue on after death, they are the ways in which every individual may evade the mortality that hangs over him: If the mortality of man confirms his powerlessness, his ability to create things that will endure, that will even stand as a contribution to the eternal, robs death of its absolute power. It relieves man of his absolute powerlessness before the eternal, restoring his spirit, which would otherwise drown in perpetual hopelessness.

While an objective estimation should place murder as the greatest of crimes, the biblical narrative is therefore often aware that from the point of view of the murdered, whose life would in any case have come to an end someday, there may be other crimes that are more terrible. Thus the book of Kings relates the story of Navot the Jezre'elite, whose vineyard Ahav, king of Israel, determined to have for a vegetable garden because it was near his house. Ahav offered to give Navot money or a "better vineyard than this one" in exchange. But the fact that Ahav was offering an objectively good deal in the form of a "better" vineyard was of no interest to Navot, for whom such a trade was reprehensible. He had spent his life from childhood building up a vineyard, as good a one as he could make, so that it could be passed on. Should he now agree to have his life's work destroyed so that the king could have vegetables near at hand? He responds: "The Lord curse me if I should give you the inheritance of my fathers."

Like Ahashverosh, Ahav finds not having his way unbearable, and like Ahashverosh, he has advisers prepared to goad him to perfidy over such opposition to his authority. Jezebel, the queen, sends out letters in Ahav's name, sealed with his signet, ordering that Navot be killed, and then triumphantly announces that he may now go down and begin uprooting the vines. When the prophet Elijah finds the king in the vineyard, he is enraged: "So says the Lord: Have you murdered, and then taken possession as well?"[5]

Here, too, it is possible to ask how a property issue can be on the prophet's mind when a man has been murdered. And the answer is that Elijah understands the evil king's deed from the perspective of the slain man, for whom the greatest pain would not have been the ending of his life, but the erasure of all that he had achieved in it, as though he had never been – so that another with no sympathy or appreciation for what he had built could plant his own shoots there and grow these instead. Elijah understands what has happened here to be not only a crime of the body, but a crime of the spirit as well. And such is also the judgment of other biblical thinkers when they consider the meaning of property to men: Kohelet, for example, considers the fact that the product of one's labors will be inherited after death, and then mistreated by men who are likely to be fools, to be one of life's worst evils;[6] and Jeremiah, in seeking to impress upon Jerusalem the terror that is to come, depicts God as saying: "Therefore I will give their wives to others, and their fields to those who will take them."[7] Enjoyment of one's life's work by his conquerors can be seen as the most potent expression of ruin and defeat, and in fact, it is to precisely this sense of ultimate ruin that Ahashverosh wishes to appeal when he gives Haman's estate to Esther.

Recognizing this, we can now understand the purpose and effect of Haman's decree. For ten furious weeks after its promulgation, the streets of every city in the empire reverberated with scenes in which the anti-Jews worked the brutal psychology of the king's edict for all it was worth. The enemies of the Jews – not only the enemies of the Jewish people, but the enemies of every particular, individual Jew as well – swaggered about the public places, trumpeting their intentions in the face of every Jew who had ever insulted them, or edged them out for a public post, or charged them a price they believed to be too high, in accordance with the three parts of the decree: "I will have your house when you are gone, Jew"; "I will have your daughter before she dies, Jew"; "I will dance on your grave, Jew." And worse. And with the taunting began the acts of vandalism, of theft, of desecration, testing the Jews, humiliating them, preparing them.

The effect of this campaign was first on the anti-Semites themselves, as it had been in Pharaoh's Egypt, as it was in the Germany of the brownshirts. It gave the anti-Jews what they wanted more than anything else: the drunken, boundless sense of vengeful rule that is the motive heart of all great evil. It provided them with the sense of empowerment, of license, of freedom without which they would never have dared to speak as they did, and without which they could never have done as they planned to do. For many are the dark thoughts that men nurse in silence; but to act when the bitter day comes requires not only organization, but psychological preparation. Every day in the streets they prepared themselves to accept, to anticipate, to desire, to believe in what was coming.

But the greater effect was on the Jews themselves. The natural reaction of a man under attack is to become angered, to rise up in power, to fight. These are the reactions of any animal that can still hope to have power over others, at least to have power over itself. But beyond anger lies despair, the emotion that accompanies the belief in the hopelessness of one's cause, and the powerlessness of one's self. And as the campaign of humiliation gained strength and popularity in the streets, so did the Jews feel more isolated every day. As friends began to distance themselves, as those who had feared them began to laugh, as those who owed them debts of gratitude turned their backs, they began to feel the despair in the air, the hopelessness and the death. The Jews turned in on themselves, grew numb, grew powerless, grew tired of life, became objects, became dead. For many of them in those terrible weeks, their annihilation gradually became a fact, and they began to say to themselves: Tomorrow we die.

When Esther finally succeeds in extracting a grudging statement in support of the Jews from the king, Mordechai recognizes that much will have to be done to transform this shift in the palace into a different reality in the provinces. Without a dramatic act to break the momentum of events, the deterioration in the condition of the Jews and the rapidly growing power of their enemies will continue, and massacres of the Jews will take place in various parts of the empire despite everything that has happened in Susa.

Unable to revoke the king's first decree, Mordechai chooses to give force to the king's new policy by giving the anti-Semites a dose of their own methods. He constructs a decree of his own, informing the empire that the king will allow the Jews "to annihilate, to kill and to destroy the forces of every people and province that threaten them, children and women, and to take their property for plunder – in a single day in all the provinces of Ahashverosh the king, on the 13th day of the 12th month, that is the month of Adar" (8.11–12).

Mordechai's missive emphasizes the fact that the king had "permitted the Jews in every city to gather and to defend themselves" against "forces ... that threaten them," whether arising from the government or the populace (8.11).[8] But the wording of Mordechai's edict does not sound defensive at all. Being copied straight out of the first letter composed by Haman, it grants the Jews permission "to annihilate, to kill and to destroy" their enemies, to slaughter their children and women, and to seize their property. Neither the assault on the families of the forces arrayed against the Jews nor the clause concerning property has anything to do with defense in any obvious sense, nor does

the brutal hyperbole of annihilation, killing, and destroying immediately seem
to have much in common with this purpose. Indeed, Mordechai's letter reeks
of Haman's style and substance, and its language is the language of terror.
When first these formulations were sent out by Haman, their purpose was
clearly to inspire fear and despair. In this second instance, this is not less the
case: Mordechai reasons that the Jews need a shot of confidence, and that the
anti-Semites need a slap in the face to deprive them of their certainty of victory.[9] And if the Jews must stay up nights wondering whether their children
will be alive a year from now, whether someone else will be living in their home
a year from now, then the anti-Semites can afford to lose some sleep as well.

In this, Mordechai's decree is successful. There immediately follows a giddy,
surreal account of Mordechai's stepping into the streets of the Jewish quarter
after the promulgation of the decree, virtually radiating with a majestic power
that revives the languishing Jews of the capital:

> Mordechai went out from before the king dressed in royal garments of blue
> and white, with a great crown of gold and a robe of fine linen and purple,
> and the town of Susa rejoiced and was glad. The Jews had light and glad-
> ness, and joy and honor (8.15–16).[10]

Mordechai had been functioning as vizier before this point, and there is no
reason to think that his personal appearance actually changed much after his
decree had been issued. But the narrative refers to the subjective understanding
of the Jews, for whom even Haman's death could have been scant comfort. So
long as the king was determined to go through with the promised outrages, the
appearance on the street of a court Jew such as Mordechai – having once been
paraded through the streets on the king's horse, now dressed in the king's fin-
ery, in fact nothing better than an accomplice – would only have been the subject of ambivalence, and probably even scorn. Mordechai himself must have
seemed to many in those weeks a rather pathetic and grasshopperish figure,
a subservient court Jew if not a traitor. It is only with the appearance of the
decree, and the shift in the policy of the king toward the Jews, that Mordechai
in fact begins to gain the stature that until then had only been formally his.
Most of the Jews, living outside the fortress, have seen the meaning of imperial
power up close only once in their lives – when Ahashverosh invited them to
immerse themselves in his wealth and majesty in the palace, amid "hangings of
white, of fine cotton, and blue, suspended with cords of fine linen and purple
from silver rods and marble columns, divans of gold and silver" (1.6). But now
they have the chance to see this strength being wielded on their behalf by one
of their own. It is no coincidence, then, that they now perceive Mordechai as
being wrapped in the same royal tones, "in royal garments of blue and white,
with a great crown of gold, and a robe of fine linen and purple." As a result,

"the Jews had light and gladness, and joy and honor" – not merely happiness, but honor, the sense of pleasure that results from a renewed belief that they have control over their lives. And while they do not take the same pleasure in it, the anti-Semites, too, can see that there is something astonishing in this reversal of fortune.

Mordechai's brutal decree is the first step in establishing him as the leader who would destroy the enemies of the Jews, his march through Susa the second. By nightfall, celebrations had been organized, which were then repeated throughout the empire as word of Mordechai's decree reached the other provinces. And everywhere the celebrations reached, the Jews began to feel themselves reviving. At Mordechai's behest, "the Jews gathered themselves in their cities in all the provinces of Ahashverosh the king, to lay their hands on those who sought to harm them," and they began to feel the first traces of genuine strength in them.

This did not, of course, mean that the anti-Semites gave up on their plans to obey the decree of the king and destroy the Jews. Some of them only grew in their determination to carry out their plans, and the harassment of the Jewish communities of the empire certainly did not immediately come to an end because of this second decree permitting the Jews to defend themselves. But what had been a straightforward edict of annihilation had now turned into a test of strengths, with that of the Jews on the ascendant, so that wherever the anti-Semites sought to humiliate the Jews and test their mettle, they now collided with a tide of increasing confidence – the taunts were thrown back in their faces, and some of the more hot-tempered Jews responded to the hatred of the anti-Semites with blows. And with every bruising confrontation, the reputation of the Jews and their leader increased, and confidence in the inevitable fact of their destruction and its desirability withered. And as this process took place, one and all could glimpse the uncanny growth in Mordechai's physical appearance as "the man Mordechai grew greater and greater" – and this slowly began to be true of the Jew in the street in every city of the empire as well.[11] Whereas only weeks before, both the Jews and much of Persia would have laughed to know that the rabbis of later times referred to Mordechai the Jew as a dragon, now the distinct contours of the dragon's armor, its talons, its mass, its breath, and its guile all began to emerge.[12]

With this change in public image, Mordechai had the strands of power he needed to barter for greater political assets, taking his political campaign to "the princes of the provinces, and the satraps, and the governors and those that conduct the king's affairs," whose support in each province would mean the difference between life and destruction. In some cases, he immediately found himself speaking with those who were sympathetic, or who could at least read the writing on the wall. Consolidating this support and encouraging it to go public, Mordechai turned to the harder cases, seeking harsher methods of persuasion, pointing to the military preparations under way, to the support for their cause that was now the policy of the king, to the foolhardiness of the anti-Semites' plans – pushing every official who could have a hand in the business to believe that the anti-Semites could not win, that those who aided them would only suffer in the end.

And one by one, they came to believe him, for "his reputation had gone out to all the provinces, because the fear of Mordechai had fallen upon them." And one by one, those who had sympathized with the Jews began to do so openly; those who had been uncertain began to sympathize; those who had been derisive and had calculated the benefits of the coming catastrophe grew silent; and those who had preached against the Jews grew afraid. And the sense grew in Persia that the Jews were going to win.

In the end, the image of Mordechai did reach the proportions that had characterized Haman during the reign of his terror, when none of the king's servants could resist prostrating himself before him. The empire believed in the power of Mordechai, and so they believed in the power of the Jews, and "none could stand before them, for the fear of them had fallen on all the peoples."[13]

And the Jews saw this additional, remarkable effect of the law that in politics, strength attracts strength, and power attracts power: "And many from among the people of the land became Jews, for fear of the Jews had fallen upon them" (8.17).[14]

PART VIII

ESTHER 9.1–9.16

O n the 13th day of the 12th month, the month of Adar, when the king's command and his law were to be enforced, on the day that the enemies of the Jews had expected to rule over them, the situation was reversed, and it was the Jews themselves who ruled over those who hated them.

²The Jews gathered themselves in their cities in all the provinces of Ahashverosh the king, to lay their hands on those who sought to harm them, and no man could stand before them, for fear of them had fallen on all the peoples. ³And all the princes of the provinces, and the satraps, and the governors, and those who conduct the king's affairs supported the Jews, because the fear of Mordechai had fallen upon them. ⁴For great was Mordechai in the king's house, and his reputation had gone out to all the provinces, for the man Mordechai grew greater and greater.

⁵The Jews struck at all their enemies with the sword, killing and destroying, and they did as they pleased to those who hated them. ⁶And in Susa the capital the Jews killed and destroyed five hundred men – ⁷along with Parshandata, Dalphon, Asphata, ⁸Porata, Adalia, Aridata, ⁹Parimashta, Arisai, Aridai, and Vaizata, ¹⁰the ten sons of Haman, son of Hamedata, the persecutor of the Jews. But the spoils they did not touch.

¹¹That day the number of those killed in Susa the capital was reported to the king.

¹²The king said to Esther the queen: "In Susa the capital the Jews have killed and destroyed five hundred men, and the ten sons of Haman. What have they done in the rest of the king's

provinces? – and whatever your wish, it will be given you, and whatever more you may request, it will be done."

[13]Esther said: "If it please the king, let the Jews in Susa do tomorrow according to the law for today, and let Haman's ten sons be hanged on the gallows."

[14]The king said to do so, and the law was given in Susa, and Haman's ten sons were hanged. [15]The Jews in Susa assembled on the 14th day of the month of Adar as well, and they killed in Susa three hundred men. But the spoils they did not touch.

[16]The rest of the Jews who were in the king's provinces gathered together and fought for their lives, gaining respite from their enemies and killing seventy-five thousand of those who hated them. But the spoils they did not touch.

20

The Jews' War

By the 13th of Adar, the Jews have turned political defeat into political triumph, and the power to emerge from battle victorious is theirs. When the day comes, they use this strength to deal a death blow to anti-Semitic power in the empire, killing more than seventy-five thousand men, laying waste to its leadership, and establishing a deterrent against future threats to the Jewish communities of Persia. Perhaps most significant, the crushing of the anti-Semitic nemesis establishes the position of the new Jewish vizier with the king, ensuring that Ahashverosh's authority will be wielded in such a way as to protect the Jewish interest for years to come.

The narrative touches on only the most essential aspects of these final stages of Mordechai and Esther's efforts, but these are enough to understand what happened. After months of feverish diplomatic work, Mordechai had succeeded in parlaying the fact of the new decree's existence and the feeble mumblings of Ahashverosh into a widespread belief that he in fact had the influence, authority, and power to make good on it: "The man Mordechai grew greater and greater," "his reputation had gone out to all the provinces," and with that "the fear of Mordechai had fallen upon them." By the opening of the actual war, the influence of the Jews in the empire had become overwhelming. The hard core of anti-Semitic power had been isolated, as "all the princes of the provinces, and the satraps, and the governors and those that conduct the king's affairs supported the Jews." Many of those who had been willing to support the anti-Semites had switched sides or disappeared into the woodwork, and it appeared that the Jews and their allies would score a terrifying victory. Thus the "fear of them had fallen on all the peoples," and "none could stand before them." (9.2–4).[1]

Some have suggested that Mordechai now had the option of restraining the fury of the promised Jewish onslaught: There was no longer much question of a real anti-Semitic assault, and if he feared there would be an anti-Semitic resurgence if he relented, he could have opted to arrest or execute a few hundred gang leaders across the empire. Would this not have sufficed?

Mordechai obviously does not believe such a minimalist response would have been enough, and his decisions are straight out of Machiavelli's textbook of power politics:

> For it must be noted, that men must either be caressed or annihilated; they will revenge themselves for small injuries, but cannot do so for great ones; the injury therefore that we do to a man must be such that we need not fear his vengeance.[2]

Moreover, a ruler or a prince

> must not mind incurring the charge of cruelty for the purpose of keeping his subjects united and faithful; for, with a very few examples, he will be more merciful than those who, from excess of tenderness, allow disorders to arise, from whence spring bloodshed and rapine .... And of all princes, it is impossible for a new prince to escape the reputation of cruelty.[3]

In other words, a minimalistic response to a genuine threat all but ensures two undesired consequences, both of them deadly: (i) The defeated enemy nurtures the hope of revenge, and continues to be an active threat as he seeks an opportunity to reassert his challenge; and (ii) the mildness of the response encourages others to take advantage of what can be perceived to be hesitancy or weakness on the part of the ruler. The only hope to avoid future outrages is thus the assertion of overwhelming power in the first instance.

And this is what Mordechai chooses to do: "The Jews struck at all their enemies with the sword, killing and destroying, and they did as they pleased to those who hated them. And in Susa the capital the Jews killed and destroyed five hundred men – along with Parshandata, Dalphon, Asphata, Porata, Adalia, Aridata, Parimashta, Arisai, Aridai and Vaizata, the ten sons of Haman .... The rest of the Jews who were in the king's provinces gathered together and fought for their lives, gaining respite from their enemies and killing seventy-five thousand of those who hated them" (9.5–10, 16).

Throughout the empire, the Jews enter into battle with the anti-Semitic forces, in most cases with the active assistance of the allies who have rallied to support Mordechai's position. Abandoned by most of their former supporters among the people and in the government, the anti-Semitic inciters and those who had actively advanced their cause are brought low in province after province.[4] The carnage is so great that (i) the anti-Semitic basilisk is in fact beheaded, its life and leadership burned out of the body politic; and (ii) the lesson is learned by all future challengers to the safety of the Jews and the power of Mordechai in the king's court. Nowhere in all the vast reaches of the Persian empire does there any longer exist a leader capable of inspiring the peoples to rise and harm the Jewish communities, nor can anyone imagine becoming one while Mordechai's influence persists.

But there is a third reason for the decision to go to war that perhaps even surpasses the others in importance: (iii) the position of the king himself toward the Jews and toward Mordechai as their leader.

When last Ahashverosh had expressed an opinion on the subject of saving the lives of the Jews of Persia, he had managed to leave no question as to how little the subject concerned him. Pushed by the queen, the best he had been able to do was to reply that he had already done something good for the Jews once ("Behold, I have given Haman's house to Esther, and he himself has been hanged on the gallows"), and that although there was nothing else to be done ("an edict written in the king's name and sealed with the king's ring cannot be revoked"), Mordechai and Esther were free to try if they so chose ("And you, write concerning the Jews as seems good in your eyes") (8.7–8). If this answer does not in itself suffice to transmit a message of disdain and disregard, one need only compare it to the account of Darius' response when confronted with similar circumstances in the book of Daniel. Upon learning that he has unwittingly issued an irreversible royal edict that will result in the death of his Jewish vizier in the lion's pit that night, Darius is "much distressed," labors futilely until sunset to rescue him, spends the sleepless night in fasting, rises at dawn "in anguish" to see what has become of his servant, and in the end orders that the advisers who pushed him to issue the murderous decree be tossed to the lions themselves.[5]

Ahashverosh is indeed a scoundrel. Not only is there no reason to believe his present professions of sympathy for the Jews, but his original complicity in the plan to destroy them, especially when combined with his subsequent statements on the subject, suggests that there is every reason to fear for the future. Who is to say that some turn of events will not take the Jews out of favor and return Ahashverosh to the original course he and Haman had set? With these facts constantly before him, Mordechai has another, crucial reason to bring the war against the enemies of the Jews to its spectacular conclusion: *Strength attracts strength, and power attracts power. Thus the weak, to the degree they can make themselves seem strong, can attract the support of the strong, thereby becoming strong in reality.*

Ahashverosh has made it clear that he is not the slightest bit inclined to become the protector of the Jews so long as they are a diffuse and contrary minority, and therefore "it is of no benefit for the king to tolerate them" (3.8). If Mordechai is to make the reversal of the Jews' fortunes complete – and if he is to lend this reversal a measure of stability and permanence – he has no choice but to make it perfectly obvious to Ahashverosh that the Jews are strong, and that it is in fact of very real benefit to him to tolerate them, to ally himself with them, and to protect them against future threats that may arise.

This, the final transformation in the king's relationship with the Jews, is depicted in an exchange between Ahashverosh and his Jewish queen at the height of the tension on the day of the war. Reports from the provinces have not yet begun to arrive, but the dimensions of the catastrophe that has befallen the anti-Semites in Susa have already become known. For the first time in the narrative, we see Ahashverosh initiating a conversation with Esther, and telling her: "In Susa the capital the Jews have killed and destroyed five hundred men, and the ten sons of Haman. What have they done in the rest of the king's provinces?"

Immediately after this, there tumbles from the king's lips a statement that one is tempted to mistake for a non sequitur. He says to Esther: "– and whatever your wish, it will be given you, and whatever more you may request, it will be done" (9.12).

The change in the man is obvious when one considers what he has said on the three previous occasions on which he has used this expression in speaking to Esther in the past: upon her first forbidden approach to him in the throne room, and at the two banquets of wine that she prepared for him. On all three previous occasions, the king responded to the queen's approach with a variation of the formula: "Whatever your wish, it will be given you. Whatever your request, up to half the kingdom, it will be done" (5.3, 5.6, 7.2).

Ahashverosh's largesse on this occasion differs from these earlier gestures. The king now seeks out Esther to find out what she wants in the absence of any initiative on her part. Indeed, his words in the Hebrew text are packed into the same verse as Ahashverosh's previous thought – about the number of anti-Semites who must have been killed throughout the empire – and the association between the two is unmistakable. With visions of blood dancing before his eyes, and afraid as to what may happen next, Ahashverosh's relationship with his Jewish queen undergoes a final, dramatic revision. It is Esther who now embodies power in the king's eyes, and it is he who offers his favors – his service – in an effort to gain favor with her. Their relationship is finally and completely reversed: Esther, who had come into Ahashverosh's bedchamber five years earlier in search of a way of winning him over so as to avoid the life of a discarded harem girl, now finds the king anxiously seeking to win her pleasure.

In this context, Ahashverosh demonstratively (or perhaps unconsciously) drops the hedge setting an upper bound on her request to "only" half the kingdom, the implication being that she can now ask for the entire kingdom if she so wishes. In practice, once it is the king that is seeking her favor, he does not even need to make this offer explicit, for it has already been granted. In fact, Esther asks for much less: "If it please the king, let the Jews in Susa do tomorrow according to the law for today, and let Haman's ten sons be hanged on the gallows" (9.13).

Like the king, Esther has no way of knowing what has happened in the rest of the empire, and news from the farthest provinces will not be available for weeks.[6] In the best case, the war in the provinces will have come to an end that night with the anti-Semitic menace eradicated. In the worst, the war will have to be extended by a decree from the palace. Her request is that the Jewish reign of arms in Susa be allowed to continue until there is news of what has happened at least in those neighboring cities from which reports can arrive after a day's ride. The point is that in the capital, the initiative should remain in Mordechai's hands until he is able to determine what should happen next. The Jews and their allies are therefore permitted to continue holding the streets of Susa at sword-point for another twenty-four hours, flushing out of hiding another three hundred of their enemies. Moreover, the bodies of Haman's sons, in life the very symbol of continued anti-Semitic power and the possibility of revenge, are transformed into a symbol of Jewish effectiveness when these grisly relics are put on display for potential opponents to consider.

By the time the streets of Susa have grown quiet after the second day's battle, reports have begun to arrive from other cities and towns. Everywhere, the victory of the Jews has become a rout. Men have been hounded out and struck down, the specter of the massacre of which Haman had dreamed is dead, the decree that has hung over the heads of the Jews for so long has been lifted. And the day on which the enemies of the Jews had hoped to rule over them has been transformed, miraculously, into a day of honor and glory, with the Jews themselves achieving rule over those who hated them.

21

The Morality of the War

All this is considered a triumph by the narrative itself and by later Jewish tradition. But contemporary readers often find it difficult to look upon the account of the Jews' war against their enemies in this way, tending to lose interest in the story after the death of Haman. This is despite the fact that Haman is hanged well before the actual turning point in Mordechai and Esther's struggle to save the Jews, and long before the actual war itself, which is the event that in fact brings the Jews redemption.

There is good reason why the account of the Jews' bloody and overwhelming victory, which in other societies would be remembered and savored with pleasure, is often underemphasized, passed over in discussion, and even, in some cases, avoided as if it were an object of shame. The liberal societies of our time are founded on the principle of nonviolent resolution of disputes. The doctrines of the social compact, the rule of law, the voluntary division of labor, and the mutual benefits of contractual exchange – all these are the basis not only for our political order, but also for a prevailing consciousness, whose hold is all the stronger as one approaches the more educated populations within Western society. Individuals who have grown up in this culture have few life experiences to suggest to them that there is any real need for force, violence, and war; and their educators strain to inculcate in them the belief that it is a virtue to "outgrow" the use of force. On such a view, reason and appetite are the only familiar and appropriate springs of human action. And all that is sought by reason and appetite – food, possessions, sex, and knowledge – can be obtained in quantities by most members of an industrialized and free society without recourse to force, and even, it is thought, without the subjugation of any individual by any other.

For those who see the world this way, the functioning of the human spirit, which, for lack of understanding, they refer to using pejoratives such as the "lust for power," is a mystery. They tend to deny the existence of a real need for power and control within themselves, and they sincerely profess incomprehension when such needs manifest themselves in others. Thus a great many individuals, recognizing no need for power, force, and war in themselves, come to consider these things to be objectively undesirable. Then evil, to the extent that it continues to exist as a concept at all, comes to be associated with power, force, and war and with those who have recourse to them.

Among Jews, such disregard for power and force is always strongly present. It was the prophets of Israel who introduced the ideal of an end to violence among nations into the world, with Isaiah calling for swords and spears to be beaten into agricultural implements, and Jeremiah going so far as to call for a "new covenant" to be instilled in every breast at birth, so that men should no longer desire iniquity.[1] Jews have always been exposed to these ideas, and the history of the last centuries, in which they were largely cut off from the experience of armed conflict and high politics – and driven into ever-deeper familiarity with the realm of ideas – did much to refashion the Jews as a caste of dream-thinkers and idealists, for whom every step toward the establishment of societies based on the principle of nonviolent resolution of disputes has served to reconfirm the idea that power and violence are simply unnecessary.

For such readers, the story of Esther up until Haman's demise is supposed quaint and harmless. Unable to understand the terrifying contest of spirit and rule that leads to Haman's execution, they find in it nothing more than a dead coincidence: As it happens, the king's wife turns out to be a Jew, and so Haman's plot is foiled. The fact that Mordechai and Esther then go on to orchestrate a rampage that soaks the empire to its farthest reaches in blood is for them an embarrassment and a mystery. What need was there for this? What rejoicing and holiday could there be in this? What moral teaching could there be in this?

Yet the narrative itself is unambiguous in making the power and control that the Jews consolidated in the bloodletting a cause for celebration – and one of the book's central *moral* themes. The summary that immediately precedes the account of the war therefore touts the fact that "on the day that the enemies of the Jews had expected to rule over them, the situation was reversed, and it was the Jews themselves who ruled over those who hated them" (9.1). The passage that caps the war footage speaks of the relief gained in "killing seventy-five thousand of those who hated them," making the morrow "a day of feasting and gladness" (9.16–17). And the summary that accompanies Mordechai's official interpretation of events underscores the fact that Haman's "evil plan, which he had intended against the Jews, should be turned on its head, and they hanged him and his sons on the

gallows" (9.25) – where "turning the evil plan on its head" means the liquidation of all those who planned to perpetrate the massacre against the Jews.
Moreover, it is impossible to miss the effort of the narrative to associate
the war with Saul's campaign against Amalek, in which it was considered
a moral imperative to kill every member of that tribe. This in itself invokes
even harsher images from the earlier periods of the Bible, in which it could
be considered a command from God to destroy an entire people, or even, as
in the case of Joshua, to drive out all the peoples of an entire land.

The difficulty in reconciling the overt militarism of Esther and other biblical
war accounts with a defensible morality is not, however, a modern invention.
These difficulties were raised at least as early as the time of the rabbis. R. Mani,
for example, suggests that moral qualms may have played a part in Saul's failure to carry out the war against the Amalekites as prescribed, the Jewish king
asking himself prior to the battle: "If the people have sinned, what have the
cattle done? And if the adults have sinned, what have the children done?" But
in this telling, at least, the grim decision to carry out the war is sealed when a
voice from heaven, the traditional arbiter of truth in such discussions, comes
forth and tells him: "Be not overly righteous."[2] In contrast, R. Mani refers to a
later incident in which Saul's men lay waste to the priestly town of Nov, which
the king believes to be guilty of treason, killing women, children, and livestock.
Here, too, the voice from heaven intervenes, this time to cry out: "Be not overly
wicked."[3] On this view, the biblical narrative cannot condone warfare against
innocents, and doubts in this regard are well in order – but then, there are also
apparently cases in which these doubts must be set aside.

The trouble with all such speculation is that one simply cannot be a good
person or a good Jew in our own age – or in the period of the rabbis, either,
for that matter – and "understand" genocide. Being good is today very closely
allied with the revulsion we have learned toward the killing of children, the
aged, and other noncombatants in war, and it is clear that our own moral sen-
sibilities are in this sense "higher" than those that drove the wars of liquidation
in Joshua and Samuel, and even the Jews' war in Esther. On the other hand, one
only need think of the foolishness of certain pacifists, ecologians, vegetarians,
and abstentionist sectarians who insist that the use of force, the expansion of
industry, the killing of animals, or sexual intimacy are inherently immoral, in
order to recognize the possibility of wandering lost in endless, false, and dangerous "higher" moralities whose pursuit bears no fruit other than destruction.
As the saying of Kohelet has it: "Be not overly righteous, and strive not to be
too clever, for why should you destroy yourself?"[4]

Is there not some terrific hypocrisy in this, that we take such pride in the
moral heights we believe ourselves to have attained in comparison with the
past; yet we find ourselves appalled and annoyed at the demands of so many of

those who, in their sanctimoniousness, their naïveté, their utter irrelevance to the world and its doings, hawk their ever-more-suffocating formulas, providing, where good and truth should have been, only strangulation?

Whenever we recognize in ourselves this aversion to the grisly warrior moralizer, this shuddering at the ghostliness of the priests, our moral vertigo, which prevents us from "understanding" much more than a certain adjustment in our own behavior in either direction – whenever we see this, it begins to appear as though the accepted belief in the linearity of this scale, from the so-called higher moralities down to the supposed nonmoralities of the lower worlds, is ill thought out, and even greatly mistaken. Indeed, the fact that either pole repels suggests that there is not one ideal of morality, but two, with our truth lying in the balance. And upon examination, this proves to be the case: that behaviors derive their normative qualities – their "should," their "ought," their divine command – from two separate directions or ideals, each vying with the other and against it, which must be kept distinct for religion and ethics to be able to speak coherently: the ideal of *morality* and that of *purity*. Let us consider what these are and how they affect our question.

Man's consciousness is challenged by objective conditions that prevent him from living in an inertial introspection, conditions that continually pull him, often against his will, toward action in the world. These conditions are essentially two: (i) the needs and urges of his body; and (ii) the needs of others, of his family, his people, and his world. It takes little experience to discover that these two influences are fundamentally and irreconcilably contrary to one another, producing antithetical impulses within philosophy and religion – the one being held as a virtue to the degree that it is minimized, the other being held a virtue to the degree that it is maximized:

(i) *Purity.* The needs and urges of one's body and spirit have always been seen as demanding that man pull away from ideas and truths to occupy himself with eating, digestion and excretion, infatuations and sex, clothing and shelter, natural and chemical intoxications, sleep, discomfort and illness of various kinds, honor and anger, phobias, depressions and other impairments of the spirit, and death. They are a bottomless pit, into which all life's energies and abilities easily disappear without a trace. After a lifetime preoccupied with the pursuit of them, man finds that he has nothing to show for his efforts other than having worn out a body that had started its career fresh. It has therefore been considered a virtue to minimize one's concern for the needs and urges of the body and of the spirit to whatever degree possible so as to free the mind for its confrontation with higher things. This virtue, when found in men, has been called *purity* or *holiness* – the Hebrew word for holiness being *kedusha*, meaning "separation," from the body, the concerns of men and the world. And its most basic ethical form is the command of the books of Moses: "Holy shall you be."[5]

(ii) *Morality.* The needs of the world, on the other hand – the protection of innocent life, the dissemination of truth and the establishment of justice, the alleviation of suffering, the development of productive talents and capacities, the facilitation of happiness, and the attainment of peace – all these have been held to be the noblest of efforts, and the pursuit of them has been held to be a virtue. Yet if they are to be pursued to any worthy effect, they demand the greatest possible concentration of the individual's worldly resources, the maximal use of his body and his spirit to attain high levels of experience and skill, reputation, respect and wealth, allies and power, in order to have a hope of achieving whatever betterment of the world can possibly be achieved. And this virtue has been called *morality* or *justice* – the Hebrew word for justice being *tzedek,* meaning "that which is right," its purport being one of involvement with the concerns of men and of the world. And here, too, the books of Moses speak in the language of a command: "Justice, justice, shall you pursue."[6]

The crux of the contradiction between these two ideals is man's relationship to power. Purity requires that man renounce power; but morality requires that man have power in order to pursue right. This is true on the individual level, in which one can only give to others if one has something to give. But it is even truer when one considers moralities of scale, which require vast amounts of political power, economic power, and military power. Without power, there is no police force capable of defending the innocent, no court capable of doing justice, no army capable of wresting peace from the aggressor, no surplus capable of feeding and clothing the poor, nor of paying to teach truth to the young. Morality requires power, and morality on a vast scale requires power on a vast scale.

For the saint, the man of perfect study and prayer, power is essentially exorcised as a motive, and so the entire world of spiritual blemishes – the obsession with honor and wealth, tantrums and rages, depressions, competitiveness, cruelty – all these are not found in him. But power is lost to him as a tool: He may give charity from what he has, but the good he can do is of necessity circumscribed; he may wish to do right in the world, but he has few resources and does not really know how. For the hero, the man of great deeds, the endless game of accumulating power and the preoccupation with wielding it, of learning the rules and building alliances, of consolidating the wins and recovering from the losses, of gradually growing to the point where one is in fact able to move an immovable world – all this leaves him relatively little time for contemplation, for study and thought, for prayer. He may include such activities in his daily routine, but he finds it difficult to concentrate as the world presses in on him, demanding that he return to it. The saint and the hero may be religious men both. Yet the saint makes a token effort toward power and leaves the rest to God, while the hero leaves nothing to God until he himself reaches exhaustion.

Purity and morality are untranslatable ideals, a vertical axis against which man measures how inwardly removed he is from the world, and a horizontal one measuring the degree to which he outwardly affects it – so that it is forever difficult to advance in one direction without doing damage in the other, a dilemma that appears in Jewish tradition again and again. Thus David, Israel's greatest king, was responsible for the moral achievement of uniting the fragmented Jewish tribes and leading them to victory against the enemies that had caused them such suffering; yet the Bible held that these very acts disqualified him from building the Temple in Jerusalem because he had "shed much blood upon the earth"[7] – so that the construction of the sanctuary was left to his son Solomon.

Even more difficult is the rabbinic story told of the arrest of R. Eleazar ben Parata and R. Hanina ben Teriadon, who are to be brought to trial for their activities by the Roman authorities. R. Hanina was a well-known representation of saintliness, of whom it is said that his only sin was that he once allocated Purim alms as though they were regular charity, a mistake that he then corrected by replacing the misapportioned alms with money from his own pocket.[8] Yet according to the Talmud, R. Hanina tells his cellmate: "Happy are you who have been arrested on five charges but will be delivered. Woe is unto me, who have been arrested on one charge but will be condemned. For you have occupied yourself with study of *tora* as well as deeds of kindness, whereas I have occupied myself with *tora* alone." When R. Eleazar is brought before the tribunal and accused, this worldlier rabbi refuses to give a straight answer, dodging and maneuvering until he succeeds in confounding the court, eventually winning his release. But when R. Hanina is asked by the court why he occupies himself with *tora* though it is against the law, he replies with words of purity: "Because I was commanded to do so by the Lord, my God." Having confessed his guilt, he and his wife are put to death, and his daughter is consigned to serve the Romans in a brothel.[9]

Lest the point somehow be missed, the Talmudic account refers in this context to the opinion of R. Huna: "He who only occupies himself with the study of *tora* is as if he had no God."[10] That is, even divine assistance depends on making sacrifices in purity in order to gather ability in the ways of tribunals, dissemblances, and occupying armies. And if there were ever an exemplar of one who benefits from such assistance, it is Joseph, who spends his life immersed in and becoming expert in the politics and impurity of Pharaoh's court. As the oft-repeated dictum of R. Jose ben Hanina has it: "As the waters cover the fish in the sea, so that the evil eye has no effect on them, so too does the evil eye have no effect on the descendants of Joseph."[11]

From the earliest times, the response of the Jews to the conflict between
the demands of purity and the moral need to achieve power in the world
was for each individual to strike a balance between them: seeking power
in the world for six days of the week and seeking purity by withdrawing
in the seventh; seeking worldly power through sexual relations and raising
up heirs, yet maintaining purity through the institution of marriage and
periods of monthly abstinence; seeking power through the consumption of
meat, yet striving for purity in the choice of the livestock and the manner
of their slaughter, as well as periodic fasts; and so forth. Yet to maintain an
entire nation on course along this middle path, it was thought necessary to
appoint individuals whose work would be the embodiment of each ideal, the
possibility of embodying both at once apparently being intolerably remote.
Thus from the time of Moses, the Jews instituted what amounted to a division of labor between the judge and the priest, between the man of morality and the man of purity – and even between Judah and Joseph, the tribes
responsible for the pursuit of justice and national well-being, and Levi, the
tribe of purity. Similarly, when the Jews entered the land, rabbinic tradition
suggests that three strategic necessities became incumbent upon them as a
nation: that they appoint a king, build the Temple, and destroy Amalek –
these representing, the establishment of justice (the king, Amalek) and purity
(the Temple) in Israel.[12]

The idea that the political and military leader is essential to morality and
religion – that he is, in other words, an important moral and religious figure in his own right – sits uneasily with our tendency to believe that politics
is "immoral" or amoral, an opinion that has been handed down to us from
antiquity.[13] The last centuries have seen endless confusion on this score, as
moral thought, which in the time of the prophets had been inseparable from
human exploration of the political realm, has become the preserve of men who
have removed themselves from the affairs of the world, the better to pursue
"pure reason" and similar projects. Contrary to their own protestations, such
individuals are not particularly adept at formulating moral systems, precisely
because they have so little experience with what is required to achieve anything
in practice. Kant, in particular, insisted on the equation of morality with the
eradication of self-interest – that is, he insisted that morality was identical with
purity – and thus was forced by his own reasoning to conclude that worldly
actions are perhaps never actually moral.[14] But this has not prevented generations of his disciples from applying this misguided standard to the actions
of governments and politicians (all of which actions are "self-interested" in
that they are taken to enhance the power, interests, and cause of that government or politician), and determining them all to be, for this reason, tainted and
"immoral."

Lending plausibility to an argument that would otherwise have little to recommend it is this: Politics is "dirty." That is, people who are not known to lie, cheat, deceive, break agreements, blackmail and black list, to engage in dual loyalties and false loyalties, in campaigns of espionage and character assassination, in bribery and incitement to violence, suddenly find themselves doing so and more when political power is at stake. There is an objective sense in which what is accepted and even necessary in the political arena is neither necessary nor acceptable among family or friends, nor even among rival businesses. Politics is dirty because it is in fact impure, relative to the world of family, synagogue, school, and business in which most individuals spend most of their lives.

But this does not make it immoral. There are many activities that are impure in this sense: The modes of behavior accepted in the bedroom, the graveyard, the operating room, the slaughterhouse, the lavatory, and the battlefield are none of them activities suited to relations of family, synagogue, school, and business. This is not because any of them are inherently immoral, but because they are impure. They are activities that focus attention on the body, its various organs, their functioning and malfunctioning, their decay and mortality – whereas family, school, and business are relatively pure, allowing us to focus on the minds of those who are with us, their hopes, insights, and personalities, and the unique human relations in which we are engaged with them. The house of prayer and *tora* study is held to be purer still, and here even much of what takes place in the realm of business, school, or family life is held in abeyance for a time so that we may attend more carefully to God and to his teaching.

This ability to distinguish spheres of greater purity from other, lesser ones is what allows mankind to step into civilization, leaving behind the physical organs and bodily fluids, decay and illness, the corpse, and death itself, in order to enter into a "safe space," a bubble that is "separated" from the world, in which it is possible to concentrate on things that are at once more essential and more personal. When we enter into such times and such places, the appearance of things associated with impurity break the spell of the higher being that we strive to be, and so such intrusions are proscribed and even deplored.

The same may be said concerning the accepted behaviors of politics. Here, too, many of the activities are brutal, and in fact they have often been referred to as "naked power," verbal actions whose meaning is pure force, acts of the spirit that are in their essence violence, whether accompanied by physical blows or not. Yet in order to achieve power to do good, one must be experienced, talented, and expert in the ways in which power is in fact allocated and applied. One must know war as it is waged by others, and be able to wage such wars more effectively than they. One must know finance as it is waged by others, and be able to build an economy more effectively than they. One must be able to gain influence and wield it as it is wielded by others, but be able to use this influence more effectively than they. Power is a matter of beating one's opponents at their own game and using the results for good. Participating in the ways of the political world as one finds it is not inherently immoral, any more than the activities of the lavatory are immoral. In neither case does a habitually pious person desire to behave in such ways. He does it neither for pleasure nor for some kind of personal gain, but because there is presumably no choice. And it would be absurd if each time an individual took it upon himself to achieve right and justice, even at the expense of his own personal purity, he would also have to be castigated for being immoral besides.

Indeed, the biblical narrative and subsequent rabbinic tradition reserved the appellation of *tzadik*, meaning "the righteous," for precisely those figures whose lives are spent in outward political and moral action, immersed in power and evil, but who nonetheless manage to maintain a level of relative purity in these circumstances. This is the meaning of the oft-repeated Talmudic appellation, "Joseph the righteous":[15] It is not, as is often supposed, that Joseph surpasses others among the Jews in the purity of his life. Rather, the significance of his great act of self-discipline – the refusal of the Egyptian temptress – is in the fact that he is able to maintain any standard of purity at all in the polluted realm in which he flourishes, and despite the ways in which he must accommodate this realm to attain success. Others referred to as "righteous" are of this sort as well: Noah, who saves mankind from the flood, is referred to as righteous in the books of Moses despite the fact that in his time "the evil of man was great upon the earth, and the whole nature of the thoughts of his mind was only to evil all day long";[16] Lot, who risks his life and that of his family to save perfect strangers from the mob, is referred to as righteous in the books of Moses despite living amid the depravity of Sodom;[17] Jacob, who wrests control of his father's inheritance from his powerful brother and makes a fortune at the hands of the Mesopotamian idolaters, is called righteous by the rabbis despite spending the best years of his life serving his father-in-law surrounded by immorality and idolatry;[18] and Mordechai, who saves the Jews of Persia, is called righteous by the rabbis despite likewise living amid the iniquity of the Persian court.[19]

Of course, the fact that the political world is a sphere of lesser purity does not legitimize every means to any political end. One cannot make great sacrifices in one's purity and humanity where the ends being pursued are immoral or unimportant. The political struggles of municipal zoning boards, for example, or the notorious politics internal to academia, cannot justify relinquishing civilized behavior. In high politics, on the other hand, it is, as Joseph says, "the preservation of the multitude of men alive"[20] that is in fact at stake, so that it can always be reasonably argued that departures from our accustomed standards of purity are justifiable, and even obligatory. Left to the hands of others who would use the power of the state for their own gain, the law would serve the few, the country would engage in oppression and unjust wars, and thousands would die for nothing. Indeed, it is the political world, with all its impurity, that makes it possible for the civil world of daily life to exist as it does. It is politics that musters the ugly power necessary for higher society to live oblivious, just as the body marshals the resources needed for the mind to do its work, although most of the time the mind is unaware of what is taking place beneath it. If the political world should one day fail in its impure task when faced by malevolent challenges from outside society or within, the bubble of civilization in which we spend most of our adult lives would come crashing down into the lava of impurity below.

There is no point in attempting to count the strata of impurity upon which our world floats, and upon which it depends for its existence. But it bears emphasizing that the impure sphere of politics floats like a bubble on top of other, yet impurer worlds: The realm of wars, both foreign and domestic, is one such, in which even today nations use the most gruesome means in order to survive – means that would be unthinkable even in an arena such as that of domestic political life. And beneath this lies another, even fouler world, which exists now only in the farthest reaches: that of the idolaters, in which murderous violence was acceptable even within the family, and in which no safety truly existed anywhere. It was this realm in which the genocides of antiquity took place: in which Rome put all of Carthage to the sword and sowed the soil of its lands with salt so that no human being should ever be able to persist there again. And it was in this world, according to the hideous exigencies of its wars, that Joshua entered the land with an imperative to secure a stable Jewish nation and faith:

> You will beat them and you will utterly destroy them, you will sign no treaties with them, nor will you show them any mercy. And you will not make marriages with them: You will not give your daughter to his son, nor will you take his daughter for your son. For they will turn your son away from following me, and they will serve other gods .... You will destroy their altars, and break down their images, and cut down their asherim, and burn their idols with fire .... The idols of their gods will you burn with fire. Do not desire the silver and gold that is on them nor take it for yourself, lest you become ensnared by it, for it is a horror to the Lord, your God. You will not bring a horror into your house, lest you become accursed as it is, but you will loathe it and abhor it, for it is an accursed thing.[21]

The point is all too clear: "They will turn your son away," "lest you become ensnared," "lest you become accursed as it is." Without an end to the murderous

Canaanite presence in the land, the moral life of the Jews, so we are told, cannot come into existence – for the Jews would rapidly become Canaanites themselves: perverse, murderous, idolatrous. Indeed, the subsequent narrative tells precisely this story. It tells of how the Jews, having failed to live up to the imperative of driving the Canaanites from the land, sank into a thousand years of assimilation into the ways of the idolaters.

The modern world is quick to decry this war against the Canaanites. But if we are honest, we will admit that contemporary warfare has resorted to the categorical destruction of innocents for less. The "counter-value" warfare waged against Hiroshima and Dresden was not aimed at saving the United States, or even Western civilization. The war had long since turned in favor of the Allies. Yet these enormities were deemed necessary to bring the war to a speedier conclusion. Japanese and German children were considered worthy of destruction to save the lives of American servicemen. The premise of the war against the Canaanites is, if anything, less cynical, since it assumes what was clearly not the case when the decision was taken to use the first nuclear weapons: that the possibility of Jewish civilization – indeed, of moral civilization itself – could not persist without the banishment of the worst level of impurity from the land.

That there may be a place in moral argumentation for such acts is not easily assimilated. Within the confines of our own world, the rules are different: One may not take the life of an innocent person to save one's own life under any circumstance.[22] When the individual violates this principle, it is rightly understood as the greatest of crimes. Yet most of us can glimpse our own descent into the realm in which our accepted norms of behavior dissolve in contemporary scenarios in which the free world is faced with annihilation, or in which the State of Israel stands to be destroyed in war with the Arabs or Iran. Would we refuse to order a nuclear strike in such a case? The harsh truth is that the immorality of such a strike, killing countless innocents to save a civilization, cannot be deduced from the immorality of murdering an innocent individual to save another.

From this it is evident that the political arena is not merely "dirty." In certain cases, it leads rapidly into a pollution in which man is transformed into a beast of the lowest grade: not merely killing individuals for his own survival, but destroying cities and bringing nations to ruin. This, at any rate, is what we find in the most horrifying of the biblical accounts of ancient warfare, which assume that there can be an imperative to wage war of this kind if the world has fallen into otherwise irreparable evil.[23] It is the curse of politics that in certain cases such monstrous acts of impurity may be considered the most moral option given the paucity of alternatives. But, of course, it is always possible instead to preserve one's own purity and allow the world to fall ever further.

Mordechai's war is fought in the world of his time and place. It is fought by its rules because any other choice in that time and place would have been folly. Thus if one were to ask why so many men had to die on the day of the fighting if the results were by then practically assured, the answer is just that which we have read in Machiavelli's politics. Without decisive action against an enemy that had been preparing to murder all of the Jews, Mordechai would have guaranteed himself a reputation of hesitancy and mildness – a reputation that would have breathed new life into the anti-Semitism of the empire and left the king doubting the Jewish vizier's abilities. And if one were to ask why Haman's ten sons had to die, it is wishful thinking to argue that every one of them was active as a leader in the camp of the anti-Semites, although some of them were exactly that. Rather, their deaths are sought, as was accepted in the course of warfare and politics in antiquity, to prevent Haman's enmity from leaving heirs, as well as to degrade his memory and emphasize the enormity of his defeat. The book of Daniel tells of Darius issuing a parallel order for the destruction of those who persecuted Daniel, along with their families: "And the king commanded, and they brought those men who had accused Daniel, and they cast them into the lion's den, they, their children and their wives."[24] In Herodotus, Artabanus, uncle to Xerxes, similarly offers to wager his life and those of his children on the outcome of a war he opposes: "If things go well for the king, as you say they will, let me and my children be put to death. But if they fall out as I prophesy, let your children suffer, and you too, if you come back alive."[25] And if one insists that Mordechai should have conducted the war without resorting to the impure norms of Persian politics, even though such a nod to purity might have jeopardized the endeavor, the first answer must be that of Kohelet: "There are righteous men who perish through their righteousness, and there are the wicked who flourish by their wickedness. Be not overly righteous."[26]

Yet harsh as is Mordechai's onslaught, he nevertheless does demand that the Jews carry on their war on a purer level than that which they expected to have waged against them. Thus Mordechai's decree, copied more or less verbatim from Haman's, speaks of the death of children and women, as well as the appropriation of all the property of their enemies, all with the intention of inspiring counterterror in the enemy camp. When the day itself is described in the narrative, however, there is no suggestion that the Jews followed through with these threats. No casualties are mentioned among the dependents, and indeed, the text repeatedly emphasizes that the Jews did not even touch their enemies' property (9.10, 15, 16).

The issue of respecting the property rights of one's enemies and their families is one that has its roots in the earlier stages of the plot, when Haman first approaches Ahashverosh with the hope of convincing him to destroy the Jews.

In making his case, he seeks to engage every interest of the king's to which he can appeal, including a possible financial interest: "If it please the king, let it be written that they be destroyed, and I will weigh out ten thousand talents of silver into the hands of those who have charge of the business, to bring it into the king's treasuries" (3.9). This is an outrageously large sum, in the range of what Herodotus reports to have been the income in silver of the entire Persian empire for a year,[27] and the only imaginable source for such a fortune would have been the plunder of the Jews' property. Yet Ahashverosh, ever eager to demonstrate his power by wasting state moneys, assures Haman that: "The silver is given to you, and the people, to do with them as you see fit" (3.11), thus clearing the way for the vizier to offer the Jews' property as an incentive to the murderers.[28] In so doing, he greatly expands the circle of those who will potentially be willing to do the work of annihilation, including not only those who hate Jews, but those who want their property.

All of this is in contrast to the wars against the Canaanites and Amalek, in which plundering was proscribed. In the case of the Canaanites, the fear was principally that in claiming the property of the idolaters, the Jews would end up with idols in their homes to which they would be inevitably drawn. But in the case of Saul's effort to destroy Amalek, there is no mention of idols, and the issue, once the plundering takes place, seems to be completely different: "But Saul and the people took pity on Agag, and on the best of the sheep, and the oxen, and the fatlings, and the lambs, and all that was good, and did not destroy them, but everything that was of little value and poor, they destroyed." When confronted by the prophet Samuel, Saul explains: "I have transgressed the instruction of the Lord and your words, for I feared the people and listened to their words."[29] For this crime, of giving in to the desire of the people for plunder, Saul is stripped of his kingdom.

At stake in the argument over the right to plunder is the motive for destroying Amalek. In Samuel's eyes, Amalek's history of unlimited terror, bloodshed, and evildoing justify what is otherwise a horrendous act.[30] But if the Jews begin claiming Amalekite cattle for themselves, the war will turn out to have been fought, in fact, for another reason altogether. Far from engaging in an act whose purpose is to make the world safe from Amalek's predations, they are in that case just engaging in an act of murder for the sake of stealing, itself a very great evil.[31] Samuel instructs Saul to kill, horribly, so that a better life may become possible for mankind, but his fighting men want to kill for plunder. In Samuel's eyes, the choice is between right and evil, and Saul chooses the latter.

The distinction between just war and murder is today referred to as the "purity of arms," and this is what is at issue, too, in Esther, in which Mordechai's war against the Persian anti-Semites is recounted as a revisiting of

the Amalekite war in the book of Samuel.[32] Here, the emphasis on not touching the property of the anti-Semites is intended to indicate the purity of the
cause. Men are killed because they had been planning to murder the Jews, and
as a preemption against future threats. The fact that this is understood by the
Jews to be the sole motive raises their warfare to a level of purity much higher
than that of Haman, and higher too than that which had been practiced by
their forebears in the time of Saul. It is for this reason that the tradition refers
to Mordechai as "the righteous": because in raising the Jews to an impressive
degree of purity amid the fearsome acts required by the politics and warfare of
his place and time, he provided the kind of political leadership for which the
Jews should hope in every generation.

PART IX

ESTHER 9.17–10.3

This was on the 13th day of the month of Adar, and they gained respite on the 14th day, making it a day of feasting and gladness. ¹⁸And the Jews of Susa assembled on the 13th and f14th, and they gained respite on the 15th, making it a day of feasting and gladness. ¹⁹That is why the Jews of the villages, who live in unwalled towns, celebrate the 14th day of the month of Adar as one of gladness and feasting, a holiday and one for sending foods to one another.

²⁰Mordechai recorded these events and sent letters to all the Jews in all the provinces of Ahashverosh the king, near and far – ²¹charging them that they should keep the 14th and 15th days of Adar every year ²²as days on which the Jews gained respite from their enemies, and as a month that was transformed for them from sorrow to gladness, and from mourning to holiday, and to make them days of feasting and gladness, and for sending foods to one another, and for giving gifts to the poor.

²³The Jews undertook to do as they had begun, and as Mordechai had written to them.

²⁴For Haman, the son of Hamedata the Agagite, persecutor of all the Jews, had planned to destroy the Jews, and had cast a *pur*, that is a lot, to terrify and destroy them. ²⁵But when she came before the king, he did decree in his letters that his evil plan, which he had intended against the Jews, should be turned on its head, and they hanged him and his sons on the gallows.

²⁶So they called these days Purim, after the *pur*, and because of all that was in this letter, and all they had seen in this regard, and

what had happened to them. [27]The Jews enacted and undertook, upon themselves and upon their descendants, and upon all those who might join them, that they should not fail to keep these two days, according to their writings and according to their season, each and every year. [28]And these days are remembered and performed in each and every generation in every family, in every province, in every city. These days of Purim will not fail from among the Jews, nor will their memory perish from among their descendants.

[29]Esther the queen, the daughter of Avihail, and Mordechai the Jew, wrote with all due emphasis to enact this second letter of Purim: [30]Letters were sent to all the Jews, to the 127 provinces of the kingdom of Ahashverosh, with words of peace and truth, [31]enacting these days of Purim in their season, as Mordechai the Jew and Esther the queen had enjoined them, and as they had undertaken for themselves and for their descendants with regard to the fasts and their lamentations. [32]And Esther's decree enacted these matters of Purim and it was written in the book.

[1]Ahashverosh the king levied taxes on the land, and on the islands of the sea. [2]And all his acts of might and power, and the account of the greatness of Mordechai, whom the king had promoted, are recorded in the book of chronicles of the kings of Media and Persia. [3]For Mordechai the Jew was second to Ahashverosh the king, and great among the Jews, and popular with the multitude of his brethren, seeking the good of his people and speaking peace to all his descendants.

22

The Festival

The Jews had achieved a frightful victory. In every land, the forces that had sought to eradicate them were uprooted. Having at the outset appeared beyond help and hope, the Jews had over the course of less than a year mustered the political and military strength to defeat some of the greatest men in the empire. By the end, the plan for their annihilation had been "turned on its head," and "Mordechai the Jew was second to the king, seeking the good of his people" (9.25, 10.3). The Jews had positioned themselves to secure their own safety and to exert a decisive influence on the politics of Persia for years to come.

The book of Esther records the reaction of the Jews to the end of the nightmare. Feelings of relief and gladness contributed to the eruption of celebrations and feasts in every province in which Jews had been delivered from their enemies. Many Jews apparently expressed their joy even on this first occasion by sending gifts to one another, as a spontaneous response to the new gift of life they had all been given.

But it rapidly became evident that the events had a more profound significance than the immediate deliverance itself, and Mordechai and Esther moved to instate the victory as days of holiday in the annual cycle of Jewish festivals – to be "remembered and performed in each and every generation, in every family, in every province, in every city," so that the days marking the ultimate effects of Haman's *purim*, the lots he cast in his attempt to seal the fate of the Jews, "will not fail from among the Jews, nor will their memory perish from among their descendants" (9.28). According to the narrative, Mordechai and Esther each send out a letter in the years subsequent to the events themselves, asking that the Jews observe the days on which the original celebrations had taken place as a festival, and giving legal force to practices that had been spontaneous among those delivered from death on the first Purim.

All of this is rather unusual for a biblical text. All of the other Jewish hol-idays that merit explicit imperatives in the Bible are already commanded in the books of Moses, many centuries before the events described in Esther. While the subsequent accounts are filled with victories and deliverances of various kinds, none of the heroes of these other biblical stories ever tries to create a holiday that "will not fail from among the Jews." Mordechai appears to have been the first Jewish leader since Moses to establish such a festival.[1]

In addition to the question of why Mordechai and Esther should have insisted on so unusual a move as the establishment of a religious festival, the text itself focuses on a rather peculiar aspect of how this new holiday was leg-islated into Jewish tradition. It is clear that Mordechai and Esther favored its establishment, and that as the leaders of the Persian Jewish community, they used all their influence to make sure that the holiday was observed throughout the empire, with Mordechai "charging them that they should keep the 14th and 15th days of Adar every year" (9.21–22), and Esther later writing "with all due emphasis to enact ... these days of Purim in their season" (9.29–31). Yet the narrative insists on mentioning, no fewer than three times, that the estab-lishment of the festival was actually in the form of an "undertaking" (9.23, 27, 31) – that is, that despite Mordechai and Esther's lobbying, the acceptance of this commitment among the Jews was voluntary.

Both the motive for the establishment of Purim and the importance of its voluntary acceptance can be understood best against the backdrop of the polit-ical context in which Mordechai and Esther found themselves responsible for the well-being of the Jewish people. The exile in Babylonia and its Persian successor was not a consequence of the first massive deportation of Jews from the land of Israel, but of the second: A century and a half before Mordechai's family had been exiled by the Babylonians, the northern kingdom of Israel had been forcibly removed from its land by the Assyrians. The result of the Assyrian exile had been the rapid obliteration of much of the northern ten tribes, which, when dispersed throughout the East, had succumbed to the peoples around them and disappeared.[2] By the time of Mordechai and Esther, the magnitude of the catastrophe that had befallen the Jews of the northern kingdom had become clear, and the burning question was how to prevent this new exile from disappearing as well.[3]

We know that the pressures and temptations of a cosmopolitan society such as Persia were immense. Like Daniel and Nehemia, Mordechai found himself deeply involved in the mainstream of Persian political life. Like Daniel, Esther bowed to Persian culture by adopting a gentile name. The hatreds of the soci-ety caused Esther to hide her Jewishness, as Mordechai, to judge from the fact that he later "reveals" his Jewishness to the courtiers, seems to have done as well. True, the Jews of the Babylonian exile were stronger in their observance of Israelite traditions than had been their brothers in the northern kingdom, and they had among them greater intellectual and spiritual leaders. And yet the issue was alive and well: In the face of anti-Semitism, and of the difficulties of keeping Jewish law in an empire that occasionally persecuted its practitioners, and with every door open if one's Judaism were hidden away or renounced altogether, would not the Jews of Persia eventually disappear as well?

The fact is that in Persia, being a Jew became – for the first time in history – a matter of choice, and a choice that had to be faced by every individual.[4] In Egypt, the Jews had been a slave caste living in segregated Jewish ghettos. In Canaan, they had lived as tribes surrounded by alien cultures with which they were constantly at war. And once the Jews had established themselves as a kingdom, every individual's identity as a Jew became even more secure. In the thousand years since Sinai, the Jews had strayed from observance of the law of Moses time and time again, but their identity as Jews had never been subject to their own volition. It was only after the dispersal throughout Babylonia and Persia that an individual born as a Jew found himself in immediate, constant, and personal contact with other possible identities – and had to choose for himself whether Jewishness would be something he would maintain, or something he would hide.

This explains why the great talmudist Rava argued that the Jews had actually accepted the law of Moses twice: under duress at Sinai, and voluntarily "in the days of Ahashverosh."[5] Sinai was the founding of a Jewish people whose members have no real alternative but to be Jews, and to take part in the unique history of their people. The Persian empire represented the refounding of the Jewish people on an entirely different basis: Since each Jew was from birth exposed to other options, his entry into the history of his people would perforce be voluntary.[6]

Thus while on the surface of it the voluntary undertaking of the Jews at the end of the Esther story is clearly with regard to the festival of Purim, there is an important sense in which Mordechai did consider his campaign to secure widespread voluntary observance of Purim to be tantamount to a quest for renewed acceptance of the covenant of Moses. Until the Babylonian exile, the dispersion of the Jews in foreign diasporas had ended only in two ways: enslavement and persecution in Egypt, and absorption and dissolution in Assyria. Either way, the meaning of the diaspora for the Jewish people had been death. In Mordechai and Esther's time, the greatest challenge for the Jewish leadership was to create the conditions under which the unwanted dispersion might mean something else.

Purim created the opportunity for life in exile to mean something different. In telling the story of the Jewish people's success in Persia, it added a cosmopolitan message for Jews far from their homeland and their God: If the Jew will stand up for himself and fight for his faith, the diaspora can allow power and life – not only for individual Jews, but for the Jewish people as a whole. Indeed, just as Purim had brought "many from among the people of the land to become Jews" when it first took place – out of respect, fear, and enthusiasm for this success – Mordechai understood that in its retelling it would deepen this sense of pride and purpose among the Jews of the dispersion in future generations; that the ambitious and strong would remain Jews only if being a Jew were a badge of strength, for power attracts power, and strength attracts strength. More than any other festival, Purim would express to the Jews that it is worth fighting to be a Jew, because even in exile the fight against Israel's enemies was one that could be won. As the rabbis declared in the centuries that followed:

> "And it will be to the Lord for a memorial" (Isaiah 55.13). This refers to the miracle that the Holy One, blessed be he, performed on this occasion [Purim], the like of which there had never been before. For was there ever in history such a miracle, that Israel should wreak vengeance on the other nations and do with their enemies as they pleased?[7]

For any Jew in the exile who could hear this message, Judaism would cease to be something that had to be hidden away in fear. Even in the exile, a Jew could make use of the tools of politics and power to become "second to the king, ... seeking the good of his people."

The successful establishment of Purim therefore suggests a second great deliverance that is infrequently mentioned in connection with the political achievements of Mordechai and Esther, yet which ranks with the more visible triumph over the enemy, Haman the Agagite. In establishing a celebration of Jewish victory and power in the annual calendar of the Jews of the dispersion, Mordechai and Esther opened the way to an exile that, though bitter, might ultimately offer triumph and life to the Jews.

It is thus no coincidence that Mordechai required the Jews to make the days of Purim "days of feasting and gladness, and for sending foods to one another, and for giving gifts to the poor," all these legal provisions of the holiday being ones that inspire a sense of well-being, control, and power. In the narrative, all three laws of the holiday – feasting, granting gifts, and giving charity to the poor – appear as expressions of royalty and rule on the only occasions that Ahashverosh feels himself to be fully in control of his personal life and his realm: the 180-day feast and the wedding feast (1.3–5, 2.18). Indeed, even the grotesque activities associated with the festival in later times – drunkenness, comedy cabarets, and masquerades of various kinds – are every one of them designed to allow cruder individuals to share in the sense of power that Purim originally sought to instill in the Jews of the Persian diaspora.

23

Politics and Faith

Over a thousand years and a thousand pages, the Hebrew Bible relates the history of God as he appeared to the Jews and among them: as creator and mentor, as redeemer, warrior, and fortress of refuge. Only in Esther does the trail grow faint, the pen weary, the sense of things irrevocably blurred. History continues, but the Bible ends. It is the Jews who are sent into exile from their land, but it is God for whom there no longer seems to be any place. What does Esther have to teach us that we do not already know – of the emptiness and grief of the old tale as it drags on, with man now the only actor, with the enemy now facing us across the stage, squinting with pleasure to have found us so alone?

What can be the meaning of a book of the Bible in which there is no mention of God, however so incidental, if not to inform us, two thousand years before Nietzsche, that the evidence of God's actions in the world has ceased – that the earth has been unchained from its sun, that it has grown darker, colder?[1] For this much, one has no need of Esther, which, coming as it does at least a century after the reduction of Jerusalem, can seem hardly more than a bitter redundancy. Had not Jeremiah, speaking of the end of the eternal city, already written that all that had been achieved in the creation had now been ruined?

> I saw the earth, and behold it was void and unformed, and the heavens with no lights in them .... I saw, and behold there was no man, and all the fowl of the skies wandered away. I saw, and behold, the fruitful field was the desert, and all its cities vanquished."[2]

Had not even the books of Moses foretold this same end, of the departure of God from among men?

> My anger will burn against them in that day, and I will abandon them and hide my face from them, and they will be devoured and many evils and

> torments will befall them, so that they will say on that day: "Are not these
> evils come upon us because our God is not among us?"[3]

What more is there to add to the horror of God's absence after these words?

The truth is that in the great Hebrew tale of the formation of the world and
its abandonment, as it seems, by its maker, Esther ranks barely as a postscript.
It is no part of this story. If anything, it contradicts it and drains it of meaning. For what is left of Jeremiah's pathos once one has feasted and drunk with
Mordechai and Esther – in celebration of the possibility of Jewish rulership
and power without Jerusalem? In celebration of the possibility of Jewish victory without God? If taken at face value, the events in Esther serve as a denial
of all that the earlier writings had come to teach.

Yet for all this – indeed, because of all this – Esther is the classic text of
Jewish continuity: It speaks of a different place and a new time, of Jews with
no land and no revelations from on high, and yet the story line is eerily familiar: Amalek, the arch-idolater and anti-Jew returns to seek dominion, the Jew
stands to resist evil against all odds, the people return from their daydreams
and wanderings to unite behind their truth, and for all his worldly might, the
enemy is brought low, leaving the Jews free to rule themselves under new conditions that permit them what they desire most, "words of peace and truth"
(9.30). Esther is a world removed from the story told in the rest of the Bible,
but it is not a different story. It is the same story, that of Moses, that of Saul,
told again in a different bible, of which Esther is not the last book, but the first.

To understand this, we must return to the dictum of Rava, who argued
that the Jews accepted the *tora* twice, once at Sinai when there was no choice
but to accept, and again "in the days of Ahashverosh," when they accepted it
voluntarily.[4] For the first thousand years of Jewish faith, the insular nature of
the community of Jews meant that the word of God could hardly be escaped.
A Jew could observe the law or fail to do so, but he lived in a community that
was bombarded by the thought of the priests and the prophets, and so always
had to reconcile his behavior with the knowledge that somewhere, somehow,
someone was judging him according to the covenant. Thus Jeremiah could
testify to the people on the eve of the destruction of Jerusalem that they had
heard God speaking to them night and day since their fathers had left Egypt
eight hundred years earlier:

> On the day I brought them out of the land of Egypt …. This thing I com-
> manded them, saying: Obey my voice … and walk in all the ways I have
> commanded you, that it may be well with you …. From the day that your
> fathers came out of the land of Egypt unto this day, I have sent to you all
> my servants the prophets, sending them to you from morning until night.
> But they did not listen."[5]

What changed in Persia was not only that prophets ceased to frequent the marketplaces, but that the majority of the Jewish people was for the first time well beyond earshot. Even had prophecy survived the catastrophe of the exile, the mere fact of being dispersed to the ends of the six-score Persian provinces would have meant that most Jews would never have an opportunity to hear a prophet in their lives. When added to the constant pressure of foreign concerns and ideas that was the daily grist of exile, the heightened sense of God's speaking – commanding, berating, imploring – dissolved and was gone, so that the rabbis concluded that "whoever lives outside the land of Israel can be considered as though he has no God."[6] With dispersion, God's voice quite literally ceased to be audible to most Jews. And if they wished to keep listening, the responsibility would of necessity be theirs to find a way to hear it.[7]

While the collapse of the Jerusalem had been political in nature, its fundamental meaning was therefore theological. In Persia in the days of Ahashverosh, God had "hidden his face" from man, had ceased to appear. But this did not mean that the world somehow ceased to need instruction or direction. God's withdrawal from man was met with no commensurate extinguishing of the voice of evil. If anything, the opposite could be said: Not since Pharaoh had Israel been so helpless before a nemesis as monstrous as Haman. In the aftermath of the destruction and the exile, the world continued as before, revolving around its flaw, and the same eternal task remained to be done. But now there was only one force that could bear the responsibility for doing it – man himself.

Many have tried to read the book of Esther as though nothing had changed from the preceding age, as though God's absence were merely a literary device in a story otherwise laced with divine intervention: The enemy is set to destroy the Jews, but by means of a series of inexplicable coincidences – the king happens to be married to a Jewess, for example – his efforts are brought to naught and he perishes himself. Every coincidence is thus understood to be a minor miracle, and the overall effect is not much removed from the deliverance from Egypt: The Jews would have perished had it not been for the active intervention of God.[8]

Yet this reading obscures more than it explains. For the great events depicted in the book of Esther are not instances of clever convergence that are otherwise inexplicable and so have to be as attributed to hidden divine activism. Rather, they follow directly from the initiatives of Mordechai and Esther, who repeatedly choose to risk everything for the sake of right and truth: Mordechai's decision to stand against Haman's elevation; his willingness to violate the king's law to draw public attention to the Jews' anguish after the decree has been issued; Esther's decision to go in to the king, knowing that she may die before even having explained herself; her maneuvers to undermine the king's trust in Haman; her final, face-to-face confrontation with her enemy; her second approach to the king; and Mordechai's subsequent work in turning the officials of the empire to assist in his cause. It is these actions that bring about the fall of Haman and permit the ultimate reversal of the decree – and it is glaringly clear that all of these are, according to the most straightforward reading of the narrative, the political initiatives of men, and no one else. The book of Esther presents matters in this light because this is the way things looked to the Jews in their dispersion in the days of Ahashverosh.

A number of events suggest that Mordechai and Esther understood this shift in responsibility from God to man, and were willing to shoulder it in full – taking initiative not only in political actions, but with respect to the difficult moral determinations needed to give normative force to these actions. Thus it is Mordechai, and no earlier Jewish source or authority, who determines that prostrating himself before Haman is an evil so great that it is worth risking his life and his people over; Esther willingly maintains the king's favor despite the Jewish prohibition violated by such liaisons; and Esther also declares a three-day fast that entails the obliteration of the festival of Passover that year.[9] Moreover, Mordechai and Esther's campaign to institute a new Jewish festival seemingly flies in the face of the injunction in the books of Moses forbidding any effort to "add to the law."[10] The rabbis said of this unprecedented human incursion into the legislation of God's law: "Forty-eight prophets and seven prophetesses prophesied to Israel, and they neither took away from nor added anything to what is written in the *tora*, except for the reading of Esther."[11] There can be no question that in all of these initiatives, ultimate values were at stake – idolatry and tyranny, life and death, the survival of the Jewish people and of the *tora* – and that without the religious and moral responsibility Mordechai and Esther were willing to accept in the crisis, all would have been lost.

And herein lies the key to Esther. The most remarkable aspect of the book is not God's absence itself, but the fact that this absence does not induce defeat and despair. Mordechai and Esther prove that even in the grim new universe of the dispersion, the most fearsome evils may yet be challenged and beaten – so long as man himself is willing to take the initiative to beat them. Thus while Esther adheres faithfully to the message of earlier Jewish teachings in terms of the outcome of the story, it heralds a dramatic shift in the burden of responsibility for this outcome. Man may still find out what God wishes of him, but he will not be given the answers; he will have to seek them. Man may still participate in the actions of God in history, but he will not be called to them; he will have to initiate them. And man may still see God's justice and peace brought into being in the world, but it will not be handed to him; he will have to build it. Thus R. Assi taught: "Why was Esther compared to the dawn? To tell you that just as the dawn is the end of the whole night, so is the story of Esther the end of all miracles."[12] Where before, the story of man had been conducted in darkness, with an occasional sign from heaven illuminating the night, now these signs have gone. There is yet to be light in the world, but this light must be brought as it was brought to the Jews of Persia – by Esther. As the rabbinic tradition told it:

> At night, despite the fact that it is night, there is light from the moon and the stars and the constellations. When is it truly dark? At the dawn. The moon disappears and the stars disappear and the constellations go as well. There can be no darker hour than this one. Then it is that the Holy One, may he be blessed, answers the world and its inhabitants, bringing forth the dawn from the darkness, and illuminating the world. And why, then, is Esther compared to the dawn? Like the dawn whose light is about to break forth, at first it comes little by little, and then it bursts forward and arrives, and then it intensifies and grows great, and then it is excellent and ever stronger. So too was the deliverance of Israel by Esther.[13]

Esther is the dawn because that light which comes to the Jews comes from her, of her own creation and her own power. Neither the seething firmament of the old Jewish night, nor the astrological fatalism of idolaters such as Haman casting their lots, will now be the final arbiter of events. For Esther is herself a star, if only she wills it, a sun in her own right.[14]

In Jewish tradition, the ideal of man acting as God acts is summarized in the exhortation of Moses in Deuteronomy to "walk in all his ways,"[15] which is to say that, as later interpreters put it, man should "behave in the same ways in which God directs his world – and these are righteousness and justice."[16] If the Jews succeed in this, Moses promises that the result will be strength and greatness in this world:

> You will inherit nations greater and mightier than yourselves .... No man will be able to stand before you, for the fear of you and the dread of you will the Lord your God cause to fall on all the land.[17]

And it is possibly the most radical expression of what the book of Esther seeks to instill in the Jewish people that precisely the words of this Mosaic promise are the ones used to describe the victory of Mordechai's forces over the anti-Semites: "No man could stand before them, for fear of them had fallen on all the peoples" (9.2). The unavoidable implication of this passage is that Mordechai and Esther saw the promise of Moses fulfilled in their day because they had, in fact, succeeded in "walking in all God's ways." That is, although God evidently did not speak to Mordechai or to Esther as he had spoken to their forefathers, they had nonetheless been able to discern his ways and walk in them as their forefathers had done, although now at their own initiative and on their own authority.

That the covenant of Moses still lives, so long after the fact and so deep in the exile, is certainly a profound and comforting message. Yet there is something frightening in this message as well. For in accepting it in the form in which it appears in the book of Esther, does not man seek to usurp the place of God, deciding right and wrong for himself and seeking to chart the course of history himself? And does not man thereby reconcile himself to a godless world, to atheism?

It seems that even in Mordechai's time, the Jews were not all so comfortable with the activist line he advocated in thought and deed. It is significant, for instance, that in Mordechai's decision not to prostrate himself before Haman, he acts alone. No other Jews join him in refusing to pay obeisance to the vizier. Indeed, as far as we know, the Jewish community as a whole remains silent up until the day of the actual decree ordering their extermination – at which time the mourning and fasting in sack and ashes finally begins (4.3). Even after this, no Jews seem to join Mordechai in his protest at the palace gate. Other than the fasting, there is no discernible Jewish activity whatsoever until two months later, when the decree allowing the Jews to defend themselves is issued and Mordechai sets to work organizing them into a fighting force. On the religious front, too, the issuing of the second letter of Purim "with all due emphasis" (9.29) strongly suggests a protracted struggle within the Jewish community over the acceptance of the new holiday. No wonder, then, that the rabbinic tradition interpreted the book's closing comment concerning Mordechai's being "popular with the multitude of his brethren" to mean that he was accepted only by the *majority* of his brethren – and opposed by many others.[18]

In this argument, history has weighed in on the side of Mordechai. Again and again in the centuries that followed, the demand for human responsibility and initiative evident in Esther allowed the Jewish people to survive where a more passive understanding of man's proper role in history would have resulted in annihilation. Politically, Mordechai created the mold from which came, for example, the successful revolt of Mattathias ben Johanan and his sons against the Seleucid Greeks – and in this case, too, the military and diplomatic daring of the Jewish leaders was accompanied by intellectual and religious responsibility, as evidenced by the Jews' decision to wage battle on the Sabbath, for if not, "they will only destroy us the sooner from the earth."[19] Intellectually, Mordechai's courage marked the beginning of the rabbinic period and the creation of the Talmud, on the remarkable thesis that the *tora* was now in the hands of man and that, even if such were available, "we pay no attention to voices from heaven."[20] Ultimately, it was the flexibility and authority afforded the Jewish leadership by this stance that permitted Judaism to survive the Roman catastrophe and beyond.

These facts, however, only strengthen the challenge that was mounted in his own time against Mordechai's faith. If man can be such a success on his own, where is there room for God?

For the answer one must look back to Mordechai's understanding of politics, as he expresses it to Esther when she must decide on her own fate and that of her people. He tells her: (i) "Who knows whether it was not for such a time as this that you came into royalty?"; (ii) "if you insist on remaining silent at this time, ... you and your father's house will perish"; and (iii) "relief and deliverance will come to the Jews from elsewhere" (4.13–14). Each of these elements represents for Mordechai an essential principle of political action – principles that, when taken together, establish man in his new role, and define the relationship in which he now stands with his God.

(i) *The principle of investment.* It takes only a moderate familiarity with politics to see that, contrary to what is often supposed, there are no "coincidences" in the book of Esther. Every significant event from the moment that Esther is ushered into the care of the king's harem keepers is orchestrated by Mordechai or by Esther. This is not to say that they can foresee every event precisely enough to have authored it move for move and line for line. No political actor can see ahead with this degree of precision. In politics events are directed, instigated, orchestrated. And so they are in Esther: They are the consequence of purposive action on Mordechai and Esther's part, which succeeds in forcing reality in a given direction. Thus while even the most skilled politician cannot know for certain what will cause the king to suspect his vizier of evil intent, Esther considers it probable that the insinuation of some sort of gathering interest between herself and the vizier will do the trick. If so, it is certainly no coincidence when the event she considered in advance to be probable takes place as predicted. In politics, as in all human affairs, this is how causation works.[21]

Moreover, a gifted orchestrator of political events will have that which is *unpredicted* work in his favor much of the time as well. Esther does not know that Mordechai's life has been put in immediate jeopardy when she moves to provoke the king's fear of Haman at the first banquet of wine. Yet it is the king's subsequent irritation with the vizier that saves Mordechai's life. Had Esther stayed her move another twelve hours, Mordechai would likely have been put to death the next morning. But Esther's ignorance of her opponent's exact moves does not change the fact that it is her purposive effort that saves Mordechai's life. Since strength attracts strength, while damage invites further damage, she can assume that if she succeeds in weakening Haman's position in one way, he will be harmed in any number of unpredicted and additional ways – a lesson the rabbis emphasized by adding that Haman, as he was leading Mordechai through the streets on the king's horse, also suffered having a

filthy chamber pot emptied on his head by his own daughter, who believed her
father to be the rider.²²

The degree to which probable and even unpredicted events fall in the desired
direction is not a matter of chance. By far the most important factor is the
degree to which the political player has invested in potentially useful assets in
the relevant arena before the start of a given effort or campaign. Mordechai
does not know precisely what will be the consequences of instructing Esther
to hide her lineage, or of saving the king's life. He only recognizes that these
moves are likely to strengthen the position of the Jews generally, and so decides
to invest against some future struggle he cannot foresee. They appear in the
narrative not because they were his only political efforts, but because they
are the ones that, with hindsight, can be seen to have contributed directly.
Unreported are the thousands of other such investments that Mordechai and
Esther made over the years, but which happened in the end to be of little
importance in this particular conflict.

With regard to all of these moves, Mordechai's attitude was that which we
recognize in his famous exhortation to Esther: "And who knows whether it
was not for such a time as this that you came into royalty?" – that is, one can
never be certain of the purpose of any specific investment in one's political
position until great events have played themselves out. A political player who
excels at his craft is one who treats every minor and apparently meaningless
turn of events as an opportunity to affect the greatest of events that lie buried
in the mists of the future, saying: Who knows whether hiding Esther's Jewish
identity will not assist her in deflecting suspicion later on? Who knows whether
saving the king's life will not prove useful at a later point? Over much time and
in the aggregate, these purposive strengthenings of one's position, the constant
imposition of will, purpose, design, and meaning on the raw material of hap-
penstance, tend to be the critical prerequisites for victory on the day the actual
battle breaks – although only when the story is retold in the aftermath is it
possible, sometimes, to see why.

In this, Mordechai was seconded by Machiavelli, who two thousand years
later prescribed this political method as the means of ensuring against the rages
of fortune:

> I would compare her to an impetuous river that, when turbulent, inundates
> the plains, casts down the trees and buildings, removes earth from this side
> and places it on the other. Every one flees before it, and everything yields to
> its fury without being able to oppose it. And yet though it is of such a kind,
> still when it is quiet, men can make provision against it by dykes and banks,
> so that when it rises it will either go into a canal or its rush will not be so
> wild and dangerous. So it is with fortune, which shows her power where

no measures have been taken to resist her, and directs her fury where she knows that no dykes or barriers have been made to hold her.[23]

The book of Esther is in accord with Machiavelli's teaching up to a certain point. Mordechai, too, believes in the building of "dykes and barriers" against unforeseen eventualities: He builds his home and his life in the fortress of Susa rather than in the Jewish quarter. He allows Esther to leave her home and enter the court. He spends his days in calculated discussion with the courtiers to gather information and build connections. He instructs her not to reveal her lineage. He teaches her to gain favor with everyone. He saves the life of an ungrateful king. In every case, Mordechai understands that where there is an investment to be made, it is an investment that must be made. And ultimately, it is these investments that yield the resources necessary to save the Jews in their hour of need.

(ii) *The principle of boldness.* The political campaign may be understood as the advance of an infantryman against a sniper whom he cannot see, and whose location is known to him only as a general direction. If he tries to rush against the sniper from his initial position, he exposes himself at his weakest and gives the sniper every opportunity to take careful aim and bring him down, while he himself stands little chance of reaching his goal. By means of calculated advances, ducking from one place of cover to another, he slowly improves his own understanding of the enemy's identity and location, while at the same time decreasing the risk that he will have to take in the final charge against the sniper's nest. But there is always a limit to how much time and effort can be invested in improving the position from which he will make his final assault. In the end, he must attack with what he has, either because it becomes too dangerous to wait any longer, or because he has simply reached the limit of what he can do to prepare, and usually for the former reason rather than the latter. At this point, every additional hesitation becomes a menace, and he must gather up his strength to begin the final, open assault – in which his opponent will know with certitude that he must fight for his life, and against whom.

There is no end to the investments that may be made in anticipation of action yet to come. But when the time comes, one must leap into the open, or all the preparation is as though it had never been. When faced with Haman, Mordechai must make his public stand and refuse, before the watching eyes of the empire, to prostrate himself. When faced with the decree, he must take his protest to the streets of the capital; and Esther must enter to see the king, demand the elimination of her enemy, and push for its repeal. No amount of careful investment can bring these moves to life without the decision to come out from hiding and attack. In the final analysis, only the willingness to risk everything can bring about victory: "If you remain silent at this time, ... you and your father's house will perish."

This, too, is the subject of a colorful figure in Machiavelli, who similarly argues that boldness is a virtue that no amount of planning can replace: "It is better to be impetuous than cautious, for fortune is a woman, and it is necessary, if you wish to master her, to overcome her by force; and it can be seen that she lets herself be overcome by the bold rather than by those who proceed coldly."[24]

These principles, that of investment and that of boldness – the accumulation of assets, and their expenditure on effecting change – are two fundamentals of all political action. Yet every politician knows that there are three stages in any move, in any campaign, and not two. One invests, one throws oneself into the abyss, and then one falls. To land on one's feet and in a better place is, of course, the goal. But how one gets there is another issue, for which is required another principle of political action.

(iii) *The principle of faith.* Although they are separated by nearly twenty centuries, Mordechai lives in a world much like that of Machiavelli. God has hidden his face, and it appears that the course of human events runs on inexorably without purpose and without guidance, either from heaven or earth. In such a world, there is little hope that any man can achieve any good at all, and it is against such a nihilistic view that both Mordechai and Machiavelli set forth their principles of investment and boldness. With these, even a man utterly alone in an endless, godless anarchy can hope to project his own direction onto the tides of history, at times emerging the victor. But there is a third principle that fails to appear in Machiavelli, thereby crippling his politics and stunting his world: the principle of faith, expressed by Mordechai in the assertion that without Esther's intervention to save the Jews, "relief and deliverance will come to the Jews from elsewhere."

There have been those who claimed that this "elsewhere" is itself a literal reference to God, relying on a word-play imposed on the Hebrew text that, although terribly strained, permits such a reading if one insists upon it. In this case, Mordechai is made to say: If you remain silent at this time, relief and deliverance will come from God.[25] But neither Mordechai nor the narrative need such a device to introduce God as Esther's understudy. For this, a direct reference would have been perfectly serviceable. Rather, the point is that God seems not to appear to his people in Susa – neither before Esther's decision, nor after it. Nor is there reason to believe he would have been more in evidence had she remained silent and relief had come from another source. Who or what, then, is this "elsewhere"?

Let us consider Mordechai on the day the vizier issues the decree condemning the Jews of Persia to death. At this point, he has not yet spoken to Esther, and the truth is that reaching Esther is manifestly not his first thought. He neither rushes immediately to the palace to find her, nor does he send word to her in writing. Instead, he dons mourning clothes and goes on a protest march through the city, shouting and crying up at the windows of the homes belonging to the officials of the empire, many of whom he has known in various capacities during his years as a courtier. Thus Esther may or may not be the best card Mordechai can hope to play in the confrontation that has now erupted between him and Haman, but it is certain that he does not believe her to be his only card. Esther is one of a large number of people who have an interest in preventing Haman from seizing power in the empire and in preventing the king from abolishing his system of advisers, and it is to all of these that Mordechai seeks to appeal. Even when he sits before the palace gate, he does not immediately send a message to her, but continues to address his protest to the many powerful men who are moving in and out in pursuit of their own business.

The fact is that Mordechai does not have any way of knowing whence relief and deliverance will come at this point. And every person who has a role in the court of any kind and who tries to communicate with him in his distress receives the same message that Esther hears, although tailored to speak to him personally: Do not think you will escape because you are not a Jew. If you remain silent at this time. Who knows whether it was not for such a time as this. Deliverance will come.

At this stage, Mordechai has no idea that deliverance will come from Esther. He knows it must come from somewhere, and if not from the particular individual with whom he has only just spoken, then from "elsewhere." Only once events have run their course can he know that this "elsewhere" is, as it turns out, the queen. But had Esther failed in her task, then the story would hardly have mentioned her, if at all, and deliverance would have come from another person, another political factor, whose name we have no way of knowing, and who may not even have been known to Mordechai yet.

What permits Mordechai to have such confidence that he is willing to speak so readily and certainly about the existence of an "elsewhere" capable of bringing salvation? First, he believes in the investments he has made, over years establishing a series of defenses – such as the hidden presence of a Jewish queen in the palace, such as the favors owed him by the king and others – for just such a time as this. Second, he believes in the boldness of his own attack, of his public refusal to recognize Haman as having absolute authority. Taking Haman off guard within weeks or even days of his coming to power, this counteroffensive is launched well before Haman's position is consolidated and stable, and is certain to result in some kind of ill-planned responses – like the issuance of an unprecedented decree of annihilation against the Jews, and the construction of the seventy-five-foot gallows. Mordechai knows he has prepared for this battle and that his open assault was launched in time. He believes that under such conditions, the chances of success are good, even though the cause might appear hopeless at first glance.

But all this is still within the realm of what Machiavelli understands as digging canals and acting impetuously, none of which affords him certainty that "relief will come from elsewhere." For Machiavelli is in this sense a "modern" thinker: He believes in the existence of an objective world outside of man, which is in its essence a dry and unyielding surface on which he plays and dies. Reality does not respond to his actions, does not concern itself with his actions. At best, it may be forced to submit to them. Whether fortune is a river or a lady, Machiavelli's prince wages his battle against her rages alone. He can count on the provisions he himself has made against her, the favors he has done and the allies he has acquired, the advice he has sought out and heeded, the resources he has set aside for bad times, and the contingency plans that he has laid against the possibility of catastrophe. Yet all of these are merely extensions of his own reach. Other men may be useful to him, but only in the sense that other things are useful: One may manipulate them according to the internal rules that govern them, and according to the dictates of one's own will. The prince ultimately believes in no one and nothing but himself, the only thing warm and alive on the cold tundra of a dead, objectified universe. Since reality is dead, it can respond to man in only two ways: It can ignore him and let him perish, or it can be forced to yield to his actions and his conscious will so that he may live. In either case, it is for him of necessity an opponent, an enemy.

But for all that is strange and new in Esther, Mordechai nevertheless understands reality from a point of vantage different from Machiavelli's, one in which all that is of interest and significance to man is to be gained by means of appropriate orientation and action within the subjective world in which he in practice thinks, lives, and acts. In this world, reality is warm and alive, a love and a friend. It supports man from underneath and above, consisting not only of objects to be manipulated, but having direction and tendency of its own as well. It gives to man his life and his consciousness, the capacities to imagine and create, to learn and to remember, freedom to make judgments, and strength and spirit to stand for them, a body responsive to his spirit, an environment that feeds it and nurtures it year upon year, and daily resurrections from sleep, forgetfulness, and pain. But more than this, reality is filled with other minds, other men, familiar and unfamiliar, who are not objects but wills, whose relationship to the subjective is responsive and giving: from those who, unbidden, choose to bring one into the world, to those who, unbidden, seek to carry on one's struggles and ideas after death. These others have their interests, but many of them are in fact interested by eternal truths, so that the more one approaches the dedication to these truths, the greater is the host of wills, future and past, that stand behind one's every effort. For those such as Mordechai, who live listening to the urgings of these wills and crying out to them in turn, it is never unexpected when one such as Esther breaks ranks with the cold and the hard, the wood and the stone, and, moved by the truth, responds – taking the initiative to be second to the true King and to pursue his interest; walking in all his ways that she may grow righteous and strong; piercing the blackness and illuminating the night. As was said by R. Eleazar in the name of R. Hanina, the moment of Esther's decision to dress in royalty and go in to see the king was also that in which she also cloaked herself in the spirit of God.[26]

Mordechai's certainty in the assistance of hidden others such as Esther is what moved the rabbis to portray him time and again as a teacher and friend of the children, and as drawing his power from them. Thus in one parable of Resh Lakish, the day of the decree finds Mordechai walking utterly alone, while Haman celebrates with his advisers and allies. Yet even as he faces the sting of the worst, Mordechai immediately understands that his hope lies with the children. He runs to a group of them coming from school, and they repeat to him the words of Isaiah: "Take counsel together, and it will be brought to naught. Speak the word, and it will not stand, for God is with us."[27] When Haman asks him: "Why are you so glad over the words of these children?" Mordechai replies: "Because of the good tidings they have given me, that I need not fear the evil design that you have formed against us."[28]

Perhaps most telling is the argument of the rabbis that it is not Esther's efforts but those of the children that result in Ahashverosh's nightmares on the fateful night when he turns against Haman:

> Having made the gallows, Haman went to Mordechai, whom he found in the house of study with the schoolchildren before him in sackcloth, studying the *tora* and crying and weeping. He counted them and found twenty-two thousand children there.
>
> He put them in iron chains and set guards over them, saying: "Tomorrow, I will kill these children first, and then I will hang Mordechai."
>
> Their mothers brought them bread and water, and said to them: "Children, eat and drink before you die tomorrow, and do not die of hunger."
>
> But they put their hands on their books and swore by the life of Mordechai, their teacher, saying: "We will neither eat nor drink, but will die while still fasting."
>
> They all wept piteously until the sound of their cries ascended to heaven, and the Holy One, may he be blessed, heard the sound of their weeping at around the second hour of the night. At that moment, the compassion of the Holy One, may he be blessed, was stirred .... He took the letters containing their doom, which were signed with a seal of clay, and tore them, in so doing bringing fright upon Ahashverosh in the night.[29]

Here the intention is not to detract from Esther's heroism, but to understand her might as part of another cause, broader and deeper – the turmoil of the Jewish children, Esther herself among them, fasting, praying, hoping, weeping, straining for the deliverance. As Mordechai does not truly walk alone because she is there for him, hidden in the palace, so too are these others with him, in their tens of thousands. As Esther had once been a child, learning at his feet and taking his teachings to her heart so that on that black day she might be ready to stand with him, so too are there always those others who, while not yet visible, are nonetheless there for him, with him. Elsewhere. Elsewhen. So that he need not fear the evil design of a transient and perverse creature, an idol, an impotence, which, even if it should hang him and take Esther as well, still would not succeed in laying a hand on that which is eternal, which it wishes to destroy first of all, but cannot.

As Mordechai wanders through the streets of the capital, his cries echo up and out among the arches and balconies and parapets of a city made of stones, begging for an answer. The truth is that he seeks a response not only from among the Jews, not only from among men, but from anywhere his voice may reach – his cries, whether he calls them such or not, are a prayer.[30] And when it comes, when Esther decides that she cannot permit this prayer to go unanswered, it is not only for the Jewish children that she responds, and not only for the righteous among men, although these voices are to be found in hers as well. Esther answers for all of reality, for God himself, whose direction and tendency it has been to provide such Jewish children in every generation, and to provide them with the strength to redeem Israel again and again. It is she herself who decides, but in so doing, she becomes God's answer to Mordechai's cries: "Then it is that the Holy One, may he be blessed, answers the world and its inhabitants, bringing forth the dawn from the darkness, and illuminating the world."

The world is in the first instance formless, directionless, anarchical, liquid, void, an utmost darkness. Not much has changed since Genesis: Man's place is perpetually to live in ships on the surface of the water, on the edge of the abyss.[31] Machiavelli's politics, and especially that of Nietzsche after him, looks out across the waves and calls on man to cease from his despair: He must impose that order which he himself decrees. He must recognize the vastness of the sea, and yet for all this, weigh anchor, engage those oarsmen whom he can command, and strive with his every fiber to give his craft direction and purpose, that it may make its way a distance across the emptiness, of its own power, before the end of it.[32] But Mordechai speaks to us of another politics, and a greater one: of one in which a spirit blows unseen over the surface of the water, allowing it direction, tendency, order, rule, purposiveness, light. Perhaps this is no great wind. One can hardly feel it when one walks about the deck.

Indeed, it is so still that when man disregards it, his ship may lie dead on the sea for a thousand years in spite of it, as though it did not exist. And yet he need only hoist a sail to see how this wind fills the world, as it has since creation. And if he has correctly aimed his craft, he then feels it shudder into motion as God answers.

In Esther, God has ceased to call man in the streets and the marketplaces. He has withdrawn from dictating political action and decreeing divine law. His shout is no more, and so our own shouts drown out his voice as a matter of course. But this does not mean we act in isolation. Beyond the investments and acts of boldness and might the individual can muster, there is infinite strength in a living reality that seeks to move in the same direction, and that can respond tenfold, ten-thousand-fold, if our aims are toward the true and eternal, toward that which is commanded. Reality does not need to be conquered, but it needs to be incited, ignited, pushed to erupt with all its latent powers in directions that man cannot possibly predict with accuracy, yet for which we are all of us responsible. We do not play against reality, but with it. We believe that if we do our part, everything that is possible according to powers that can be mustered on earth, there will be others, there will be "elsewheres" that react to our cries and our acts and do theirs. If we do our part, God will do his.

After every holocaust, and certainly the one in our time, it must be asked again whether all this is not nonsense. If there had been a Mordechai to witness the consequences of the German war against the Jews, would not he have recognized that "relief and deliverance" simply does not come on every occasion, that God does not initiate and that frequently he also does not do his part?

To this there can be two answers, both possible, but neither pleasant. The first is that in Germany, as in all the previous enormities in the history of the Jews, God did respond. Relief and deliverance did come, in the form of the United States, in the form of the Soviets, and the life of the Jews as a people and as an idea was indeed saved. No one has ever claimed that relief and deliverance would come to every Jew in every case, as it did not come to all of Israel who lived and died in Egypt. The second is that God did not do his part because we did not do ours – that there were too many such as Mordechai who were placed to invest for the crisis, but who did not bother to do so, and that there were too many such as Esther who were placed to act boldly to stem the tide, but who chose to remain silent at that time. We chose not to initiate, we chose not to walk in all his ways. And as we were not merciful, so he was not merciful.

And the truth is that these two answers are much the same. While Mordechai insisted that relief and deliverance would come from somewhere, eventually, it seems that it was not his intention to say that if Esther chose to remain silent, it would be without terrible consequences. "You and your father's house will perish." And if the many choose to remain silent, they and many, many more may also perish before God can, with the feeble tools we have left him, find a way of bringing relief and deliverance to the remnant.

And one must wonder whether this is not the most terrible punishment that has come of the world after the exile, in which God's face remains hidden and the initiative has gone over to man in all things – that man may walk in God's ways in this as well: that as he hides his face, so too do we hide our face. And then even God cannot respond to the cries of his children.

May we in our own day learn these teachings, that they may be in our hearts and in our hands, that we may merit the lifting of the evil that has been decreed by reason of our folly and our ignorance, our impiety and our inaction, and that the Jews should have light and gladness, joy and honor as in days past.

AFTERWORDS

24

A Missile over Tel Aviv

The book of Esther is not about coincidence or luck. No extraordinarily unlikely events just happen to intervene to save the Jews of Persia from destruction. Haman's fall from power and the frustration of his plot to murder the Jews are depicted in the narrative as being entirely the result of human initiative: Mordechai and Esther use conventional political means to bring all this about. And, indeed, nothing but conventional political analysis is needed to understand all of the events that bring about this outcome.[1] God is not explicitly mentioned even once, although there are undeniable implicit references to God. These implicit references teach that God is *nistar*, that he is "hidden" from view, but that his will and justice can be recognized as entering history by way of the deeds of the human beings in the story, who act throughout without special knowledge of what his plans or purposes might be.

But the story of Esther is not always told this way. A number of recent commentaries read the book of Esther precisely as a story constructed around an astonishing set of coincidences,[2] turns of events that happen to work out favorably for the Jews, but are "inexplicable by natural causality."[3] Far from orchestrating Haman's demise by conventional political means, Mordechai and Esther are seen as triumphing because they are enveloped by a "mysterious grace" that arranges everything so they will succeed.[4] True, there are no grandstand miracles in the Esther story like the parting of the Red Sea in Exodus. But the coincidental turns of events in the plot are supposed to serve the same function, the author subscribing to the view that "a coincidence is a miracle in which God prefers to remain anonymous."[5] As Jon Levenson writes:

> If the term "theology" means anything in reference to the book of Esther, this is its theology. That Ahashverosh could not sleep one night would be trivial, except for the coincidence that the records read to him as a

soporific happen to open to the report of Mordechai's unrequited bene-
faction. Similarly, that the king asks for advice as to how to repay a loyal
courtier would hardly be worth mentioning, except that Haman – in
another strangely coincidental turn – happens to be entering the court at
that moment.[6]

Readings of this kind differ from the one I have presented in the kinds of
causes they ascribe to the events in the narrative: Whereas I have suggested
that Esther's premeditated actions are the cause of the king's inability to sleep
and his request to review the records concerning the attempt on his life, these
readers prefer to see a mysterious grace at work. And whereas I understand
Haman's early-morning visit to the king to ask for Mordechai's life as having been caused by Mordechai's ongoing public campaign against the vizier,
these readers see this same event – and especially its timing at just the moment
Ahashverosh has begun to reevaluate the wisdom of relying on Haman so
extensively – as inexplicable by natural causality. These and quite a few other
links in the chain of events need to be examined to determine whether they
are really as inexplicable and mysterious as Levenson and other commentators
have insisted, or whether it is reasonable to see them as resulting from moves
in a conventional contest of power between Haman and his Jewish adversaries.

But before we can settle questions concerning the causes of specific events in
the Esther story, there is a larger issue that has to be dealt with. Many of those
who read Esther as a book of coincidences assume that the author of Esther
subscribes to a very particular kind of theology – a way of thinking about
God's relationship to events that dictates the sort of role he has to play in the
narrative. I would like to examine this assumed theology, which I believe is neither sensible on its own terms, nor very helpful in reading the Bible. Once it is
out of the way, it will be much easier to make sense of the plot and the theology
of Esther, as well as much else in Scripture besides.

How is God's action in the world related to the events described in the story
of Mordechai and Esther? One option is to read this story as including two different kinds of events that need to be distinguished from one another: (i) those
that are the result of natural causation, including the normal actions of human
beings; and (ii) acts of God, which interrupt the sequence of naturally caused
events. At most times and places, the affairs of the world consist of events of
the first kind, being carried forward exclusively as a result of an uninterrupted
sequence of natural causes, one thing following from another in accordance
with natural laws that are supposed to govern all things. But on occasion, there
will be certain special events that are, as far as the natural order is concerned,
"uncaused," amounting to the breaking and rerouting of these sequences of
natural causes and the violation of the natural laws that otherwise govern
them. The result is abnormal, extraordinarily improbable events that change

the course of a given drama so that justice can enter the world, whereas the natural run of affairs would apparently have yielded only evil. These are the miracles that are so often associated with God's action in the world, including the various purported coincidences in the plot of the Esther story.[7]

This is a not uncommon way of thinking about God's relationship with events. We find versions of it among theologians and their academic detractors, as well as among the broader public. I offer an example of such a standpoint drawn from my own recent experience, and I'm sure readers can come up with many others. In the middle of the last war between Israel and Gaza, there was a widely circulated story told by an officer on an Israeli missile battery. Tel Aviv had been bombarded for weeks by missiles, but these had either been shot out of the sky by these missile crews, or else had been aimed so poorly that the batteries did not need to respond to them. But at a certain moment, the missiles falling on Tel Aviv overwhelmed the capacities of the battery. A single explosive charge was able to penetrate Tel Aviv's defenses and was left falling directly toward the center of the city. The officer watched helplessly as the missile plummeted toward the buildings. Suddenly, a wild gust of wind swept in from the east and blew the missile out into the ocean, where it landed harmlessly among the waves. "I witnessed this miracle with my own eyes," he said in his account. "It was not told or reported to me. I saw the hand of God send that missile into the sea."[8]

I did not myself witness the event in question, so I do not want to go too far in judging the reactions of the officer to what he saw. Nevertheless, I was and still am struck by how preposterous it is. Here we have an officer operating a piece of machinery that, for the first time in human history, is able to shoot twenty or fifty armed missiles a day out of the sky, and in so doing save the lives of all those in the buildings below. Yet he is impressed that he has seen the hand of God because of a single missile thrown aside by a freak gust of wind! Even at first glance, there should be something absurd about this. Why should the inspiration and difficult work over so many years that created these missile systems be any less the result of God's action in the world than the appearance of a strong gust of wind? To be sure, a wind from God can bring about salvation in the Bible, as in the parting of the waters at the Red Sea. But in the Bible, it is at least as common for remarkable success in conventional military, political, or economic undertakings to be described as being from God. This is said of Ishmael ("God was with the lad as he grew"), Joseph ("The Lord was with him, and the Lord caused all that he did to succeed at his hand"), David ("And David had success in all he did, for the Lord was with him"), Nehemia ("I told them of the hand of God, which was good upon me"), and many others.[9] And if we consider these cases with care, we see that such references to divine action rarely refer to anything that would today be categorized as "supernatural."

On the contrary, what is usually being described is instances of protracted hardship, where the challenges that had to be overcome were immense and the talents employed prodigious, the extraordinary performances of extraordinary men and women whom God is said to have rewarded with success. The Israelite prophet or historian, in other words, recognized God's hand in just the kinds of trials and hardships over decades that faced Israel's engineers as they labored to produce these unprecedented missile batteries and to bring them, ultimately, to successful deployment in battle. And I do not doubt that if our prophets had seen this, they would have described God as having been with Israel's engineers and soldiers in their work as well.

If the prophets and scholars who composed the Bible were able to see God's hand in the world of exceptional human labor and achievement, why could our young officer not see this? The answer is that his vision is constrained by the very metaphysical distinction we encountered earlier. His way of looking at the world is defined by these same mutually exclusive categories: natural causation, which, he has been taught to believe, is what brought about the design and creation of these missile batteries and the performance of the soldiers manning them, including himself; and divine causation, which he thinks it is fitting to apply to the freakish gust of wind that played a role in the battle. But why should he or anyone else say that strikingly unusual human achievements are the result of "natural causation," whereas strikingly unusual atmospheric events are the result of "divine causation"? This is entirely arbitrary. And it is not clear what is gained by it.

The elimination of exceptional human efforts from the inventory of God's possible ways of acting in the world should already serve as a warning that there is something profoundly wrong with the distinction between natural and divine causation. But this is not its only undesirable effect. Another is that the rigorous distinction between natural and divine causation leads inexorably to the notorious view of God's action in the world as existing only in the gaps that remain in the sequence of events caused in accordance with nature. (This has been described as the theology of the "God of the gaps."[10]) Since divine action has been defined in opposition to natural causation, the inevitable result is that God is thought to be visible only where our ignorance of the causes of things leads us to perceive gaps in the natural, law–governed sequence of events. For example, we see that the world is filled with a vast variety of animal and plant life, but we do not understand how these creatures can have developed eyes and wings and other remarkable adaptations that permit them to survive and flourish. Or we experience human beings, ourselves and others, as possessing a structured consciousness of the world, and we do not understand how something composed of dead matter can be conscious of the world. Since we do not know what are the causes that have brought eyes, wings, and human consciousness into being, we perceive gaps in the known causal architecture of the world, which are thought to suggest that God's miraculous action must have been required for these things to exist.

But as has been pointed out many times, the result of such a view is that God's presence in the world ends up playing a zero-sum game with the advancement of human understanding and science: So long as we do not understand the natural causes of a given phenomenon, God is thought to be manifestly present in the world before us. But as soon as we can propose plausible natural causes for this phenomenon, God is seen as retreating before the light of human understanding. God's presence is therefore associated only with human ignorance, whereas the ideal of a complete human knowledge of the causes of things would be one in which there is nothing left for God to cause, and human beings have arrived at a perfect atheism.

It goes without saying that past ages did not dream of such a zero-sum game relationship between the recognition of God's action in the world and the advancement of human understanding and science. The Israelite prophets and scholars who composed the Bible did not dream of such a thing because they knew of no opposition between knowledge of God's actions in the world and knowledge of the natural causes of things. In Hebrew Scripture, the regularities that are observed in nature are the result of God's commands. So any knowledge of the natural causes of things is knowledge of the things that God has commanded – an improvement in our understanding of God's actions, and therefore in our knowledge of God himself.[11] Such a biblical standpoint comes to an end when natural causation is defined in opposition to divine causation, forcing God out of his biblical position as Lord over a natural order that he created – and into his more recently conceived role of peering into the natural order through the gaps in it.

Many readers, however, mistakenly suppose that this later opposition between natural and divine causation already exists in Scripture. A frequent mistake is to assume that when the biblical text explicitly invokes God's name to tell us that he is acting or speaking, we have divine causation, whereas when we are told that a human being is acting, we are in the realm of natural causation. It is this assumption that leads to readings of Esther such as the following:

> Haman's being hoist with his own petard conforms to a more general biblical pattern in which the punishment fits the crime .... Here, however, there is no mention of divine causation. It is Harvona and Ahashverosh, and not God, who bring about the condign punishment. In this, Esther may show the influence of wisdom literature, which sometimes speaks of an inherent [i.e., natural] correspondence of deed and consequence, even apart from divine intervention.[12]

Notice the way in which the rigid distinction between natural and divine causation is imposed on this passage in Esther. The subject here under discussion is the fact that Haman, ironically, ends up being hanged on the very gallows that he himself had earlier erected in order to do away with Mordechai (7.10), and whether it was human beings who brought about this ironic outcome or God. God's name is not explicitly mentioned, and so it is proposed that it was "Harvona and Ahashverosh, and not God, who bring about the condign punishment." In addition, since it is human action and not God that brings about this punishment, this passage in Esther is then said to reflect the influence of biblical "wisdom literature," such as certain passages in Proverbs, in which justice is likewise supposed to come into the world exclusively through natural causation.[13]

At this point, the distinction between natural and divine causation is being used to sort entire sections of the Bible into two piles, with some parts of the Bible supposedly viewing worldly reward and punishment as taking place by natural causation, while others require "divine causation" to get the same job done. But is there any reason to think that the authors of Scripture intended to draw such a distinction? Or that they would have embraced it if it had been proposed to them? This is exceedingly doubtful, and it only becomes more so when one examines the biblical passages that are being sorted in this way. This, for example, is the particular verse in Proverbs that is invoked to help us understand the natural (and not divine) causation that is thought to be in evidence when Harvona and Ahasherosh decide to hang Haman:

> He who digs a pit will fall into it himself. He who sets a stone rolling, will have it turn back upon him.[14]

On the other hand, the description of Haman's execution in Esther is thought *not* to have been influenced by passages such as the following from Exodus, in which Moses reports God himself as taking responsibility for bringing justice of this kind into the world:

> You will not afflict the widow or the fatherless child.
> If you afflict him in any way, if he cry out to me in any way, I will surely hear his cry.
> My anger will burn, and I will kill you with the sword, and your wives will be widows, and your children fatherless.[15]

The proposal here is that the verse from Proverbs teaches us that justice enters the world without God's involvement, whereas the passage from Exodus teaches the opposite: that justice enters the world because God makes it happen. But the truth is that none of this makes any sense. Our ability to understand these texts is only impaired by their being refracted through the lens of the distinction between natural and divine causation, forcing each one to become an example of one of these two categories of causation and not the other. In fact, the passage we have just read from Exodus, in which God promises those who abuse the widow and the orphan that "I will kill you with the sword, and your wives will be widows, and your children fatherless," teaches us nothing at all concerning the existence of an opposition between natural and divine causation. On the contrary, while God says that it is he who will do the killing, the sword in question is a sword wielded by human beings acting out of human motives. The sword is wielded, in other words, as a consequence of both natural *and* divine causes. And its effect – that it makes widows and orphans of the wives and children of men who have themselves dared to oppress the widow and the orphan – is offered by Moses as a natural principle, decreed by God, governing the political order.

In the same way, the passage from Proverbs suggesting that "He who sets a stone rolling, will have it turn back upon him," teaches us nothing concerning the existence of an opposition between natural and divine causation. On the contrary, the rolling stone moves as it does as a consequence of both natural *and* divine causes: One cause is the man who set the stone rolling out of human motives; and the other is God, who, as the broader context in Proverbs makes plain, has established it as a natural law governing the world that harmful forces will harm those who have unleashed them.[16]

These passages are typical of the worldview of the biblical authors, and the same things can be said of innumerable passages throughout the Bible, which relies constantly on the assumption that the purposive actions of human beings can, at the same time, also be an expression of God's action in the world.[17] In attempting to try to force the various events described in Scripture to be either the result of natural causation or a consequence of God's miraculous intervention in the natural order, contemporary readers irreparably distort the meaning of these texts, thereby making it impossible for their theological standpoint to be heard. The same is true of the passage from Esther in which Haman is hanged from the gallows that he erected for Mordechai: No conclusion of any kind can be drawn from the mere fact that Ahashverosh and Harvona are described as being the cause of Haman's execution, whereas God is not named as the cause of this turn of events. If we wish to resolve the question of whether the narrative depicts God as having caused Haman's hanging, we will have to find another approach to the problem.

I have suggested that readers who see the story of Esther as revolving around a series of coincidences or chance events tend to rely on a particular kind of theology to make this view work: They assume that behind these coincidences are acts of divine will that break the natural sequence of events, redirecting matters so as to bring about an outcome that the human actors could not have attained by themselves. But a theology of this kind is neither defensible on its own terms, nor does it sit well with the tradition of Jewish theological inquiry captured in the Bible. The book of Esther was written in the wake of a vast tradition of biblical texts in which a single action or event is simultaneously attributed to both a human cause and to God. Far from distinguishing natural from divine causation, this tradition sees the natural functioning of the world as itself an expression of God's actions, and the justice that is found in the world is, likewise, understood as an expression of the natural functioning of the world and of God's action. Far from seeing dramatic, unusual, and unexpected instances of justice as "violations" of God's order, such wondrous events are, on the contrary, the most powerful expressions of God's order.

For this reason, the possibility of God's involvement hovers over everything that happens in the Esther story, despite the fact that God is never mentioned by name. What is needed is to determine the standpoint of the book of Esther with regard to the earlier biblical traditions concerning God's relationship with the events of human history. Does the Esther narrative refrain from invoking God's name because it is has broken with the kind of view of God's action in the world that we have seen in Exodus and Proverbs? Or is the book of Esther a rearticulation, or a clarification, of the understanding of the prophets for an age in which the voice of the prophet has grown still?

25

God and Emergence

Our discussion has pointed to two radically different ways of understanding what is meant when we say that God acts in the world. These can be summarized as follows:

God's Actions Intervene in Nature. Natural causation is opposed to divine or "supernatural" causation. Every event is either caused by nature or it is not. Interruptions and violations of the sequence of natural causes can result in events that have no cause in nature. These interruptions or violations are said to be God's actions, also called miracles.

God's Actions Emerge from Nature. There is no opposition between divine and natural causation. Natural events are seen as being in accordance with laws or regularities that have been imposed by God. A given event can thus be said to have been brought about by human action or physical causes, and also to have been caused by God at the same time. Worldly justice is similarly understood to be the result of a law or regularity imposed by God. What we see as wonders or miracles are unusual or striking instances of justice appearing in the world. These wonders take place through human action or physical causes, with God's action in the world being emergent upon these causes.

The second of these two ways of understanding God's action in the world is today less familiar to us, but it is one that appears frequently in Hebrew Scripture. On this view, God's actions do not live in the gaps between sequences of natural events. Instead, God's actions, as well as traits that are attributed to God such his justice, mercy, love, and anger, are properties that are *emergent* upon the actions of human beings and the physical things that are visible around us. By this I mean that the relationship between God's actions and the more conventional human and physical causes that we recognize in the world is much like that between higher and lower levels of description in science: We rightly consider a table or a glass of water to be real things to which we attribute causal properties. But at the same time, we also suppose that a table is solid and that water is wet because of the actions of the molecules that make up the table and the water – and because of the actions of the atoms that make up these molecules, and so on – which are governed by causal laws of their own. This does not mean there is any way fully to reduce the causal sequences in which large-scale objects such as the table or the water are involved to those of the molecules below. This is impossible. But we can explain at least some significant properties of the table, the glass, and the water in terms of the actions of their constituent molecules and the laws that govern them. In the same way, descriptions of God's actions cannot be reduced entirely to specific human actions and physical events that we can identify. That is, we will never be able to give an absolutely complete account of a specific act of God in terms of human and physical actions that together constitute it. Nevertheless, it is possible to explain at least some significant aspects of God's will in terms of the actions of human beings and physical causes that make up God's action in the world in a particular time and place.[1]

The emergence of God's actions from the conventional events of the human world is a commonplace of Hebrew Scripture.[2] It is central to the Joseph narrative, in which God forges Israel into a nation capable of receiving the law by means of the Israelites' enslavement in Egypt, but these events are at the same time depicted as resulting from the quite human motives and deeds of Joseph's brothers, of Joseph himself, and of the Pharaohs. It is essential to the story of the Exodus as well, in which God redeems Israel through Moses, a man whose birth and training in the Egyptian palace are portrayed as resulting exclusively from human actions. But nowhere in the Bible is the emergent character of God's will more carefully examined than it is in Esther, a work whose theological concerns are focused on this subject. God is never mentioned explicitly in Esther, just as he did not appear in an unequivocal way to the exiles in Persia after the decline of prophecy. The theological purpose of the narrative is to suggest that God's seeming absence from the world is, at least in part, a consequence of man's own preoccupation with a certain level of reality: that in which the political crises and other pressing issues of the day are taking place. If we look to the higher levels, however, we will see that God's actions are strongly in evidence, being emergent upon those of the human actors who are explicitly named in the story, just as the properties of a table or a glass of water emerge from the molecules of which it consists.

A number of indications or hints are imbedded in the narrative to ensure that readers recognize that this is what the author of Esther had on his mind. Let us take a look at a few of these.

First, we should think again about the name that Mordechai gives his adopted daughter when she enters into the palace to serve the Persian king. Readers have always recognized that Esther is a name of Persian origin, as opposed to the Hebrew name Hadasa, which the heroine of the story received from her parents. This new name, derived from the Persian word *stara*, meaning "star," is meant to appeal to the followers of astrology in the fortress of Susa, so that Esther may enter easily into the world of the palace and move about in it without friction.[3] But this is not all there is to this name. An emergent property of the name Esther is that, although of Persian origin, when transliterated into Hebrew characters it looks as if were constructed from the Hebrew root *satar* (סתר), meaning "to conceal" or "to hide." Indeed, the sequence of letters that make up the name Esther bears an unmistakable resemblance to the Hebrew word *astir* (אסתיר), meaning "I will conceal" or "I will hide."[4] This Hebrew word opens out onto two additional levels of meaning: It can be read as Mordechai's watchword, referring to his strategy of concealing the fact that he and Esther are Jews, turning both of them into hidden instruments of Jewish political will in the Persian court. But beyond this, the word *astir* is also associated with the hiddenness of Israel's God, who in Deuteronomy tells Israel that if they turn away, their fate will be to lose touch with God's presence, for "I will surely hide [*haster astir*] my face on that day."[5] Indeed, the prophet Ezekiel uses just this word in describing God's return at the time of Israel's redemption and the return of Israel to their land ("And I will no longer hide [*lo astir od*] my face from them"[6]).

Thus beneath the principal Persian meaning of the name Esther, we find references to two additional layers of reality, that of the Jewish political figures who have concealed themselves in the palace, and that of that the God of Israel, who has hidden himself in the world of the Persian exile. The fact that Esther's name is constructed to allude to these other levels of reality is already a strong indication that emergent properties in general, and especially God's emergence upon mundane reality, is an important part of what the author of Esther is interested in discussing with his readers.[7]

A second indication that God's emergence is at issue in Esther is the peculiar way in which the fasting and supplication of the Jews is presented throughout the story. This fasting and supplication has a central position in the key theological passage in the book – Mordechai's speech urging Esther to intercede with the king and Esther's reply to him. Here, again, is this exchange in its entirety:

> Mordechai said to reply to Esther: "Do not imagine in your heart that you, of all the Jews, will escape because you are in the king's palace. For if you

insist on remaining silent at this time, relief and deliverance will come to
the Jews from elsewhere, but you and your father's house will perish. And
who knows [*mi yode'a*] whether it was not for such a time as this that you
came into royalty?"

    Esther said to respond to Mordechai: "Go assemble all the Jews present
in Susa and fast for me. Do not eat and do not drink for three days, night
and day, and I and my maids will fast as well. Then I will go in to the king,
though it is against the law. And if I perish, I perish [*veka'asher avadeti
avadeti*]" (4.13–16).

In this passage, we encounter the most glaring absences of God's name in the
entire Esther narrative – for example, in Mordechai's declaration that even if
Esther does not act to save her people, "relief and deliverance will come to the
Jews from elsewhere." But it is easier to approach the problem by considering
the fact that God is not mentioned even as Esther requests that the Jews of Susa
fast for her for three days. The Jews had actually begun fasting and putting on
sackcloth and ashes before this, as soon as word of the decree of annihilation
had reached them. As we are told: "In every province, wherever the king's command and his law reached, there was great mourning among the Jews, and fasting and crying and wailing, many of them lying in sackcloth and ashes" (4.3).
Mordechai's own sackcloth and ashes, although also directed at the courtiers
in the king's gate (4.1–2), is part of this larger act of fasting and mourning that
the Jews of Susa have initiated. Esther only intensifies this enterprise, already
under way, asking that all of the Jews in Susa join in, and that they now take on
the extraordinary burden of a fast continuing for three days and nights. And in
all of these references to fasting and sitting in sack and ashes, not a word is said
about the God at whom all of these actions are presumably directed.

    Yet despite the absence of God's name, the reader is expected immediately
to recognize that the Jews of the empire, including Esther and Mordechai, have
joined together in rituals of grief and contrition whose purpose is to petition
God to avert the evil that has befallen them and save their lives. We know this
because the passage we have just read in Esther is purposely designed, using
parallel circumstances and parallel language, to refer to various other passages
in the Bible in which just such petitions to God are described.[8] Look, for example, at the following passage in which the people of Nineveh fast in sack and
ashes in Jonah:

> And the people of Nineveh believed God [would destroy the city], and they
> proclaimed a fast and put on sackcloth, from the greatest of them to the
> lowest. And the thing reached the king of Nineveh, and he rose from his
> throne and he removed his robe from upon him, and covered himself with
> sackcloth, and sat in ashes. And he proclaimed and published throughout
> Nineveh, by decree of the king and his nobles, saying: "Let neither man nor

beast, herd nor flock, taste a thing. Let them not feed, nor drink water, but let them be covered with sackcloth, both man and beast, and let them cry mightily to God. And let every man turn from his evil way, and from the violence that is in their hands. Who knows [*mi yode'a*] whether God will not turn and relent, turning away from his fierce anger, that we perish not [*velo noved*]?"[9]

The analogy to Esther is perfectly clear. Here, too, a decree of annihilation has been issued, upon which the people begin a spontaneous fast in petition to God. This is then followed by the order of the king, who joins the fast himself and requires universal participation in the fast, sackcloth and ashes, and repentance in the hope of averting the evil decree. The parallel to Esther is emphasized by the king's choice of words, which mirror those of Mordechai and Esther: The king's speech includes the same Hebrew expression that Mordechai employs in order to invoke the possibility that God may change his mind and forgo the destruction of the city (*mi yode'a*, "Who knows?"); and concludes with the same Hebrew word for "perish" (*velo noved*, "that we perish not") with which Esther concludes her speech as well (*veka'asher avadeti avadeti*, "and if I perish, I perish").

There are other relevant parallel passages as well. When David pleads with God to save the dying child that was born to him and Batsheva, he too fasts and throws himself on the ground, and he also employs language similar to that which we have already seen in the speeches of Mordechai and the Assyrian king in Jonah:

> And David petitioned God on behalf of the child, and David fasted, and when he went to retire he slept on the floor ... "For [David] said: Who knows [*mi yode'a*] whether the Lord will not be gracious to me, that the child may live?"[10]

In the same way, we find the prophet Joel telling the people of Judah to fast and repent to try and avert their downfall at the hands of the vast foreign armies God has brought upon them. And he too uses the same linguistic construction in referring to the hope that God will change his mind and relent:

> "Turn to me even now," says the Lord, "with all your heart, and with fast-
>   ing, and with weeping, and with lamentation." ...
> Turn back to the Lord, your God ....
> Who knows [*mi yode'a*] whether he may turn and relent, and leave a bless-
>   ing behind him?[11]

In addition to the fasting, crying, and contrition, all of these passages specifically involve petitions to God to deliver human lives that have already been condemned, as is the case in Esther. And all of them use the same set phrase to introduce a distant hope that the fasting and contrition may succeed in persuading God to change course and save the lives that hang in the balance (*mi yode'a*, "Who knows?"). The fact that the text in Esther refers to these other texts in this way leaves no doubt that the Esther narrative, too, portrays the Jews as crying out to God and pleading for their salvation, even though this is not said explicitly.[12] In other words, the Jews of Susa petition God to save them, but this petition to God is left to emerge from the actions that are explicitly described in the text and from the specialized language that is used to describe what is taking place. This device again suggests that the issue of God's emergence upon conventional actions is on the narrator's mind, and at issue throughout the story.

I would like now to look at a third instance of such emergent reference to God, which is only slightly more subtle. There is one sentence in Esther that can arguably be said to serve as the thesis of the whole book. This is Mordechai's statement to Esther, quoted earlier: "Who knows whether it was not for such a time as this that you came into royalty?" It is here that we find the proposition that the queen must desist from the accumulation of favor in the court, and throw whatever favor she has gained onto the political balance in an attempt to steer the course of the empire. If this key sentence also alludes to God's emergence, we can be satisfied that we are being urged to view the entire story of Esther as one in which God's actions emerge from the human decisions and actions that are described in the narrative.

Now, I have already said that the "Who knows?" (*mi yode'a*) construction at the head of this sentence is a set phrase that refers to petitioning God in the distant hope that he will reverse a decree of death. But the matter is a bit more complicated than this. For while all four examples of such sentences that we have examined do indeed refer to God's salvation, closer inspection reveals that they do so while having very different subjects in the subordinate clause:

JONAH:
"Who knows whether *God* will not turn and relent ...?"

DAVID:
"Who knows whether the *Lord* will not be gracious to me ...?"

JOEL:
"Who knows whether *he* [i.e., *God*] may turn and relent ...?"

MORDECHAI:
"Who knows whether it was not for such a time as this that *you* [i.e., *Esther*] came into royalty?"

The first three of these sentences are framed in such a way as to raise a question that is directly about God: *Who knows whether God will change his mind so that we may be saved?* The last one, on the other hand, is framed so as to raise a question about Esther: *Who knows whether Esther does not have a role to play in saving us?* In fact, since Esther has already told Mordechai that she will not act, this text is even more striking, in that it can be read as: *Who knows whether Esther will change her mind so that we may be saved?* Mordechai's formulation thus involves a dramatic shift in focus from what God will do to what Esther will do, yet again underscoring the concern of the narrative to present every aspect of this story as taking place at the level of human responsibility, human decisions, and human actions.

Yet it would be a mistake to interpret this shift of focus as indicating that in this story Esther is in place of God, and that if one understands the actions of the human players, one knows all there is to know.[13] That Esther is not in place of God, but is rather playing a role in a larger story in which God is himself the principal actor, is elegantly alluded to in the expression that Mordechai uses to conclude the sentence "Who knows whether it was not for such a time as this that you came into royalty?" – the Hebrew phrase *higa'at lamalchut* ("that you came into royalty"). The word *lamalchut* literally means that Esther "came into kingship," or that she "came into the kingdom." This expression is parallel to the one used when Esther goes in to see the king, when she "dressed in royalty" (Hebrew, *vatilbash malchut*) (5.1), literally meaning that she "clothed herself in kingship."[14] Whose kingship is she clothing herself with in this passage? Which kingdom is it that she has come into now? On the surface, we see that Esther has come into royalty by becoming queen to the Persian king, Ahashverosh. But immediately beneath the surface of these passages is another meaning, emergent upon this one, as the rabbis recognized: By coming into worldly royalty, Esther has placed herself in a position to act in the service of another king entirely. The secondary meaning of Mordechai's question, emergent upon the first, is this: Who knows whether it was not for such a time as this that you have come into the service of the true king, of God?[15]

No, Esther does not replace God as the actor and cause to whom Mordechai's plea of "Who knows?" refers. Mordechai sees that while God's salvation may in the end be emergent upon that which is brought about by Esther, it may also arrive through the actions of others whose role cannot possibly be foreseen ("relief and deliverance will come to the Jews from elsewhere"). And Esther, too, is aware that her own decision and her own actions, crucial though they may be, can nonetheless amount only to a part in this story. We know this from the way in which she responds to the proposal that it is "for such a time as this that you came into royalty." It is just these words – which on the surface of them refer to the immense power that Esther can wield as queen of Persia – that induce Esther to tell Mordechai: "Go assemble all the Jews present in Susa and fast for me. Do not eat and do not drink for three days, night and day, and I and my maids will fast as well." Esther herself immediately turns the spotlight that has been shined upon her back upon God.

There is no mysterious grace that envelops Esther in this story, arranging things so that they go her way. If there had been, Esther would not have been forced into the harem of the king on pain of death, and she and all her people would not now stand condemned to die. She herself sees this with a scorching clarity. She faces failure, humiliation, and death. They come quickly to her now. And if, by her strength and her cunning, she does succeed in delivering the Jews, it will be because God has delivered them, as he has delivered her.

26

God Casts No Shadow

In a recent work, Michael Walzer proposes that there is no philosophical investigation of the political order in the Bible, no independent human search for the good of Israel and of the nations in Scripture. The reason for this absence, he writes, is that there can be no genuine investigation of the political realm where human beings live out their political lives "in God's shadow." This is a chilling image, suggesting that wherever God appears in the Bible, his very presence casts a dark pall over the things that are of this earth, suppressing and suffocating man's potential to establish himself through a reasoned and independent inquiry into the nature of the political order and of man's best course in it. And in fact, this is more or less what Walzer believes. As he writes:

> God is a 'man of war' and a supreme king – so what is there for human beings to do? ... When God is called a king, the independence of his royal subjects is denied. When God is called a man of war, the need for royal warriors is called into question.

On this view, the fact that God is said to be king and ruler over the earth means that kingship and rule are taken away from men, who suspend the operation of their own abilities and withdraw into quiescence in the belief that decision and action belong to God, not to them. As a result, the presence of God blots out the very possibility of political leadership among the Jews:

> The idea that any political leader could, on his own, shape the destiny of Israel is not be found in the prophets or the histories. Israel's destiny was firmly in God's hands.... In principle, God doesn't need help.[1]

Walzer is an important figure in the scholarship of recent decades, and he has devoted much time and effort to studying the Bible and the teachings of the rabbis. But in the end, his writings about God and Scripture are hostage to the same persistent prejudice that prevents so many readers in our day from being able to come to a working understanding of the politics and theology of the Bible. He is unable to free himself from the metaphysical prejudice that Scripture is committed to a thoroughgoing opposition between divine and natural causation – that is, to the view that God is one cause, independent of human action; whereas men and women are another cause, independent of God. His embrace of this prejudice is the reason that Walzer imagines every scriptural mention of God's action in the world as if it casts a shadow, creating a dark space in which no human initiative and action can survive. For if God's action and human action are mutually exclusive categories, then any mention of God doing anything necessarily requires us to subtract whatever it is that God has done from the sphere available for human activity. Again, we have a zero-sum game: Human freedom and activity begin only at the point where God's action in the world comes to an end.

There is no reason to believe that the prophets and scholars who composed the Bible thought anything of the kind. It is the imposition of mutually opposed categories of divine and natural causation, and not anything that is written in the Bible, that fills the world with these shadows – which are identical with the "gaps" in the chain of natural causation that many readers believe they find everywhere in the biblical narrative. The biblical authors were masters of metaphor and analogy, which were the principal tools they used to advance their understanding of God's action in the world. In Scripture, we find scores of different metaphors and analogies that are used to address this subject. And yet they never speak of God existing in gaps, and they never speak of God casting shadows. Nor do they say anything like these things, or anything equivalent to these things, because they mean nothing of the sort. Rather, they think of God's action in the world in a different way, which we must reclaim if we wish to understand Scripture.

Consider the metaphor of God's kingship, which Walzer sees as having blotted out the freedom of Israel's leaders to shape the destiny of their nation. In Hebrew Scripture, God's will and his laws are, in fact, often compared to those of a great king who rules over all things. But this metaphor is never employed, as Walzer supposes, to suggest that God's kingship can somehow take the place of human political leadership.[2] The opposite is the case. The biblical narrative consistently portrays God's world as having fallen into corruption and ruin through the violence and wickedness of men.[3] In this context, the metaphor of God's kingship is used to portray God as resembling a great human king, in that he requires the initiative and action of capable and daring subordinates to bring his rule and his justice into being in his realm. This is the basis for the central biblical political concept of an alliance (*brit*, or "covenant") between God and man, which is modeled on the political concept of an alliance between a great human king and the less powerful local rulers who are subordinate to him.[4] Notice that the rule of a human king is always a property that is emergent upon the actions of the less powerful local rulers who are allied to him. If these subordinate kings, governors, and ministers are successful and just, each in the specific region or area of responsibility that is under his jurisdiction, then we will consequently recognize the king's rule of his realm as successful and just.[5] And the same is true of God's kingship in Scripture, which is never considered contrary to the initiative and action of human political leaders, but always emergent upon these as they undertake to bring rule and justice into the world. We have seen an example of just this in Esther's "dressing in royalty," which is a metaphor for her taking up the service of God, the true king. And the moment in which she takes up this service, moving to establish God's kingship in the world, is precisely the moment in which she initiates political action of her own devising that will make her one of the great leaders of Israel.[6]

Or consider the prophets' metaphor of God's will as a wind that fills all things ("and a wind from God blew across the waters"[7]), pressing them in a certain direction, imparting to them a tendency toward a certain order. The existence of this direction and tendency in the world does nothing to deny man's initiative and his freedom. In acting in accordance with this direction and tendency, man can grow strong by it, contributing his own solidity and strength to the growth of the world, growth that is emergent upon man's own initiatives and deeds. Or he can deprive the world of this strength, acting in accordance with what seems right only in his own eyes, and so contributing to the dissolution of the world and its return to the chaotic waters that came before. In either case, a very great emphasis has been placed on man's initiative and action, upon which the fate of God's will for the world is understood to depend.

This is as the biblical authors saw the matter. In these and other metaphors and analogies that Scripture employs to describe God's actions, we find only God's openness to man's initiative, his longing for it, his cry and his call for it: "Why did I come, and find no man?" God says to the prophet in Isaiah. "I called out, but no one answered me."[8] Every time the prophet writes in this way, telling us that God despairs over the actions of men, or that he is angry or ashamed, or that he is filled with regret – and we read this countless times – the intention is precisely to say that God needs our help. To be sure, any individual, no matter how well placed at a given moment, is still only a thread in the tapestry of history as it will appear a few years from now. This means that if we fail, deliverance can always, in the end, come from somewhere else, as Moses eventually came to do what Joseph could not. But the narrative does not obscure the bitterness of the centuries that have been lost. These things weigh upon anyone who reads Scripture with a ready ear, as they are said to weigh upon God himself. It is not too far from the mark to read all of Scripture as one great cry, calling upon man to rise from his stupor and offer God what assistance we have to offer.

How strange it is, then, to read Walzer's conclusion that "in principle, God doesn't need help." If this is to be the conclusion, then the truly, the scribes labored in vain. The prejudices of our age have robbed many of the ability to open the biblical narratives and the speeches of the prophets and find even the first things that their authors meant for us to read in them.

For such a time, the book of Esther is a precious gift. For here we have a narrative that is, as it were, a translation of the great biblical stories of God's action in history into the language of a later time – the language of the time after the destruction of Judah and Jerusalem, when prophets no longer come forward to interpret events for us in light of God's unceasing cry, and none know how to look upon the things that come to pass and say: Look at this again, for it was here that we ourselves saw the hand of God. A time when, as R. Johanan put it, prophecy has been given over to children and to fools.[9]

In keeping with the needs of this new time, the story of Esther has been written with the name of God everywhere erased. The story has been written, in other words, as a reflection of, even a satire upon, the way in which later readers prefer to see themselves: at the center of the stage, alone. Even the Jews' fasting in sackcloth and ashes is absurdly reported without reference to the God they are petitioning, as if these were self-contained human actions, directed at nothing and no one outside of themselves. Anyone can understand that there is something terribly wrong, even grotesque, about this.

There is, however, something important that is gained by it. With the name of God everywhere removed, the narrative in Esther has described a world that is in a sense much more sharply defined than the world of Abraham or Moses. Now everything that is subtle and difficult about man's place in the world has been made simple and clear. Only man is described. Only the actions of men are said to take place. The entire story, from beginning to end, consists of the highly effective actions of human beings causing things to happen in uninterrupted, seamless chains.

We read how Esther spoils her appearance to arouse the king's pity, how she orchestrates two intimate banquets with Ahashverosh and Haman to prick the king's jealousy and his fear of conspiracies against him, and how Mordechai continues to goad Haman. And the actions of Esther and Mordechai have their intended effect: Seeing that the edict of destruction has not staunched Mordechai's attack on him, Haman realizes he must have Mordechai put to death. Seeing that something is taking place between Esther and Haman that cannot but augur ill, Ahashverosh permits a thread of suspicion to enter into his mind, keeping him awake at night and bringing him to review the attempt on his life and the manner in which Haman was subsequently promoted.

Haman approaches the king to have Mordechai executed, but his move arrives a few hours too late. Esther's blow has landed first, and now the king's mind is turned only to probing Haman's loyalty. Asked how the state should honor a man who has served the king well, Haman shows that he cares nothing for honoring anyone but himself, unrolling a fantasy of usurpation that greatly strengthens the king in his view that Haman cannot be trusted. Haman's subsequent public embarrassment is thus the outward sign that the king is no longer willing to back Haman unequivocally, as before. Recognizing this, Esther understands that the moment has come to launch her final attack on the vizier – an attack that succeeds only because the king is now receptive to it, his thoughts already having been turned against Haman, his most trusted advisor, during the night and in the course of the day. Even the king's vicious misinterpretation of Haman's having fallen on the queen's couch in supplication for his life has the same cause: It was Esther herself who, the day before, had put it in the king's mind that Haman might have a sexual interest in her. That this thought now falls from the king's mouth in the context of a decision to have Haman executed is no surprise, but the final proof of Esther's success.

This is an impressive and intricate sequence of events. But all of it takes place within the boundaries of a conventional political stratagem, well conceived and finely executed. That is, it takes place entirely in the world of human political intrigue, with events following upon others that have been caused by human agents locked in a battle for the king's favor and for control of his political agenda. There is no need to suppose that any "supernatural" events have been inserted into the chain of causation, because every event we see from the moment Esther determines to go in to the king is either a direct action by Esther or Mordechai, or else something that falls out from their actions as if in a line of dominos. No "astonishing set of coincidences" has taken place, and so there is no need to invoke God to fill in gaps between political events. It is only Esther herself, with an assist from Mordechai, who has created this entire weave of political events, culminating in Haman's downfall. And the same is true for all other events in the story of Mordechai and Esther, which, as we have seen, are readily accountable by means of the normal operations of human nature and human politics.

But the fact that Haman's downfall and the ultimate reversal of his decree are every bit the political handiwork of Mordechai and Esther, and the fact that God's name has been erased from this story and from this picture of the world, does not yet create a picture of a world without God in it. What it creates is, rather, a picture of a world without prophets, without men and women who know how to recognize God's voice and see his hand in the course of events. But the world is the same world, whether or not there are any prophets in it to give God's name to things. God is still there, as he was before. He is still the cause of events in this story, just as he was the cause of events in the previous stories. Even with God's name removed, the plain meaning of the Esther narrative is that the young queen and the Jews of Susa petitioned God to strengthen her hand in her approach to the king, and that God answered their cry, granting Esther success in all her efforts. Another way of saying the very same thing, in the idiom of the prophets, is that God raised up Mordechai and Esther to save Israel, and that God delivered Haman and his allies into their hands.[10] And indeed, with regard to this very story, the rabbis went on to teach that Jews must thank God for the miracle he performed for us at the time of the first Purim in the following words: "You, in your many mercies, brought [Haman's] plans to naught, and brought ruin upon what he had thought to do, and turned retribution back upon him."[11]

I opened this work by referring to the teaching of the Talmud, according to which it is to the book of Esther that one turns to learn about miracles.[12] Why did the rabbis choose this work, in which God's name does not appear and everything that takes place results from the actions of human beings, to teach us how to understand the miracles in Scripture? Because Esther is written so as to ensure that the following teaching cannot be missed: God's salvation is not a thing that exists in the world without reference to the actions of women and men. God's salvation is emergent upon the salvation that Esther and Mordechai bring about through their own efforts in the politics of Susa. If one looks for it anywhere other than in these political endeavors – for example, if one's eye is fixed on the fasting and the sackcloth – then one will still have *witnessed* a wonder and a miracle, for one will still see that the Jews have been spared, when the warrant for their destruction had already been sealed and delivered. But one will not have *understood* what this miracle was, or what it is that God did for the Jews.

I have said that the book of Esther is a translation of the great biblical stories of God's action in history into the language of a later time. I wish to be clear about what this means. Esther teaches us to recognize God's action in the world by showing us how God's action is emergent upon human and physical causes. And it teaches this in a way that can be grasped by a generation for whom this manner of understanding things is no longer immediately intuitive, and to whom, for just this reason, it must be taught. Esther is, in other words, concerned to preserve or revive what was intuitive in the time of the prophets and scholars who wrote the earlier works of Scripture, to recover for a later generation the way in which their forefathers had seen God's action in the world.

Of course, there is always something lost in translation, and this is the case here as well. A text that erases God's name cannot say the same things that are said in a narrative in which God is portrayed as speaking directly with Israel and acting through evident wonders. But even taking this into account, the success of the translation persists, and its significance remains. Esther teaches that God's action in Scripture was always recognized as being emergent upon human and physical causes. Thus God sends Moses to speak before Pharaoh, and an east wind parts the Red Sea – because God's actions do not exist apart from the human actions and physical causes from which they emerge.[13] In this way, Esther serves not only as a handbook of politics for Jews who must learn to live and flourish in the exile, but also as a guide to the theology of Israel's Scriptures for an age that needs to be initiated into this discipline once more.

Notes

Introduction

1 Shabbat 88a.

2 Jerusalem Megila 1.5.

3 According to the rabbis, the books of Ezekiel, Proverbs, and Ecclesiastes are associated with wisdom; Jeremiah, Job, and Lamentations with an understanding of punishment; Psalms and Song of Songs with piety; Kings with greatness; and Isaiah with consolation. Esther, the last book mentioned, is associated with miracles. See Brachot 57b.

4 More space is devoted in rabbinic literature to commentary on Esther than to any other work in the Bible besides Genesis. This enthusiasm for Esther was not always shared by the Christian Church, whose embrace of the book, Frederic Bush writes, "has been a cold embrace indeed." Bush mentions as representative Martin Luther's remark that "I am so hostile to this book [2 Maccabees] and Esther that I could wish they did not exist at all, for they judaize too greatly"; and Otto Eissfeldt's comment that "Christianity ... has neither occasion nor justification for holding on to it." For these quotations and further discussion, see Bush, *Word Biblical Commentary: Ruth and Esther* (Nashville, TN: Thomas Nelson, 1996), pp. 332–333. Recent years have, however, seen a pronounced change in this regard, with both Christian scholars and popular Christian authors increasingly turning to appreciative readings of Esther.

Note that the book of Esther found in many Christian Bibles is based on the Septuagint Greek version, which diverges in significant respects from the standard Hebrew version of Esther (the "Masoretic" text) that I discuss in this work. Many Christian Bibles also group Esther together with the historical works at the front of the Old Testament, rather than in the Writings at the conclusion of Scripture. For an examination of the Greek versions of Esther in the context of historical Christian anti-Semitism, see Tricia Miller, *Jews and Anti-Judaism in Esther and the Church* (New York: James Clarke, 2015).

5 According to the Babylonian Talmud, Bava Batra 14b, the last books of the
   Bible are Esther, Ezra (read as a single, unified work together with Nehemia) and
   Chronicles. Jewish Bibles today insert Daniel between Esther and Ezra.

6 Deuteronomy 31.17–18, 32.20.

1. Submission and Rule

1 Khshayarshan I, whom the Greeks called Xerxes I. Xerxes ruled the Persian empire
   from 486 to 465 BCE, a century after the exile of the Jews of Judah and the destruction of Jerusalem in 586. This would place the months of the great feast at the
   beginning of Esther in the year 483 and the first Purim in the year 473.

2 Megila 11b.

3 Megila 11b.

4 This account of Ahashverosh's feasting, as well as much of what follows, is
   intended as satire, depicting the government of Persia as "overblown, pompous,
   over-bureaucratized, and, for all its trappings of power, unable to control events."
   Jon Levenson, *Esther: A Commentary* (Louisville, KY: Westminster John Knox
   Press, 1997), p. 12; also Bush, *Ruth and Esther*, pp. 314–316. Such criticism fits
   well within the broader context of the Bible's view of kings and their governments.
   See Abravanel, commentary on 1 Samuel 1.8; Yoram Hazony, *The Philosophy of
   Hebrew Scripture* (Cambridge: Cambridge University Press, 2012), pp. 140–160.

5 Esther Raba 2.2.

6 Genesis Raba 68.13.

7 Genesis 1.26. In philosophy, *thymos* is best known as the middle part of Plato's
   three-part description of the human soul. See Plato, *Republic* 439e3–8; M. F.
   Burnyeat, "The Truth of Tripartion," *Proceedings of the Aristotelian Society*
   (2006), part 1, pp. 1–22; Joshua Weinstein, *Plato's Three-Fold City and Soul*
   (Cambridge: Cambridge University Press, forthcoming).

8 It is the desire for control at the hands of others, as a substitute for one's own control, that produced the golden calf when the Jews felt that Moses was no longer
   determining events, that led them to demand to return to the certainty of Pharaoh's
   bondage when they came to the desert, and that in the end led them to demand that
   a king be set over them because they could no longer stand the uncertainty of living
   with only God to rule them. See Exodus 32.1; Numbers 14.3–4; 1 Samuel 8.4–9.

9 Joseph is described as "a man in whom is the spirit of God" at Genesis 41.38. Of
   Betzalel, it is said that "he has filled him with the spirit of God in wisdom … and
   in all manner of crafts, and to contrive works of art." Exodus 35.31–32. Regarding
   Caleb, we are told that "because he had a different spirit … him will I bring into
   the land." Numbers 14.24. And Joshua is called simply "a man in whom there is
   spirit" at Numbers 27.18.

10 Compare Plato, who argues that great virtue can be achieved only if the power
    of the spirit is devoted to achieving that which is dictated by reason. This is what
    Plato refers to as "justice" in the soul of the individual. *Republic*, 441d–e.

11 Or David on Esther 1.1 suggests that Ahashverosh should be viewed as an "axe in
    the hand of the wielder." However, this does not mean that Ahashverosh has no will

of his own, or that he is simply malleable in the hands of others. See my discussion in Chapter 4, n. 6.

12 Yalkut Shimoni 1048.

13 Thus Zechariah associates alcohol with might and confidence on the battlefield. See Zechariah 9.15, 10.7.

14 In the Bible, being merry with wine is often a sign of impending doom, as in 1 Samuel 25.36; 2 Samuel 13.28; Jeremiah 13.12–14. Levenson, *Esther*, p. 47.

15 Megila 12b.

16 Exodus 7.22f.

17 As Ibn Ezra comments on 2.14, it would be an insult to the king for another man to sleep with a woman who has shared his bed.

2. Political Favor

1 The corresponding years during the reign of Xerxes were devoted to his invasion of Greece, an adventure that ended in humiliating defeat for Persia.

2 This search for virgins for the king is described in language parallel to that which initiates the search for a virgin to warm the bed of David in advanced old age. But what is proposed to David when he is no longer able to function is here proposed to Ahashverosh as a way of attending to his personal needs in the prime of his life. See the comment of Judah Hanasi, Megila 12b; Aaron Koller, *Esther in Ancient Jewish Thought* (Cambridge: Cambridge University Press, 2014), pp. 62–63.

3 The verse in which Mordechai is introduced (2.6) uses the Hebrew root for "exile" (*galah*) no fewer than four times. Levenson, *Esther*, p. 56. The destruction of Jerusalem had taken place in the year 586 BCE, a century before the events described in Esther. Jechonia had been exiled with thousands of Jews from Jerusalem a decade earlier, in 597. It is Mordechai's great-grandfather Kish (2.5) who is said to have been exiled from Jerusalem together with Jechonia.

4 The comparison between fallen Jerusalem and the helplessness of virgins is made explicitly by the prophets. For example: "Hear this word which I take up against you: A lamentation, O house of Israel. The virgin of Israel is fallen, she will rise no more. She is forsaken on her land, there is none to raise her up." Amos 5.1–2.

5 This distinction between Ahashverosh's citadel or fortress and the rest of the city appears in the commentary of Abraham Ibn Ezra, and it has gained many adherents since, especially in the wake of modern archaeological excavations at Susa that have contributed to making this distinction plausible.

6 Gersonides argues that Esther hides her Jewishness so that she may have a chance of becoming queen. Had she not done so, she would have been forced into the harem anyway.

Some recent commentators have followed the medieval exegete R. Isaac Arama in arguing that the supposition that Esther's identity could have remained hidden is a significant flaw in the narrative. On this view, it is inconceivable that a queen could have been appointed without an inquiry into her lineage. It therefore must have been known that Esther was Mordechai's adopted daughter, and the fact that Esther was a Jew would likewise have become known, at the latest, when Mordechai refuses to bow to Haman and explains that it is because he is a Jew (3.4). Similarly, Mordechai's daily walk past the harem while Esther is in training (2.11) and his communicating with her on issues of importance after she becomes queen (2.20, 3.22) would surely have made their relationship clear to onlookers. See, for example, Adele Berlin, *The JPS Bible Commentary: Esther* (Philadelphia: Jewish Publication Society, 2001), p. xvii; Levenson, *Esther*, p. 61.

I am not persuaded that there is a significant problem here. The question turns on whether Esther could have prevented the king's servants from learning she was Mordechai's adopted daughter when she first enters the harem. The narrative speaks explicitly to this point, telling us twice that she does not reveal "her people or her kindred" (2.10, 2.20) to her handlers, the word *moladeta* ("her kindred") indicating that she hides not only her identity as a Jew but her relationship to Mordechai as well. This seems to be one reason that the narrative emphasizes that Esther has two names: In her home, she apparently used the name Hadasa and was known as Mordechai's daughter (2.7). But when she enters the harem, she adopts a different name, calling herself "Esther, daughter of Avihail" (2.15). When asked about her family, she says that they are dead (2.7). There would have been additional questions put to her, and if we wish we can speculate concerning the story that Mordechai and Esther contrived in order to answer them. Esther must have said that she had no other living relatives; she may have said that she grew up as the ward of, say, a servant of her parents; and so on. But such guesswork contributes little to our understanding of the text. What we need to know is that Esther entered the harem using an assumed name, and that this was part of a concerted effort to conceal both her identity as a Jew and her relationship to Mordechai, one of the courtiers.

Regarding Mordechai's walks by the harem compound to learn what was happening to Esther, it seems we are to understand that he was able discretely to gain information about her in the same way that he was able to learn about the conspiracy to assassinate the king (2.21–22) and about Haman's financial offer to king in exchange for the destruction of the Jews (4.7). Presumably, he was able to gain such information by bartering favors or distributing bribes, although other possibilities can also be imagined. Again, we do not know the details, but there is nothing impossible in this. Similarly, the fact that on at least one occasion the queen passed the king information in Mordechai's name only demonstrates that as queen she was acquainted with some of the courtiers, and that it was not unusual for her to speak with them if a matter were sufficiently grave. In short, Esther's concealment of her identity as a Jew and as Mordechai's adopted daughter would have been difficult, but certainly not impossible.

7 From the Persian *stara*, meaning "star," which is *aster* in Greek. According to R. Nehemia, the name Esther is identical to Ishtar, the Persian queen of heaven, associated with the planet Venus. Megila 13a. This is the same goddess known in the Hebrew Bible as *Ashtoret*, the goddess of the Phoenicians. Esther adopts this

name because it is likely to be pleasing to the Persians in the court, but it is also a play on the Hebrew *nistar*, meaning "hidden." For discussion of this Hebrew meaning of Esther's name, see Chapter 25.

8 The massive gate building revealed in archaeological excavations of Susa is discussed in Bush, *Ruth and Esther*, pp. 372–373. It is also evident that Mordechai was not among the more prominent figures in the court, since his refusal to bow before Haman goes unnoticed until it is reported by some of the courtiers. Michael Fox, *Character and Ideology in the Book of Esther* (Grand Rapids, MI: Eerdmans, 2001 [1991]), p. 42.

9 The term "vizier," which I use here, is of later origin. But other terms such as "prime minister," favored by some scholars, are not less anachronistic.

10 This is evident from the well-developed anti-Semitic theory Haman presents to the king to justify genocide, as well as the king's agreeable reaction (3.8–11); the fear of people of "Jewish descent" pervasive among Haman's advisers (6.13); the trouble members of the court make for Mordechai upon learning that he is a Jew (3.4); and his admonitions to Esther not to disclose her descent in the palace for fear that it would endanger her well-being and position (2.10, 2.20).

11 Darius I, who ruled Persia in 522–486 BCE. Darius was Xerxes' father.

12 Genesis 34.24–31, 35.22.

13 Rashi on Genesis 37.2.

14 Genesis 37.2. Rashi understands "their evil report" to refer not to a report against the younger brothers but rather to be the report of the younger brothers against the older sons of Leah. In this case, Joseph took the lead in trying to build a coalition of the younger brothers and Jacob against the older brothers – all the more reason for them to have hated him.

15 Genesis 37.3.

16 Genesis 39. 3–4.

17 Genesis 38.21–23, 47.13–26.

18 Genesis 45.16–21.

19 Daniel 1.15, 17.

20 Daniel 11.1.

21 Daniel 6.3.

22 The text explains that "the king thought to set him over the whole realm," as a result of his success as a triumvir. There follows an account of the conspiracy against Daniel by his political opponents, who oppose the promotion. The conspiracy ends with Daniel's salvation and the death of his enemies, as well as with Darius' proclamation recognizing the authority of the God of the Jews. But we are told nothing of Daniel's subsequent political career other than that he "succeeded in the reign of Darius." The implication seems to be that he received his promotion. Daniel 6.4, 26–29.

23 In the medieval period, Jews such as Hasdai ibn Shaprut, Shmuel Hanagid, and Isaac Abravanel were famous for their positions in the courts of gentile kings, among many others. On the influence of the Esther story on Jewish courtesanship, see Barry Dov Walfish, *Esther in Medieval Garb: Jewish Interpretation of the Book of Esther in the Middle Ages* (Albany, NY: SUNY Press, 1993).

24 R. Judan, in the name of R. Benjamin ben Levi, attributes the similarities between Joseph and Mordechai to the fact that they are of common lineage, both of them being descended from Rachel. Genesis Raba 87.6.

25 Genesis 40.22.

26 See Orit Avnery, *Liminal Women: Belonging and Otherness in the Books of Ruth and Esther* (Jerusalem: Hartman, 2015), p. 105.

27 Esther Raba 6.8.

28 R. Eleazar's comment is recorded in Megila 13a. The dishonor in having one's household speak in another language is raised by Ahashverosh's adviser Memuchan, who suggests that the king decree "that every man should rule in his own house and speak in the language of his own people" (1.22). Nehemia, too, is particularly distressed that the Jews' gentile wives are raising their children without knowledge of Hebrew: "At that time, too, I saw Jews who had taken wives from Ashdod, Ammon, and Moab. And their children half spoke Ashdodite and did not know how to speak the language of Judah, rather speaking the language of various other peoples. I fought with them and cursed them, and beat some of them and pulled out their hair, and made them swear to God, saying 'You will not give your daughters to their sons, nor take their daughters to your sons nor to yourselves.'" Nehemia 13.23–25; compare Deuteronomy 7.3. The capacity to put all men at ease by speaking to them in their own tongue also appears with regard to Joseph and Mordechai, whom the rabbis describe as being able to speak seventy languages. See discussion in Chapter 4.

29 Playing on the fact that her given name is Hadasa (Hebrew, myrtle), he asserts that her complexion was greenish. Megila 13a. But the majority opinion among the rabbis was that Esther was physically beautiful as well, following the plain meaning in the narrative. Megila 15a.

30 Megila 13a. Other rabbinic adages on the subject of Esther's sexual virtues are even more graphic. See, for example, Yoma 29a.

31 Megila 16b suggests that Mordechai was opposed by some among the Jewish leadership. Rashi's commentary brings what has become the traditional understanding of the reason for this opposition: "Because Mordechai neglected *tora* and went into rulership."

3. The Enemy

1 For examples of such bowing, see Genesis 23.7, 27.9, 43.28; Exodus 18.7; 1 Samuel 24.8; 1 Kings 1.23, 31.

2 Some recent commentators have concluded that Mordechai refuses to bow because of "tribal and racial enmity" between Israel and Haman's people, the Amalekites. Thus Mordechai's action contains nothing other than "ethnic pride. He simply would not bow down to a descendant of the Amalekites." See Bush, *Ruth and Esther*, pp. 379, 384–385, 387; Fox, *Character and Ideology*, p. 44; Berlin, *Esther*, p. 35. I do not see how this can be accepted as an answer to the question at hand. As a general matter, it is difficult to think of any scriptural precedent for making

a hero out of a Jew who endangers his own life and those of others, breaking the king's law in the process, for no reason other than tribal and racial spite. To make a convincing case that this is what is taking place here, one would need either strong textual proofs from Esther or weighty evidence from parallel texts. As far as I can tell, commentators endorsing this reading have neither. The biblical tradition prior to Esther explicitly describes Israel's enmity against Amalek as resulting from this tribe's moral perversity and idolatry, as Talmudic and later rabbinic commentators recognized. See my discussion in Chapter 8; Walfish, *Esther in Medieval Garb*, pp. 178–180. Moreover, the fact that Haman is willing to murder an entire nation because one man will not bow to him (3.5–6) is in itself proof enough of the man's moral perversity, and of the fact that he is referred to as an Agagite not only because of his ancestry. True, the reader has the measure of the evil that is in Haman only after his edict to murder all the Jews has been announced, just as many at the court did not recognize what kind of a man he was until this point. But the narrative assumes that Mordechai recognizes Haman's moral perversity and his idolatry long before this and that this is the reason he is not willing to bow before him. This may be because Mordechai has more information than others do. But it is more likely that he is simply able to recognize the evil in the man based on his past statements and deeds, whereas others are blind to it. We have seen in the last century, and even in our own day, how political leaders and the public can fail to recognize the evil that is manifestly before their eyes time and again, only to understand their mistake at great cost at a later date. Some are able to recognize the evil that has been born and is fast approaching (Pirkei Avot 2.13), even as the majority goes on thinking that nothing of significance has happened.

4. The King's Men

1 Compare Plato: "Also don't some of those who helped in setting [the tyrant] up and are in power – the manliest among them – speak frankly to him and to one another, criticizing what is happening? ... Then the tyrant must gradually do away with all of them, if he's going to rule, until he has left neither friend nor enemy of any worth whatsoever." *Republic* 567b.
2 Megila 16a.
3 In fact, the only thing we hear the other courtiers say after Haman's elevation is that Mordechai should bow down to Haman just as they do (3.3–4).
4 This view is similar to that of Malbim, who understands the narrative to be distinguishing between constitutional monarchy (the rule of the Persian king and the seven princes) and absolute rule (the sole rule of the king through his vizier). See his commentary on Esther 1.1.
5 Megila 15a.
6 This fact is at odds with a trend among recent commentators to portray Ahashverosh as being so weak that he has no control at all over events; and so malleable in the hands of those around him that he does whatever he is advised to do. See Fox, *Character and Ideology*, p. 17; Levenson, *Esther*, pp. 13, 46; Bush,

Ruth and Esther, pp. 430–1; Koller, *Esther in Ancient Jewish Thought*, p. 62. There is no doubt that Ahashverosh is of weak character. He is given to sudden rages and to their equally sudden collapse, to acting on flattery or with the aim of impressing others, to rapid and poorly calculated changes of direction, to making decisions when drunk, and so on. All this makes him a weak ruler, and a buffoon besides. But it does not mean that he is limp and malleable, always letting others make decisions for him and having no control over events. This reading obscures the quite considerable extent to which Ahashverosh is capable of setting his own course when he chooses to focus his attention – which he in fact does when he feels in danger of losing his life, his crown, or his second queen. It is Ahashverosh, and not anyone else, who elevates Haman and keeps him and his policies in power. As we are told: "Ahashverosh *promoted* Haman ... and *advanced* him, and *set his seat above all the princes* who were around him. And all the king's servants who were in the king's gate bowed and prostrated themselves before Haman, *for the king had so ordained* concerning him" (3.1–2, emphasis added). This idea of reconstituting the position of vizier and promoting Haman may have come from Haman himself, since we know he is an ambitious man given to making bold proposals. Nevertheless, the narrative is emphatic that it is the king's will that establishes Haman's authority and supports it. That all the courtiers accept this suggests that they, too, feel the firmness of the king's hand in this, as does the fact that Haman himself is never seen taking a step without Ahashverosh's consent. Even the killing of a single courtier is something that Haman and his advisers are afraid to do without getting Ahashverosh's approval (5.14). Moreover, we get to see the king "hurrying" Haman along on more than one occasion to make sure it is obvious who is in charge (5.5, 6.10, 6.14). These indications that Ahashverosh is capable of exercising a firm will when he is forced to do so are supported by others. When he begins to turn against Haman, it is the king himself who initiates the reading of the chronicles so he can gain a better understanding of what is happening in the palace (6.1). It is the king, at his own initiative, who orchestrates the humiliating scene in which Haman is set up to advise him as to how to give honor to someone else (6.6). In addition, the king's abrupt and angry departure from the room when Esther finally mounts an open attack on Haman (7.7) is an act of self-possession aimed at reducing the furor in his own mind and the effect of the drink. Moreover, just as it was Ahashverosh who elevated Haman, and no one else, it is he who decides that Haman is finished (7.7), with Harvona only supplying the means. Nor is Ahashverosh malleable in Esther's hands: The decision to promote Mordechai is in keeping with the king's judgment as to what is best for his own safety given that Mordechai had previously foiled an attempt on his life. But he refuses to take any action with regard to what is most important to Esther, which is to save her people from destruction. Certainly, the king wishes to avoid the embarrassment of a reversal of his policy. But he is also uncertain as to whether her advice on this is right. It may be that there is some truth in Haman's warnings about the danger that the Jews pose to the kingdom. And having given too much power to Haman,

Ahashverosh hesitates to make the same mistake again with Mordechai. Perhaps keeping a sword dangling over the heads of the Jews might not be a bad way to hold his new Jewish vizier in check.

7 The Talmud actually renders Shmuel's opinion as: "The king above has prevailed over the king below.". This is apparently in the tradition of using opposites as euphemisms for expressions that men of faith should never utter. Megila 15a. See Rashi's comment on it.

8 Jonah 4.11. Similarly, Jeremiah grieves for Moab at Jeremiah 48.31, 36, and calls for the restoration of the destroyed peoples of Moab, Ammon, and Elam (Jeremiah 48.47 49.6, 39). See also Isaiah 19.24–25; Amos 9.7. Compare Ezekiel 29.13–15.

9 From Jeremiah's declamations against Jehoyakim, Josiah's son, who was ruler in Jerusalem. Jeremiah 22.13–16.

10 Genesis 18.20–19.28. The flood in the time of Noah is an even earlier example. Genesis 6.1–8.22.

11 My reading follows R. Shmuel ben Imi in emphasizing that Ahashverosh's habit of consulting with his advisers is a virtue. Esther Raba 1.15. Every political figure, if he is not a fool, consults constantly with those around him, seeking insights and proposals, and for just this reason is susceptible to influence. Such consulting is the bedrock of the political order. It is not in itself an indication of weakness in Ahashverosh or in any other political figure.

12 Plato, *Republic* 488a–e.

13 Proverbs 16.14. Compare: "The desire of kings are lips saying righteousness, and he who speaks what is right will he love." Proverbs 16.13. "Whatever pleases him, he will do. For the word of the king is rule, and who will ask him 'What are you doing?'" Ecclesiastes 8.3–4.

14 To this, the school of R. Ishmael added: "Just as the hammer blow produces seventy sparks, so every word that went forth from the Holy One, may he be blessed, fragmented into seventy languages." Shabbat 88b. Compare Pirkei de R. Eliezer, ch. 24.

15 Genesis 11.1, 7–9. Compare Targum Jonathan on Genesis 11.8.

16 Accompanying this theory in the rabbinic literature is the ideal of understanding the seventy languages – that is, being able to understand and speak to the perspectives of all men. R. Johanan considered this to be a requirement for being appointed to the Sanhedrin, the highest legal body among the Jews, and such ability was also seen as a requirement for leadership in other nations. With regard to the Sanhedrin, the Talmud suggests that if three or four members out of the seventy-one on the court are so gifted, it would be an exceptional Sanhedrin. Sanhedrin 17a–b. The reference to such a requirement among the Egyptians appears in Sota 36b. Not coincidentally, the tradition sometimes ascribes the skill of understanding the seventy languages to Joseph and to Mordechai, each of whom is considered able to gain favor with others precisely because of his talent for appreciating their personal perspectives. Joseph's knowledge of the seventy languages appears in Sota 36b. Compare Numbers Raba 14.5, 19.3; Ecclesiastes Raba 7.23.1. Mordechai,

in particular, was held by R. Johanan to have gained his knowledge of the plot against Ahashverosh through a familiarity with the "language" of the conspirators, and so was able to understand their motives, although they themselves believed that they were well concealed. Mordechai's knowledge of languages is mentioned in Shekalim 5.1 and Megila 13b. Compare R. Eleazar's image attributing much the same ability to Esther. Megila 13a.

17   The passage continues: "Tomorrow two men will appear before you in a suit, a Jew and one who is a tormentor and an enemy. Can you please both of them? You will have to raise up the one and hang the other." Esther Raba 2.14.

18   A version of this balance among competing perspectives appears in the constitution of Moses, which establishes a balance among the king, priests, prophets, and tribal elders. See Deuteronomy, passim, and especially 17.14–18.22; Spinoza, *Theological-Political Treatise*, ch. 17. Plato likewise argues for "a compromise between a monarchical and a democratic constitution," in which each of four property classes are to be given equal power, since either strict equality or inequality "fill[s] a state with quarrels among its citizens." *Laws* 756–7. Aristotle mentions other theories of the mixed state. *Politics* 1265b. But in Esther, the argument is not so much one of keeping the peace, but of actually finding the best course for the state, as is evident from the connotation of idolatry attributed to the state as ruled by one man alone (see discussion in Chapter 5). Note, however, that the free play of competing interests in the palace is not a mechanism that in and of itself leads to justice and to the best course of the state. It is only a prerequisite, permitting the ruler to understand political reality in its totality so that his decisions may be informed ones.

19   The rabbis assumed that the principal effect of the decree was to damage Ahashverosh's credibility among the citizens. Thus R. Pinhas suggests that it made the king the butt of humor among the citizens. Esther Raba 4.12. Rava goes so far as to argue that the letters issued after Vashti's disobedience contributed to the failure of Haman's decree against the Jews by making the peoples doubt the seriousness of the king's subsequent edicts. Megila 12b.

20   Herodotus brings an additional illustration of the way Xerxes made decisions for the empire: In determining whether to go to war, the king receives arguments on both sides from members of his own family and the court, as well as from the representatives of various factions in Greece itself. Herodotus reports that the king changed his mind several times before finally electing to pursue the venture. Herodotus, *The Persian Wars* (New York: Random House, 1942), pp. 494–502.

5. Idolatry

1   Esther Raba 6.2.

2   Megila 19a.

3   Herodotus reports the invasion force Xerxes mustered against the Greeks to have comprised an incredible 1,700,000 men. Contemporary scholars suggest that his

numbers were off by a factor of six, Herodotus apparently calculating 60,000 men to a division, when in fact these divisions commanded only 10,000 troops. If this is correct, the 76,000 casualties reported in Esther amount to a force more than a fourth the size of Persia's land power. Herodotus, *Persian Wars*, p. 522n.

4 Megila 13a.

5 Esther Raba 6.2. Compare Sanhedrin 61b. Similarly: "So terrible is idolatry that anyone who rejects it, it is as if he accepted the entire *tora*." Hullin 5a. "The prohibition against idolatry is equivalent to all the commandments of the *tora*." Horayot 8a.

6 Avoda Zara 55a.

7 According to R. Nachman in the name of R. Mana, Jerusalem Avoda Zara 4.7.

8 An example of how idolaters perceived the locality of truth is the adoption of Jewish practices by the peoples that the Assyrians brought to settle the depopulated Jewish towns of Israel: "Then they spoke to the king of Assyria, saying: 'The nations that you have removed and settled in the cities of Samaria know not the law of the God of the land. Therefore he has sent lions among them, and behold, they do not know the law of the God of the land.'" The assumption is that the law of the Jewish God is what controls the fate of men living in the land of the Jews, but not elsewhere. 2 Kings 17.26.

9 Paraphrase of Exodus 20.2–6.

10 Exodus 5.1-2.

11 Deuteronomy 7.7.

12 Deuteronomy 12.31. The rabbis, too, wrote: "One should not leave cattle in the inns of idolaters, because they are to be suspected of bestiality. And a woman should not be alone with them, because they are to be suspected of lewdness. And a man should not be alone with them, because they are to be suspected of violence." Avoda Zara 22a. The subsequent discussion, beginning at Avoda Zara 22b, goes into the grisly details.

13 See discussion in Chapter 21.

14 Shabbat 88a.

15 Genesis Raba 38.13. Nietzsche's *Twilight of the Idols* is subtitled "How to Philosophize with a Hammer." See Friedrich Nietzche, *Twilight of the Idols and the Anti-Christ*, R.J. Hollingdale trans., Michael Tanner ed. (New York: Penguin, 1990), pp. 29–122.

6. Disobedience

1 Genesis 22.1–19, especially 21.8; Hazony, *Philosophy of Hebrew Scripture*, pp. 117–120.

2 This view appears in the Talmud in the name of R. Nahman: "'For Israel are my servants [*avadim*]' (Leviticus 25.55) – but not the servants of servants." Bava Metzia 10a.

3 In considering the reasons for Abraham's departure from Mesopotamia, one frequently meets with the proposal that he left "because God commanded it." Yet this

only raises the question of what it was that moved God to concern himself with whether Abraham lived in one place or another. And unless one is to claim that God's commands as recorded in Scripture are arbitrary and without reason, there is no choice but to return to the circumstances surrounding them in order to discern their motive: What are the reasons for Abraham's escape from Mesopotamia; what are the reasons for God's instruction to Moses to smear the blood of a sheep on the doorposts on the night of the Jews' departure from Egypt; and so forth.

4 Genesis 12.2–3.

5 For example, consider the following passage from the Hindu scriptures: "The whole world is kept in order by punishment.... If the king did not, without tiring, inflict punishment on those worthy to be punished, the stronger would roast the weaker like fish on a spit: The crow would eat the sacrificial cake and the dog would lick the sacrificial viands, and ownership would not remain with anyone, and the lower ones would usurp the place of the higher ones .... Punishment alone governs all created beings, punishment alone protects them, punishment watches over them while they sleep .... Punishment is ... the king." *The Laws of Manu*, G. Bühler, trans. (Delhi, India: Motilal Banarsidass, 1962), Book vii, sections 16–22f, pp. 219–220f.

6 Of course, this does not mean there were no lawbreakers. In every civilization, there have always been rogues and thieves willing to break the law for personal gain. Likewise, every tyranny of the ancient world sired its fair share of putsches and assassinations, usually the brainchild of a would-be usurper whose principal concern was to bring the machinery of absolute rule under his own control. But while a successful usurpation of power might be rationalized as being proof that the new rulers had the support of heaven – and could therefore claim absolute obedience as had their deposed predecessors – under no philosophical, moral, ideological, or religious system were such actions considered legitimate in principle.

7 On the shepherding imagery in the biblical narrative from Genesis to Kings, see Hazony, *Philosophy of Hebrew Scripture*, pp. 105–139.

8 Abraham challenges God at Genesis 18.25. Moses changes God's mind several times, including at Exodus 32.9-14 and Numbers 14.11–20. Jacob wrestling with God and prevailing is at Genesis 32.29; see also Rashi's comment. For further examples and discussion of man contending with God, see Hazony, *Philosophy of Hebrew Scripture*, pp. 135–138, 235, 316 n. 138.

9 Genesis 10.8–9.

10 Genesis 11.3–6.

11 Genesis 12.12.

12 Genesis 26.18.

13 Genesis 34.1f.

14 Exodus 1.17–19.

15 Regarding Pharaoh's daughter, the rabbis wrote: "Why was she called a Jewess? Because she repudiated idolatry, as it is written: 'And the daughter of Pharaoh went down to bathe in the river.' (Exodus 2.5). R. Johanan said: She went down to

cleanse herself from the idols of her father's house." The point is that at the moment she drew Moses from the water and disobeyed the will of her father, she renounced the essence of Egyptian idolatry. Megila 13a.

16 Exodus 2.1–10.

17 Exodus 2.11–12.

18 Exodus 5.21.

19 Exodus 12.3–11, 21–23.

20 Judges 8.23. See further discussion of this passage in note Chapter 26, note 2.

21 1 Samuel 8.10–20.

22 Deuteronomy 17.16–20. For the development of the ideal of the limited state in the biblical narrative from Genesis-Kings, see Hazony, *Philosophy of Hebrew Scripture*, pp. 150–159.

23 1 Samuel 14.43–45. Similarly, when Saul determines to have David killed, it is Jonathan and his sister Michal, David's wife, who resist the king to save his life. 1 Samuel 19.11f. Saul's servants also refuse his order to kill the priests of Nov. 1 Samuel 22.17.

24 1 Samuel 12.1f. The much-quoted Talmudic passage that appears to absolve David of having sinned in the affair with Batsheva (Shabbat 56a) is contradicted by a more conventional reading elsewhere that argues that David lost four loved ones prematurely as punishment for this liaison. Yoma 22b.

25 1 Samuel 15.30f, 16.1f.

26 2 Kings 9.1–10.29.

27 Jeremiah 38.2. That such defection was illegal is clear from 37.13.

28 Daniel 3.16–18.

29 Daniel 6.7–11.

30 Compare Henry David Thoreau's 1848 lecture, "On the Relation of the Individual to the State," a published version of which was posthumously renamed "Civil Disobedience." In it, Thoreau argues that if government "is of such a nature that it requires you to be an agent of injustice to another, then, I say, break the law. Let your life be a counter-friction to stop the machine .... I do not hesitate to say, that those who call themselves Abolitionists should at once effectually withdraw their support, both in person and property, from the government of Massachusetts, and not wait till they constitute a majority of one, before they suffer the right to prevail through them. I think that it is enough if they have God on their side .... [E]ven suppose blood should flow. Is there not a sort of blood shed when the conscience is wounded? Through this wound a man's real manhood and immortality flow out, and he bleeds to an everlasting death. I see this blood flowing now." Henry David Thoreau, Carl Bode, ed., *The Portable Thoreau* (New York: Penguin, 1947), pp. 119–123. On the biblical origins of modern disobedience theory, see Yoram Hazony, "The Jewish Origins of the Western Disobedience Tradition," *Azure* 4 (1998), pp. 17–74.

31 In fact, the narrative in Esther consistently describes adherence to Persian law as producing substantive outcomes that are either monstrous or trivial, whereas

real good comes of breaking this law. Koller, *Esther in Ancient Jewish Thought*, pp. 58–61.

32 See discussion in Chapter 23 and in the "Afterwords."

33 The difference between the Hebrew Bible and the New Testament in this regard is marked. While upholding the Jewish claim that the Roman emperor had no authority to determine right and wrong for his subjects, Christian scripture acquiesced in the theory that so long as men were to live in this world, their relationship to worldly power should be one of submission: Thus Peter writes: "Submit yourselves to every human institution for the sake of the Lord .... Servants, accept the authority of your masters with all due submission, not only when they are kind and considerate, but even when they are perverse. For it is a fine thing if a man endure the pain of undeserved suffering because God is in his thoughts .... [W]hen you have behaved well and suffer for it, your fortitude is a fine thing in the sight of God. To that you were called, because Christ suffered on your behalf, and thereby left you an example; it is for you to follow in his steps. He committed no sin ... [yet] when he suffered he uttered no threats, but committed his cause to the One who judges justly." 1 Peter 2.13, 18–23. Paul's views are similar: "Every person must submit to the supreme authorities. There is no authority but by act of God, and the existing authorities are instituted by him; consequently, anyone who rebels against authority is resisting a divine institution, and those who so resist have themselves to thank for the punishment they will receive. For government, a terror to crime, has no terrors for good behavior. You wish to have no fear of the authorities? Then continue to do right and you will have their approval, for they are God's agents, working for your good. But if you are doing wrong, then you will have cause to fear them; it is not for nothing that they hold the power of the sword, for they are God's agents of punishment, for retribution on the offender. That is why you are obliged to submit." Romans 13.1–4; see also Colossians 3.22; Ephesians 6.5. Translations are from *The New English Bible* (Oxford: Oxford University Press and Cambridge University Press, 1970).

34 Shabbat 88a. The text literally reads: "One for 'we will do' and one for 'we will hear,' " the two responses of the Jewish people at Sinai in Exodus 24.7.

35 Midrash Tanhuma, Mishpatim 2 on Exodus 21.1.

7. Joseph

1 Examples include Abraham's activities in the war of kings (Genesis 14.1–24) and his various dealings with Avimelech (Genesis 20.1–5, 21.22–32).

2 Ezra and Nehemia are actually a single work, which is broken up in the referencing system of chapters and verses in use today. See Sanhedrin 93b. Both parts contain much material relevant to the Esther story, but Nehemia, who was a senior adviser to the king, is of particular interest. See Tamara Cohn Eskenazi, *In the Age of Prose: A Literary Approach to Ezra-Nehemia* (Atlanta: Scholars Press, 1988).

3 Genesis 37.2–4. The Hebrew *ro'e et ehav* means "shepherds with his brothers," but it is worded so as to have a second meaning as well, that he "shepherds his brothers" rather than the sheep. See Seforno's comment here.

4 Genesis 39.6.
5 Genesis 37.6–11.
6 Even when they are all adults in Egypt, Joseph continues to attempt to impose order and unity on the brothers. See Genesis 43.33, as well as Genesis 45.24, where Joseph tells them on their way back to Canaan: "Make sure you do not fall out along the way." This entire aspect of their relationship can be understood as foreshadowing the anarchy among the tribes in the period of the Judges, in which Joseph's efforts are parallel to the demand for the imposition of a central authority at the hands of a king.
7 Other than Joseph, the only other Jew who interprets dreams in the Bible is Daniel.
8 Genesis Raba 84.14 on Genesis 37.20.
9 Sota 36b. The advances of Potiphar's wife are described in Genesis 39.10 in language that is closely parallel to the wording describing the pressure applied by the courtiers on Mordechai to bow before Haman (3.4). Mordechai's refusal to bow is motivated by his understanding that to do so would be to bow before an idol (see discussion, Chapters 5, 8). At the same time, this passage in Esther, by means of parallel language, implies that to give in to Potiphar's wife would also have been to give in to an idol – as the rabbis proposed explicitly.
10 Genesis Raba 87.5. The rabbis also believed that sexual appetite could itself be a false god, dictating all value in a person's life. In this regard, they told the story of Eleazar ben Dordia, who could not hear of the existence of a prostitute without running to her and paying whatever she asked. Avoda Zara 17a. But the idol that Potiphar's wife hangs before Joseph is more generally the success and power of Egypt, of which she is only one example.
11 This success is in contrast with his older brothers, Reuben and Judah, who are unable to overcome such temptation. Reuben slept with one of his father's concubines. Genesis 35.22. Judah becomes badly entangled because of a visit to a harlot. Genesis 38.1f.
12 Joseph's victory over Potiphar's wife is the basis for the appellation "Joseph the righteous," which is found repeatedly in the writings of the rabbis in various contexts. For example, the passage immediately preceding this dialogue reads: "Our rabbis taught: The poor, the rich, and the wicked come before the heavenly court .... To the wicked person they would say: Why have you not occupied yourself with the *tora*? If he were to say: I was beautiful and upset by sensual passion, they would say to him: Were you more beautiful than Joseph? It was told of Joseph the righteous that the wife of Potiphar tried every day to entice him with her words. The clothes she put on for him in the morning, she did not wear in the evening; those she put on for him in the evening, she did not wear in the morning." Yoma 35b. See also Ketubot 111a; Megila 13b, 16b; and discussion in Chapter 21.
13 Sota 36b. It is important to note that Joseph's brothers, Judah or Levi, for example, did not have to pass such a test to remain Jews. They were not as attracted to Egypt as Joseph was, nor were they so well suited to be of use to the Egyptian hierarchy. Thus even when they came to Egypt, they did not have to survive such a test.

14 "Why did Joseph die before his brothers? Rabi and the rabbis disagree. Rabi said: Because he embalmed his father. The Holy One, may he be blessed, said to him: Can I not protect my righteous ones? ... But in the opinion of the rabbis: Nearly five times did Judah say: 'Your servant, my father,' 'your servant, my father,' yet he heard it and kept silent." Genesis Raba 100.3.

15 Genesis Raba 100.3. Judah says this four times himself (Genesis 44.24, 27, 30, 31) and once together with his brothers (Genesis 43.28).

16 "R. Judah said in the name of Rav: Why was Joseph referred to as 'bones' while he yet lived? (Genesis 50.25) Because he did not intervene to protect his father's honor when his brothers said to him: 'Your servant, our father,' (Genesis 44.31) but made no reply to them. R. Judah also said in the name of Rav, although others say it was R. Hama ben R. Hanina: Why did Joseph die before his brothers? Because he conducted himself with rulership." Sota 13b. Both of these criticisms are aimed at Joseph's understanding of his own place in the order of the world as a result of his position in the Egyptian state: He considered it acceptable to participate in a system in which Jacob and his God, as well as the rest of the world, were understood to be servants. See also Brachot 55a.

17 Sota 13b. Compare Ezekiel's image of the people of Israel in exile to a valley filled with bones. Ezekiel 37.1f.

18 The figure of the wine cask belongs to one of the greatest of the agadists, R. Levi. Exodus Raba 20.19. See discussion in Chapter 11.

19 According to R. Hanin ben Bizna in the name of R. Shimon the Righteous, Joseph sanctified God's name in private in the trial of Potiphar's wife, as opposed to Judah, who sanctified God's name in public by admitting the wrongs he had committed against Tamar. Sota 10b. It is Judah's capacity to make the right decision publicly, even at the cost of tremendous embarrassment and potential political harm to himself, which ultimately results in Judah, not Joseph, meriting the leadership of the Jews.

20 On Joseph's adoption of Egyptian ways, see Chapter 11.

21 Daniel 6.25.

22 On Joseph's failure to ask for Israel's freedom, see Chapter 11.

23 Genesis 47.13–25. See Aaron Wildavsky, *Assimilation Versus Separation* (New Brunswick, NJ: Transaction, 1993), pp. 139–144.

24 Nehemia 5.1–16. The book of Ezra and Nehemia relates events that take place very close to the time described in Esther. Ezra sets out for Jerusalem in 458 BCE, fifteen years after the victory over Haman and his followers in 473. Nehemia's expedition begins in 445, another thirteen years later. Xerxes is assassinated in a palace coup in 465.

25 Mordechai and Esther are Benjaminites and therefore descended from Joseph's brother. Joseph and Benjamin were the only two of the twelve sons of Jacob born to Rachel. R. Johanan, in the name of R. Benjamin ben R. Levi, brings a long list of similarities in the personalities and in the plots of the two stories. Esther Raba 7.7. Compare Genesis Raba 87.6. Moreover, the book of Esther is intentionally written in such a way as to highlight these similarities through the

use of parallel wording. For example, compare Genesis 41.34–37 with Esther 2.3–4; Genesis 50.3 with Esther 2.12; Genesis 39.10 with Esther 3.4; Genesis 43.14 with Esther 4.16; Genesis 44.34 with Esther 8.6. See Moshe Gan, "The Book of Esther in Light of the Story of Joseph in Egypt," *Tarbiz* 31 (1961), pp. 144–150 [Hebrew].

8. Amalek

1 The Kish who is Saul's father would have lived some five centuries before the Kish who is said to have been exiled from Jerusalem with Jechonia and to have been Mordechai's great-grandfather. But the inclusion of this name here does suggest either an actual family relation to Saul or a figurative association. Other parallels to Saul include the deposition of Vashti in favor of "someone better than she" (1.19), which uses the same expression that is deployed when Saul is deposed as king for having failed to destroy Amalek (1 Samuel 15.28). Similarly, Saul's error was in part the fact that he allowed the Jews to take spoils in their war against Amalek (1 Samuel 15.19), whereas Mordechai makes sure that the Jews do not touch the property of the Persian anti-Semites (9.15–16). Compare Esther Raba 4.9.

2 Exodus 15.22–17.7.

3 Exodus 17.14–16.

4 Deuteronomy 25.17–19. According to rabbinic tradition, this passage must be read aloud prior to the annual reading of the book of Esther on the festival of Purim.

5 Numbers 13.18.

6 Numbers 13.26–33.

7 Numbers 13.30.

8 Numbers 14.3–4.

9 Notice also that at Numbers 14.25, God directs Israel to avoid traveling near Amalekite territory.

10 The complete passage reads: "And now, Israel, what does the Lord your God require of you, other than to fear the Lord your God, to walk in all his ways, and to love him, and to serve the Lord your God with all your heart and with all your soul, to follow the instructions of the Lord and his laws, which I instruct you this day for your good?" Deuteronomy 10.12–13.

11 Numbers 19.14.

12 Deuteronomy 10.19–20.

13 Leviticus 19.32, 25.17, 36, 43. Similarly, see Nehemia 5.15, where the governor of Jerusalem does not oppress the poor as his predecessors did for fear of God.

14 Genesis 20.11.

15 Exodus Raba 27.6. The enmity of Jethro the Midianite is established through an anachronism, but an important one: "How do you know that both the Amalekites and the Midianites were the enemies of Israel? Because it says: ... 'Now Midian and Amalek and all the children of the east' [lay in wait for the Jewish forces]." Exodus Raba 27.6 on Judges 7.12f.

16 Exodus 1.17. Joseph also uses this expression when, as vizier of Egypt, he seeks to assure his brothers that he will not arbitrarily destroy them although it is in his power. Genesis 42.18.

17 Exodus Raba 27.9.

18 Exodus 18.21.

19 Numbers 24.3.

20 Numbers 24.20.

21 Numbers 23.21, 24.5.

22 For example, Avimelech as described in Genesis 20.1–5. Similarly, Bilam at Numbers 23.7–8.

23 By the days of Hezekiah, king of Judah, the Amalekites are described as no more than a "remnant." See 1 Chronicles 4.43.

9. Anti-Semitism

1 Exodus 1.7–12, 22.

2 Genesis Raba 68.13. A related figure suggests that the anti-Semite, Haman, had been predestined to die being pricked to death on a thorn bush since the beginning of creation. Esther Raba 9.2.

3 In this passage, Resh Lakish also tells of the unspeakable cruelties that Haman describes the Jews as having committed, including the war of liquidation waged against Amalek. Esther Raba 7.13. Elsewhere, the rabbis suggested that various aspects of the Jewish tradition rendered the Jews undesirable as citizens by, for example, not working on the Sabbath and therefore failing to pay their fair share of the tax burden. Megila 13b. Similarly, according to R. Hisda and Raba bar R. Huna: "What is Mt. Sinai? The mountain from which came the hostility [sin'a] of the idolaters." Shabbat 89a. Compare Jerusalem Gittin 5.7, which suggests that the Romans had a tradition that the Jews had killed their national progenitor.

4 Composed in 1905 by the Czar's secret service and still popular in certain countries, *The Protocols of the Elders of Zion* is one of the most notorious anti-Semitic works, claiming to contain the record of a secret Jewish conspiracy to undermine the governments of the world.

5 Some readers have proposed that in declaring the inevitability of Haman's downfall before the Jews, Haman's wife and his advisers speak for Scripture, and are in fact expressing the standpoint of the biblical author. See Fox, *Character and Ideology*, p. 250; Levenson, *Esther*, pp. 20–21; Bush, *Ruth and Esther*, p. 335; Koller, *Esther in Ancient Jewish Thought*, p. 208. I do not believe we should rush to embrace this reading. Zeresh believes that the course of human events can be fated and unchangeable, as it seems Haman does as well from the fact that he attempts to ensure the successful execution of his plans by selecting appropriate dates for them by lot (3.7). Mordechai, on the other hand, holds no similar view concerning the inevitability of any particular human political effort or campaign

succeeding or failing (see 4.14, and discussion in Chapters 12, 23). In this argument between Mordechai and Zeresh, we should assume that Mordechai speaks for the author of Esther and not Haman's wife. A better reading is that Zeresh's advice concerning the inevitability of Haman's downfall is no more valuable than her advice in sending Haman out to have Mordechai hanged (5.14). In both cases, her advice is typical of the idolatrous worldview that Zeresh represents and not of a view that is to be endorsed by Jews. Moreover, we should notice that Zeresh declares that Haman is destined to fall before the Jews only after the political tide has already turned against him. But if defeat at the hands of the Jew was in her eyes inevitable, why did she not announce this at an earlier opportunity – for example, instead of sending Haman to try to have Mordechai killed? It seems that Zeresh's declaration that Mordechai cannot be defeated is another example of the way in which the different political players in the story alter their views to accommodate Mordechai's rise. Like Harvona (Chapter 17), Ahashverosh (Chapter 18), and the many other unnamed individuals who change course once the position of the Jews is ascendant (Chapters 19 and 20), Zeresh and Haman's other advisers likewise switch from believing that Haman has an easy win ahead of him to believing that his defeat is inevitable once the tide has turned "because the fear of Mordechai had fallen upon them" (9.3). As we say, they have "jumped on the bandwagon."

6 Esther Raba 7.23.

7 The rabbis say this same thing in a different way, arguing that Haman's hatred and his end on the gallows is intrinsic to the fabric of the world from the time of creation. Esther Raba 9.2; Hullin 139b.

8 Genesis 4.2–8; Hazony, *Philosophy of Hebrew Scripture*, pp. 105–110.

10. Pressure

1 "For what good are sackcloth and ashes without prayer?" Esther Raba 10.9.

2 "By the merit of the righteous women of that generation were the Jews redeemed from Egypt." Sota 11b.

3 Exodus Raba 1.26.

4 Compare Ze'ev Jabotinsky: "For there is no friendship in politics: There is pressure. What tips the balance one way or another is not whether the ruler is good or bad, but the degree of pressure exerted by his subjects. If pressure is exerted solely by our opponents, with no counter-pressure applied by us, then whatever is done in Palestine will be against us, even if the head of the government will be called Balfour, or Wedgwood, or even Theodor Herzl .... For no reformation in national conditions is attained without pressure and struggle. And whoever lacks the stamina, courage, ability and desire to fight, will not be able to achieve even the smallest adjustment [of these conditions] on our behalf." *Do'ar Hayom*, May 17, 1929. See discussion in Benjamin Netanyahu, "The Question of Jewish Power,"

in *A Place Among the Nations: Israel and the World* (New York: Bantam, 1993), pp. 382–383.

5 Exodus 3.11–12. Compare Shabbat 88a.

11. Court Jew

1 R. Sheshet emphasizes the ongoing nature of Mordechai's protest. Megila 16a.

2 Mordechai is asking Esther both to repeat Vashti's crime by defying the king's command (1.12) and to confirm Haman's charge that the Jews are insubordinate (3.8). Levenson, *Esther*, p. 89.

3 Exodus 5.21. The narrative's depiction of the slaves here is remarkable. Pharaoh and his servants stand over them with swords every day of their lives. Moreover, their willingness to slay the Hebrews has already been amply demonstrated. Yet in the slaves' eyes, it is Moses and Aaron who "are putting a sword in Pharaoh's hand" with which to slay them!

4 Genesis Raba 5.14.

5 It is no coincidence, either, that when the God of the Jews finally brings ruin upon Pharaoh, it is in the form of such ostensibly insignificant opponents as frogs, lice, flies, sores, hailstones, and locusts – that is, grasshoppers. (But compare Exodus Raba 11.4, where R. Judah understands one of the plagues to be wild animals.) In other words, the Egyptians were brought low by precisely the kinds of opponents that they had thought the Jews to be. This is clear from the fact that the account of the Israelites' increase in Egypt is described using the word *vayishretzu* – "they swarmed." As the narrative tells us: "They swarmed and multiplied and grew strong, and the land was filled with them." Exodus 1.7.

6 Genesis 43.32, 46.34.

7 Genesis 41.14, 41.28–36, 41.45, 41.42, 41.42, 41.42, 42.6, 42.15, 41.45, 50.2, 50.26.

8 Genesis 41.51.

9 Genesis 41.37.

10 Genesis 39.8–9.

11 Genesis 45.5–8.

12 Genesis 45.9–11.

13 Genesis 50.20–21.

14 Amenemhet I, quoted in Harold Nicolson, *Monarchy* (London: Weidenfeld and Nicolson, 1962), p. 20. Amenemhet I served as vizier to the last Pharaoh of the Eleventh Egyptian Dynasty, whom he probably overthrew in order to become the founder of the Twelfth Dynasty. He ruled Egypt from 2000–1970 BCE, several centuries before the time of Abraham.

15 The rabbis belittled a similar position by imagining what the Romans would say when brought before God on the day of judgment: "The Holy One, may he be blessed, will then say to them: How have you occupied yourselves? They will reply: 'Ruler of the Universe, we have established many marketplaces, we have built many bathhouses, we have accumulated much gold and silver, and all this we

did only for the sake of Israel, so that they might be able to occupy themselves with the study of *tora.*' The Holy One, may he be blessed, will then answer: You foolish ones among peoples. All that you have done, you have done only in order to satisfy your own desires." Avoda Zara 2b.

16 Genesis 47.29–31.
17 Genesis 45.19.
18 Genesis 46.1.
19 Compare: "Why did he not call Reuben or Judah? Reuben was the firstborn and Judah was king, yet he disregarded them and called Joseph. Why? Because Joseph had the means of fulfilling his wish." Genesis Raba 96.5.
20 Genesis 50.4–5.
21 The Moses story is written as a mirror image of Joseph's failure: When Moses approaches Pharaoh two centuries later with the request that the Jews be allowed to go up from Egypt for a religious rite, he refuses Pharaoh's offer to go without the children and herds. Exodus 10.9–12, 24–26.
22 Genesis Raba 100.4.
23 Genesis Raba 96.1.
24 Genesis 50.24–25. Genesis closes with this final, searing image: "So Joseph died at the age of one-hundred and ten years. And they embalmed him. And they put him in a box [*ba'aron*] in Egypt." Genesis 50.26.
25 An *agada* of R. Isaac Napaha suggests that for this reason, Mordechai should not be compared to the patriarchs, but to Moses. He tells that when death is decreed against the Jews of Persia, the prophet Elijah runs in search of assistance for the Jews of Persia. "Abraham, Isaac and Jacob then said to him: 'If they have violated the law of the Holy One, blessed be he, and their fate is sealed, what can we do?' Then Elijah went to Moses, saying: 'Faithful shepherd, how many times did you stand in the breach for Israel and avert their fate so that they should not be destroyed?' ... Moses said to him: 'Is there a virtuous man in that generation? ... Go and speak to him, so that he may stand and pray there, and I here, that we may together seek mercy from the Holy One, blessed be he.'" Esther Raba 7.13. According to R. Isaac's reading, Abraham, Isaac, and Jacob were fundamentally men of purity, living in the hill country of Canaan in order to avoid just such direct confrontations with empire and idolatry as are the subject of the books of Exodus and Esther. When it comes to the political deliverance of the Jewish nation, mired in the foulness and error of the world, the assistance they can offer is limited. For such tasks, one needs a man such as Moses – who grew up among the abominations of Pharaoh's court, who kills the Egyptian that justice be done, who confronts Pharaoh face to face where Abraham would likely have dissembled to escape difficulty, who rains plague and slaughter on Egypt and brings its armies to ruin. Such a man can confront God over the worldly fate of the Jewish people and even divert that fate once it has supposedly been "sealed." And it is to such a man that the figure of Mordechai should be compared.

This having been said, notice that Abraham's encounter with Pharaoh also includes plagues, as does Moses' confrontation with Pharaoh, as well as the forcible induction of Sarah into Pharaoh's harem, as in Esther. Genesis 12.10–20. It is the plagues that persuade Pharaoh to let Sarah go from his harem. However, Abraham's role in obtaining this outcome is rather less than that which Moses plays in the exodus.

26 Exodus Raba 20.19.

12. The Decision

1 Daniel 3.16–18.
2 Daniel 6. 7–11.
3 Apparently Artaxerxes I, who ruled Persia from 465 to 424 BCE, immediately after Xerxes I.
4 Nehemia 1.1–3.
5 Nehemia 2.19.
6 Ezra 4.6–22.
7 Nehemia 1.4–11.
8 Nehemia 2.6. Compare Moses' decision to take leave of Jethro's flocks after forty years or more of service: "Moses went back to Jethro, his father-in-law, and said to him: 'Let me go, I pray, and return to my brothers in Egypt, and see whether they are still alive.' Jethro said to Moses: 'Go in peace.' " Exodus 4.18.
9 The biblical narrative does not seem to back up Joseph on this point. Unlike his forefathers, Joseph is never depicted as having God speak to him. What understanding he does have of God's intentions seems to come from his faith in God and his dreams, which, while containing important truths, are problematic as well. Perhaps Joseph himself should have suspected this because they depict him, for example, as having his father, mother, and brothers bow down to the ground before him, although his mother had long since died. Genesis 37.9–10. As it turns out, Joseph's brothers do end up bowing before him over and over, and referring to themselves as Joseph's servants as well, but his father Jacob never does either of these things. Genesis 42.6, 43.26, 28, 44.14, 16, 50.18. R. Joshua of Siknin in the name of R. Levi disagrees with this conclusion, arguing that "Jacob, too, when he was about to die, humbled himself before Joseph and said to him: 'Now if I have found favor in your eyes.' " Genesis Raba 96.3 on Genesis 47.29. It is a fair point, although I suspect that even these words of Jacob's are laced with irony. But in either case, we do not have an example of Jacob bowing before Joseph. His dream was mistaken in this regard.
10 The expression "who knows" (Hebrew, *mi yode'a*) appears elsewhere in the Bible to mark the possibility, although not the certainty, of assistance from God. 2 Samuel 12.22; Joel 2.13–14; Jonah 3.9. See my discussion of these texts in Chapter 25.
11 See, for example, Menahot 53b.
12 Compare Daniel 6.13–17, however, in which Darius tries to rescue Daniel from death by the decree that he himself has issued, but is prevented from doing so by his advisers.
13 Psalms 115.5–8, 135.16–18.

13. The Plan

1 The rabbis handed down prayers that Esther and Mordechai were supposed to have said during the crisis. Esther Raba 8.6. Some Christian versions of the Bible follow the Septuagint in incorporating these prayers into the narrative itself.

2 Gersonides' commentary on Esther. Nehemia writes: "It came to pass ... that the wine was before him, and I took up the wine and gave it to the king, and I had never looked sad in front of him before then. The king said to me: 'Why is your face fallen, seeing that you are not ill? This can be nothing other than sorrow of the heart,' and I was exceedingly afraid. And I said to the king: 'May the king live forever. Why should my face not be fallen, when the city, the place where my ancestors are buried, lies waste, and its gates are consumed with fire?'" Nehemia 2.1–3.

3 Most translations miss the fact that Esther hesitates here and breaks off her request. See Bush, *Ruth and Esther*, pp. 404–405.

4 So long as the king trusts Haman, any promise he makes to Esther is susceptible to being rolled back afterward as the vizier presses upon him to withdraw the commitment. This means that Esther cannot afford to aim only for a simple agreement from the king to spare the Jews. Her aim must be to damage Haman so badly that he will no longer be in a position to challenge her on this issue. See Fox, *Character and Ideology*, p. 72.

14. Reaction

1 On Mordechai's escalation, see Fox, *Character and Ideology*, p. 44; Levenson, *Esther*, p. 92. Mordechai is no longer acting only on principle, as may have been the case when at first he would not bow before Haman. This further insult is designed to aggravate Haman in the hope of getting him to miscalculate and do something foolish.

2 A gallows as we conceive it may be anachronistic. Recent commentators prefer to translate the term *etz* as a "stake," on which Mordechai was to be impaled rather than hung.

3 The urgency of the matter is evident not only from the fact that Haman is to approach the king immediately in the morning, but also from the raising of the gallows even before the king agrees to the execution. Haman and his advisers realize that if the gallows is already in place, Mordechai can be quickly dispatched before the king has a chance to change his mind. Fox, *Character and Ideology*, p. 75.

4 See discussion in Chapter 4, n. 6.

15. Power Shift

1 According to R. Huna, Megila 19a, and Eliezer of Modi'im, Megila 15b; commentary of Gersonides. Gersonides adds that the king may have connected the

attention Esther has paid to Haman in inviting him to the banquet to the evident change in her appearance induced by the fast.

2 According to Abaye and Raba. Megila 15b. See also Esther Raba 10.1; commentary of Gersonides.

3 Since Haman was appointed in the aftermath of the attempt on the king's life, the vizier should have investigated the assassination attempt himself and promoted Mordechai for his loyalty and his service to the king. This would have solidified the king's power and contributed to his safety. Of course, the failure to act is ultimately the responsibility of the king. Nevertheless, the fact that Haman did not make an effort to advance Mordechai in this way raises questions as to why he did not in the king's mind. Similarly, when the king's youths answer, "Not a thing has been done for him," this can be read: *Haman has not done a thing for him.*

4 Megila 16a.

5 According to R. Nachman in the name of R. Mana, Jerusalem Avoda Zara 4.7.

6 Exodus 1.9. See discussion in Chapter 9, especially n. 5 concerning Zeresh.

16. Downfall

1 Esther avoids mentioning the Jews by name so as not to make it immediately clear to Ahashverosh that he is himself responsible for the threat to her life. See Fox's fine discussion of the rhetoric of this passage, *Character and Ideology*, p. 84. Esther's use of the word "sold" could refer to Haman's offering the king a vast sum as an incentive to have the Jews killed (3.9). But Ahashverosh turns this offer down. The Hebrew verb here (*machar*) is apparently being used to mean "handed over," as in Judges 2.14.

2 Ahashverosh's revelation is presaged by a similar scene in the Joseph story, in which Potiphar removes Joseph from administering his household when he comes to believe, unjustly, that his servant would take his wife from him. Although Potiphar hands control of all his affairs to Joseph, he feels he is still in charge so long he is secure in certain personal matters. As we are told, "He left all that he had in Joseph's hand, and he knew not what he had except for the bread he ate." Genesis 39.6. The rabbis supposed this to be a euphemism for his wife. Genesis Raba 86.6. (The use of bread as a metaphor for sex also appears in Proverbs: "By means of a harlot, a man is brought to a piece of bread." Proverbs 6.26). But when Potiphar's wife claims that Joseph has made advances, the entire fiction collapses and the master of the house is left feeling that all he has is truly in Joseph's hands, and not in his own. From here Joseph's path to the dungeon is assured.

3 Thus the rabbis compared Haman to the snake in Eden: "They set their eyes on that which was not proper for them. Therefore what they sought was not granted to them, and what they possessed was taken from them." Sota 9b.

4 Haman, obsessed to the point of murder by the Jew's refusal to bow to him, now throws himself down before the Jew to plead for mercy. Fox, *Character and Ideology*, p. 87.

17. Allies

1 Genesis 40.14–15.
2 Genesis 41.9–13.

18. The Last Appeal

1 Haman's edict is sent out on the 13th of Nisan, and Mordechai's on the 23rd of Sivan, seventy days later. Since Mordechai would not have delayed issuing his order permitting the Jews to organize to defend themselves once the king had consented to it, it is clear that Esther's second approach to the king takes place on or shortly before the 23rd of Sivan. This means that more than two months have gone by since Haman's downfall on the 17th of Nisan without any action from the king in response to Esther's first request to spare her people.
2 Assuming that Haman is hanged on the 17th of Nisan, four days after his letters of extermination are sent out.
3 In Memuchan's proposed degradation of Vashti (1.19), in Haman's initiative to have the Jews destroyed (3.9), and in Esther's request for a renewed assault on the enemies of the Jews after the first day of battle (9.13). A similar formulation appears where the king's youths suggest that Ahashverosh select a new queen (2.4).
4 "It is not, therefore, necessary for a prince to have all the above-named qualities [mercy, faith, integrity, humanity, and religion], but it is very necessary to seem to have them." Niccolo Machiavelli, *The Prince* (New York: Random House, Modern Library, 1950), p. 65.
5 See Fox, *Character and Ideology*, pp. 86–87, Bush, *Ruth and Esther*, p. 433.

19. Political Power

1 From the 23rd of Sivan to the 13th of Adar is a period of eight months and twenty days.
2 See Chapter 2, n. 10.
3 *Natural law* is a philosopher's term referring to general principles deriving from human nature and from the nature of the world that, if followed, would work to bring about human well-being and flourishing. In Jewish tradition, Mosaic law is the natural law. See Maimonides, *Mishneh Tora* Me'ilah 8.8, Temura 4.13; *Guide* 3.26, 31; Yoram Hazony, "Three Replies: On Revelation, Natural Law and Autonomy in Jewish Theology," *Journal of Analytic Theology* 3 (2015), pp. 184–193, and references on p. 184, n. 34. For other views of natural law in the Hebrew Bible and rabbinic literature, see David Novak, *Natural Law in Judaism* (New York: Cambridge, 1998), pp. 27–61; Matthew Levering, *Biblical Natural Law* (Oxford: Oxford University Press, 2008); John Barton, *Ethics in Ancient Israel* (Oxford: Oxford University Press, 2015).
4 "[M]any have imagined republics and principalities which have never been seen or known to exist in reality; for how we live is so far removed from how we

ought to live, that he who abandons what is done for what ought to be done, will rather learn to bring about his own ruin than his preservation." Machiavelli, *The Prince*, p. 56.

5   1 Kings 21.1–19.

6   "So I hated life …. And I hated all my labor in which I had labored under the sun, because I must leave it to the man who will come after me. And who knows whether he will be a wise man or a fool, yet he will have rule over all my labor in which I have labored, and in which I have shown myself wise under the sun." Ecclesiastes 2.17–19.

7   Jeremiah 8.10.

8   This part of the edict clearly emphasizes the defensive nature of Mordechai's proclamation: The Jews and their allies are only interested in fighting those who are threatening them. See Fox, *Character and Ideology*, pp. 220–225; Bush, *Ruth and Esther*, pp. 459–460, 463–464. Some scholars have pointed out that this leaves open the possibility that if the day came and there were no provincial governments and no armed bands among the peoples threatening the Jewish population anywhere, there would also be no war. I agree that the wording of Mordechai's edict leaves this option open. But the narrative offers no evidence that Mordechai or anyone else believes it is possible that such a rosy scenario will come to pass. This is not merely a result of Mordechai's assessment of who the Jews' enemies are and what they want. The fact is that the king's original decree had ordered the destruction of the Jews and that this order remains in force, creating an overwhelming presumption that there will be attempts to kill the Jews and plunder them in many places. Even after the issuing of the second edict, the Jews throughout the empire are still weak, their property is still a tempting target, and a command of annihilation is still the law of the land supported by many enthusiasts. Moreover, vengeance is now a powerful motive animating many of Haman's supporters. The idea that attacks on the Jews would fail to materialize under these circumstances seems utopian.

9   As part of this effort to instill self-confidence in the Jews, Mordechai sends out his decree in Hebrew, among other languages (8.9), something that Haman presumably did not do (compare 3.12). Recall that in Esther, being able to speak in one's own language is considered to be the basis for a sense of control and rule (1.22). See Chapter 2, n. 28; Fox, *Character and Ideology*, pp. 230–231.

10 The Hebrew *bilvush malchut* literally means "clothed in kingship" or "clothed in the kingdom." This phrasing is parallel to Esther's dressing kingship when she goes in to see the king (5.1). See discussion in Chapter 25.

11 Compare Exodus 11.3: "The man Moses was very great in the land of Egypt, among Pharaoh's servants and in the eyes of the people."

12 The rabbis describe a dream of Mordechai's in which he and Haman are depicted as dragons. Esther Raba 8.5. This dream appears as part of the narrative in some Christian editions of the book of Esther.

13 We see the same thing in Egypt when the might of the plagues instills fear of the Israelites in the Egyptians, who then wish to help the Jews: "And the Lord gave

the people favor in the eyes of the Egyptians, so that they let them have what they asked, and they despoiled the Egyptians." Exodus 12.36.

14 The reference here is to Zechariah 8.20, in which it is said that the peoples of the nations will "lay hold of the hem of a Jew [*ish yehudi*], saying, 'We will go with you, for we have heard that God is with you.'" The expression *ish yehudi* (literally, "a Jewish man") is exactly that used to introduce Mordechai when he first appears in the narrative (2.5). The suggestion is that thanks to Mordechai's achievements, Zechariah's vision of the peoples coming to Judaism will come true.

20. The Jews' War

1 The account in the narrative begins with the effects ("The Jews gathered themselves in their cities in all the provinces of Ahashverosh the king, to lay their hands on those who sought to harm them, and no man could stand before them .... And all the princes of the provinces, and the satraps, and the governors, and those that conduct the king's affairs supported the Jews" [9.2-3]); and then explains the causes ("Because the fear of Mordechai had fallen upon them. For great was Mordechai in the king's house, and his reputation had gone out to all the provinces, for the man Mordechai grew greater and greater" [9.3-4]. It must be read in reverse order to see the sequence of events.

2 Machiavelli, *The Prince*, p. 9.

3 Machiavelli, *The Prince*, p. 60.

4 The combined might of the Jews and their allies among the governors and officials of the empire was overwhelming. But this does not mean that they faced no resistance. The expression "no man could stand before them" (9.2) is to be understood as in Joshua 23.9, meaning that attempts to defeat them were futile. Levenson, *Esther*, p. 120.

5 Daniel 6.7–25.

6 Herodotus wrote in admiration of the system of relays that carried messages throughout the Persian empire, but he nonetheless reported that three months were required for a message to be carried to the farthest provinces. We can therefore set aside the concern that the second day of battles in Susa should not have been conducted because it was by then clear that "the danger no longer existed." See, for example, Fox, *Character and Ideology*, p. 225. In fact, given the delay in receiving information from distant provinces, Mordechai and Esther could not have known that the danger had passed after only the first day of battle, or even after the second. The best information we have concerning their estimates of what was happening comes from the fact that a second day of fighting was deemed necessary in Susa. This seems to have no possible meaning other than that, on the basis of the best information available, the danger was not yet known to have passed.

21. The Morality of War

1 Isaiah 2.4; Jeremiah 31.30–33.

2 Ecclesiastes 7.16.

3   Ecclesiastes 7.17. R. Mani's account appears in Yoma 22b.

4   Ecclesiastes 7.16.

5   Leviticus 19.2. Compare: "You will be a nation of priests and a holy nation." Exodus 19.6. Similarly: "The commandments were given only to purify man therewith." Genesis Raba 44.1.

6   Deuteronomy 16.20.

7   1 Chronicles 22.8.

8   Avoda Zara 18a.

9   Avoda Zara 17b.

10   Avoda Zara 17b. According to the subsequent discussion, the daughter manages to escape the house of shame, but this hardly alters the point.

11   Sota 36b. See also the opinion of R. Judah ben R. Hanina. Brachot 20a, 55b.

12   Sanhedrin 20b. A constitutional doctrine distinguishing the "crown of kingship" from the "crown of priesthood" appears at 2 Chronicles 26.16–21, and is later developed by the rabbis. See, for example, Mishna Avot 4.13; Kiddushin 66a; Jerusalem Sota 8.3. It is not easy for a people that aspires to be "a kingdom of priests and a holy nation" (Exodus 19.6) to accept that the fact that it needs men of power and rule. But much as the Jews wished to be ruled by none other than God, the unmistakable message of the centuries when they first entered the land – without a king and with their resources diffused among the tribes – was that precious little of the dream of a nation of priests can be achieved without wielding immense worldly power. Neither the construction of the Temple in Jerusalem nor the concerted effort against Amalek become possible until the Jews unite their resources by placing them in the hands of a singularly unpriestly moral figure, the Israelite king.

13   For example, Avot 2.3. But compare Avot 3.2.

14   "Now an action done from duty [i.e., a moral action] must wholly exclude the influence of inclination, and with it every object of the will, so that nothing remains which can determine the will except objectively the law … that I should follow this law even to the thwarting of all my inclinations …. [But] although many things are done in conformity with what duty prescribes, it is nevertheless always doubtful whether they are done strictly from duty, so as to have moral worth …. [Y]et whether this or that takes place [in reality] is not the question … [R]eason itself, independent of all experience, ordains what ought to take place, that accordingly actions of which perhaps the world has hitherto never been given an example … are nevertheless inflexibly commanded by reason." Immanuel Kant, *Fundamental Principles of the Metaphysic of Morals*, T.K. Abbott, trans. (Buffalo: Prometheus, 1987) pp. 25, 33, 35.

15   Yoma 35b; Ketubot 111a; Megila 13b, 16b. The passage from Yoma is quoted in Chapter 7, note 12.

16   Genesis 6.5. Noah is introduced as being righteous "in his generations," apparently because no one else was in his time. Genesis 6.9 and Rashi's comment.

17   Genesis 19.1f. Lot is the proverbial "righteous man" to whom Abraham is referring in his argument with God in the preceding passage, after God announces his intention to destroy the city in which Lot is living. See Genesis 18.23–33.

18 Genesis 29.13–31.55. Jacob is referred to as "completely righteous" by the rabbis. Ketubot 111a; Numbers Raba 14.5.

19 Megila 13b.

20 Genesis 50.20.

21 Deuteronomy 7.2–5, 8.25–26. See also 12.29–31, 13.7–19. Compare Numbers 33.55–56.

22 R. Johanan in the name of R. Shimon ben Yehotzadak, Sanhedrin 74a.

23 It is a mistake to think that the biblical narrative itself subscribes to the view that God wants such wars. The biblical history must be read in light of the teaching of Genesis with which it begins, which is explicit in suggesting that God preferred for human beings to be vegetarians, causing no harm to any living thing. See Genesis 1.29–30. God's plan is rejected time and again by men, who are perverse in their desire to shed blood. Genesis 4.8, 4.23–24, 6.11–13. Whatever norms are subsequently invoked in God's name refer to a world in which mankind has already refused consistently to walk in the ways God himself desired.

24 Daniel 6.25.

25 Herodotus, *Persian Wars*, p. 501. Even among the early Hebrews, Reuben was willing to argue for such an outcome when trying to convince his father to allow the brothers to take Benjamin down to Egypt with them: "Reuben spoke to his father, saying: 'Slay my two sons if I do not bring him back to you.'" Genesis 42.37.

26 Ecclesiastes 7.15–16. The use of the word "righteous" in this way confuses us, as it is meant to do. Kohelet achieves his effect by placing righteousness and purity on the same scale, thus producing a category of "over-righteousness" for excessive purity, with the right amount of righteousness being in the balance between the extremes.

27 Herodotus, *Persian Wars*, pp. 258–259. Under Darius' rule, Herodotus reports that the annual income of the Persian empire was 9,540 talents of silver, plus the equivalent of another 4,680 talents levied in gold. The tribute of a large province such as Egypt was 700 talents of silver annually. See also Bush, *Ruth and Esther*, pp. 381–382.

28 In trying to persuade Esther to act against Haman, Mordechai also sees fit to make mention of "the money that Haman had offered to pay into the royal treasuries for the Jews, to have them destroyed" (4.7).

29 1 Samuel 15.9, 24.

30 1 Samuel 15.2, 18, 33.

31 See discussion in Chapter 19.

32 Purity of arms (Hebrew, *tohar haneshek*) is an Israeli moral term referring to the use of weapons only in a just fashion.

22. The Festival

1 The Bible does, however, refer to a number of fasts that were instituted not long before the time of Mordechai and Esther to mark the destruction of Jerusalem in

586 BCE: "The fast of the 4th [month] and the fast of the 5th and the fast of the 7th and the fast of the 10th will be unto the house of Judah joy and gladness, and good times." Zechariah 8.19. The phrasing here is very similar to that in Esther when the Jews rejoice over Mordechai's decree (8.17).

2 The deportation and scattering of the people of the northern kingdom of Israel by the Assyrians took place in 722 BCE. The southern kingdom, Judah, of which Mordechai's tribe of Benjamin was a part, was destroyed by the Babylonians in 586 BCE. See William M. Schniedwind, *How the Bible Became a Book* (New York: Cambridge University Press, 2004), p. 45. But see the alternative view presented by Bustany Oded, *Mass Deportations and Deportees in the Neo-Assyrian Empire* (Wiesbaden: Ludwig Reichert Verlag, 1979), p. 74.

3 We know that the question of how the Jews would survive the exile was at the fore in the thinking of the prophets Jeremiah and Ezekiel, and the Hebrew Bible was itself constructed to make such survival possible and to pave the way for a return from exile. See Hazony, *Philosophy of Hebrew Scripture*, pp. 55–59; Jacob Wright, "A Nation Conceived in Defeat," *Azure* 42 (Autumn, 2010), pp. 83–101; Dale Patrick and Allen Scult, *Rhetoric and Biblical Interpretation* (Sheffield: Sheffield Academic, 1990), pp. 51–54, 77–78. Koller beautifully describes how the book of Esther reflects the shrinking of Jewish consciousness in exile into a frame pre-occupied with survival in the present. Koller, *Esther in Ancient Jewish Thought*, pp. 93–95, 126.

4 Of course individual Jews such as Joseph had faced this choice many centuries earlier. But in this new condition of exile, all Jews now had to confront it.

5 Shabbat 88a.

6 In Nehemia, the Jews of Jerusalem actually take upon themselves an oath to perform the commandments of the *tora*. See Nehemia 10.1f.

7 Esther Raba 10.10.

23. Politics and Faith

1 Friedrich Nietzsche, *The Gay Science*, trans. Walter Kaufmann (Vintage: New York, 1974), Section 125.

2 Jeremiah, 4.23–26.

3 Deuteronomy 31.17.

4 Shabbat 88a.

5 Jeremiah 7.22–25.

6 Ketubot 110b.

7 The Bible does in fact record the persistence of Israelite prophecy all the way through the Babylonian exile and on into the Persian period, including the speeches of prophets who were involved in the first attempts of the exiles to return to Jerusalem. The last of the biblical prophetic texts that can be dated with reasonable accuracy are from the 510s BCE, a generation before the reign of Xerxes and the events described in Esther.

8   The supposition that the story of Esther revolves around a series of coincidences is common in recent commentaries. For discussion, see the "Afterwords" to this volume.

9   Passover falls on the 15th of Nisan, the day Esther first approaches Ahashverosh to invite him to her banquet that afternoon. Since she had requested that the Jews fast for her from the 13th of Nisan, this means that their *seder* night went by without the central aspects of the commemoration familiar to us. It is unclear to what degree Passover was being practiced among the Jews at the time, since the narrative reports that it had only been reinstated in the time of King Josiah, in the decades before the exile, having apparently gone largely unobserved before then. 2 Kings 23.21–23. But in any case, the willingness to take responsibility for such a decision is remarkable. It bears mentioning that Nehemia also goes before the king seeking deliverance for his people in month of Nisan. Nehemia 2.1 There is a related saying of the rabbis: "In Nisan they were redeemed, and in Nisan they will be redeemed in the time to come." According to R. Eliezer, Rosh Hashana 11a; R. Joshua, Rosh Hashana 11b. But this is not true in Esther's case. The king in effect turns down her request to save her people, and the subject is not brought up again until the month of Sivan. If this tradition of Nisan being a time of good tidings for Jews was known to the author of Esther, then the Jews' approach to the king in that month would serve as an interesting complement to Haman's belief that Adar would be a good month for the enemies of the Jews. However, neither of these proposals turns out to be right in Esther.

10 Deuteronomy 13.1.

11 The reference is to the public readings of the book of Esther on the holiday of Purim, but the point is that all the legal provisions of Purim are added to the law. Megila 14a.

12 Yoma 29a.

13 Shochar Tov 22.

14 The very name of Esther, a star (see Chapter 2, n. 7), suggests at the outset that the Persians may rely on the stars as they please, but that one of the Jews may herself be the decisive star they have failed to include in their calculations. The rabbis understood the plot of Esther to be mocking the belief that astrology, even if it were a true science, could be the ultimate arbiter of history. They envisioned Haman in his vain efforts to learn of a fortuitous time to attack the Jews by casting lots: "Then he turned to examining the signs of the zodiac: ... On reaching Pisces, the sign of the fishes, which shines in the month of Adar, he found no merit in it and rejoiced, saying, 'Adar has no merit and its sign has no merit, and, what is more, Moses their master died in Adar.' He did not know, however, that Moses died on the first of Adar but was also born on the first of Adar. He said: 'Just as fishes swallow one another, so will I swallow them.' The Holy One, blessed be he, said to him: 'Fool, sometimes fishes swallow and sometimes they are swallowed.'" Esther Raba 7.11.

15 Deuteronomy 11.22.

16 Seforno on Deuteronomy 11.22. Compare Rashi's comment: "He is merciful, and you should be merciful; he performs kind deeds, and you should perform kind deeds." Similarly, the Talmud on Deuteronomy 13.5 brings the opinion of R. Hama ben R. Hanina: "What is the meaning of the verse, 'You will walk after the Lord your God'? Is it then possible for a man to walk after God's presence, for has it not been said: 'For the Lord your God is a devouring fire' (Deut. 4.24)? But it means to walk after the ways of the Holy One, may he be blessed. As he clothes the naked, for it is written 'God the Lord made for Adam and for his wife coats of skin and clothed them,' (Genesis 3.21) so too should you clothe the naked. The Holy One, may he be blessed, visited the sick, for it is written 'The Lord appeared to him by the oaks of Mamre' (Genesis 18.1; see Rashi's comment), so should you also visit the sick. The Holy One, may he be blessed, comforted mourners, for it is written 'It came to pass after the death of Abraham that God blessed his son Isaac,' (Genesis 25.11) and so too should you comfort mourners. As the Holy One, may he be blessed, buried the dead, for it is written 'He buried him [Moses] in the valley,' (Deuteronomy 34.6) so too should you bury the dead." Sota 14a.
17 The complete passage reads: "For if you diligently keep all of this commandment that I instruct you to perform, to love the Lord your God, to walk in all his ways and to embrace it, then will the Lord drive out all these nations from before you, and you will inherit nations greater and mightier than yourselves. Every place where the sole of your foot steps will be yours, from the wilderness and Lebanon, from the river, the Euphrates, to the last sea will be your border. No man will be able to stand before you, for the fear of you and the dread of you will the Lord your God cause to fall on all the land on which you walk, as he has said to you." Deuteronomy 11.22–25. See also Deuteronomy 10.12–13.
18 The Hebrew word *rov* can be understood to mean only a majority. Megila 16b.
19 "When the news [of the massacre on the Sabbath] reached Mattathias and his compatriots, they mourned bitterly for the victims and said to one another: 'If we all do as our brothers have done and refuse to fight the pagans to defend our lives and institutions, they will only destroy us the sooner from the earth.' Then and there they came to this decision: 'If anyone attacks us on the Sabbath, whoever he may be, we will resist him. We cannot all be killed, as were our brothers in hiding.'" 1 Maccabees 2.39–41.
20 In a famous passage from the Talmud, R. Joshua rejects the use of supernatural proofs in legal argumentation by relying on Deuteronomy, which says: "For this commandment that I command you this day is not hidden from you, nor is it far off. It is not in heaven, that you should say, 'Who will go up to heaven for us and bring it to us, that we may hear it and do it?' ... But the word is very near to you, in your mouth and in your mind, that you may do it." (Deuteronomy 30.11–14). R. Jeremiah argues that decisions are properly made by the majority, and that signs and wonder have no weight, because "we pay no attention to voices from heaven." Bava Metzia 59b.

21   It may be that Esther estimated her chances of succeeding as even less than this. Perhaps she felt that it was only *possible* – and not probable – that she could prick Ahashverosh into suspecting Haman's loyalty in this way. But for our purposes here, this makes no difference. Even if Esther estimated that her chances were not great, this does not change the fact that she foresaw the outcome and intentionally brought it about through her actions. Private life is no different in this respect from political life. We may wish to conclude a business transaction, or to win a certain man or woman's love, or to persuade our children to take a certain course rather than another. Whether we estimate that this outcome is probable or only possible, we do our best to attain it. On no account is it appropriate to speak of such a positive outcome as coincidence or mere chance, for this would be to deny the evident fact that this outcome was planned and brought about through our efforts.

22   Megila 16a.

23   Machiavelli, *The Prince*, p. 91.

24   Machiavelli, *The Prince*, p. 94.

25   The Hebrew *makom aher* ("another place") has been read by some to refer to God because the word *makom* has been an accepted designation for God since at least the rabbinic period. But this is far-fetched, for then what can possibly be the meaning of the other word, *aher*? Compare Esther Raba 3.10, where references to "the king" in the narrative are understood by R. Judan, and by R. Levi in the name of R. Johanan, to refer to the true king, to God.

26   Megilla 15a.

27   Isaiah 8.10.

28   The complete passage reads: "When this decree was signed and delivered to Haman, he and all his associates began rejoicing. As it happened, Mordechai was just then walking in front of him. He saw three children coming from school and ran after them. So they followed Mordechai to see what he would ask the children. When Mordechai came up to the children, he asked one of them to repeat the verse he had just learned. He said: 'Be not afraid of the sudden terror, neither of the destruction of the wicked when it comes.' (Proverbs 3.25). The second followed, saying ... 'Take counsel together, and it will be brought to naught. Speak the word, and it will not stand, for God is with us.' (Isaiah 8.10). Then the third spoke up with the verse: 'Even to old age am I the same, and even to silver hair will I carry you. I have made, and I will bear. I will carry, and I will deliver.' (Isaiah 46.4). When Mordechai heard this, he smiled and was exceedingly glad. Haman said to him: 'Why are you so glad over the words of these children?' He replied: 'Because of the good tidings they have given me, that I need not fear the evil design that you have formed against us.' Thereupon the evil Haman grew angry and said: 'I will lay my hand on these children first of all.'" Esther Raba 7.13.

29   The passage replaced by an ellipsis reads: "At that moment, the compassion of the Holy One, may he be blessed, was stirred, and He rose from the throne of judgment and rested on the throne of mercy, and said: 'What is this loud noise I hear as the bleating of kids and lambs? Moses, our teacher, stood before the Holy One, may

he be blessed, and said: 'Ruler of the universe, they are neither kids nor lambs, but the little ones of your people who have been keeping a fast now for three days and three nights, whom the enemy plans to slaughter tomorrow like kids and lambs.' At that moment, the Holy One, may he be blessed, took the letters containing their doom, which were signed with a seal of clay, and tore them, in so doing bringing fright upon Ahashverosh in the night, as it says: 'That night,' etc." Esther Raba 9.4 on Esther 6.1. Moses speaks for the children who are about to die because he was one of them himself as an infant.

30   That gentiles may serve as redeemers for Israel is suggested in the Bible itself, in Isaiah, where Cyrus, king of Persia and Medes, is referred to as God's anointed: "So says the Lord to his anointed, to Cyrus, whose right hand have I held, that I might subdue nations before him .... For the sake of Jacob, My servant, and Israel, my chosen, I have called you by your name and consecrated you, though you did not know me." Isaiah 45.1–4. Cyrus destroyed the Babylonian empire and ordered that the Temple in Jerusalem be rebuilt at his expense.

31   "In the beginning, God created the heaven and the earth. And the earth was formless and void, and darkness was on the face of the abyss. And God's wind moved over the surface of the waters. And God said: Let there be light." Genesis 1.1–3. The Hebrew word for wind, *ruah*, is the same as the word for spirit. For man living on the sea in ships, compare Bava Batra 73af; Nietzsche, *Gay Science*, Section 124.

32   This idea is implicit in Machiavelli, but becomes an explicit and crucial theme in Nietzsche, *Gay Science*, Sections 283, 289. Compare especially Section 337. For Nietzsche, the meaning of humaneness itself is to be a sun, which dies at the end of its life, but which continues giving off light even at sunset, so that "even the poorest fisherman is still rowing with golden oars."

24. A Missile over Tel Aviv

1   See my discussion of causation in human affairs in Chapter 23.

2   According to Levenson, the plot of Esther is marked by "an astonishing set of benign coincidences." Levenson, *Esther*, p. 79. See also pp. 18–19, 22, 46, 64. Frederic Bush sees the narrative in Esther as based on "a set of coincidences so remarkable that they can hardly be anything but the narrator's cipher for 'divinely arranged.'" Bush, *Ruth and Esther*, p. 418. Carol Bechtel writes that "God's presence is also felt in the book's 'coincidences' .... Without them, the story would have a very different – and very tragic – resolution." Carol Bechtel, *Interpretation, a Bible Commentary for Teaching and Preaching: Esther* (Louisville, KY: Westminster John Knox Press, 2012 [2002]), pp. 13–14. Adele Berlin likewise asserts that "the entire plot turns on a succession of unlikely events." Berlin, *Esther*, p. xxi. Michael Walzer, too, suggests that in the book of Esther, "escape from doom is a piece of luck, not likely to be repeated." Michael Walzer, *In God's Shadow: Politics in the Hebrew Bible* (New Haven, CT: Yale University Press, 2012), p. 117. Fox leaves more room for appreciating Mordechai and Esther as responsible for the unfolding of events, but he too describes the climax of the plot in this way: "By coincidence

the king could not sleep that night, by coincidence he whiled away the time listening to a reading of the royal annals, and by coincidence the reader hit upon the mention of Mordechai's discovery of the assassination plot." Fox, *Character and Ideology*, p. 81.

3 Levenson speaks of events "inexplicable by natural causality." *Esther*, p. 20. Fox, too, writes of a "logic in history beyond natural causality," and of eventualities that are "not the outcome of causally linked events." *Character and Ideology*, pp. 80, 246.

4 Levenson, *Esther*, pp. 89, 117. See also pp. 20–21. In addition to the "mysterious grace" that envelopes Esther and Mordechai, Levenson refers to their "mysterious charm," pp. 62, 89; "mysterious charisma," p. 120; and "good luck of mysterious origin," p. 16. There are also "mysteriously beneficial" coincidences, p. 64; and the king's "mysterious inability to sleep," p. 95.

5 Levenson, *Esther*, p. 19; Bechtel, *Esther*, p. 57. See also Bush, *Ruth and Esther*, p. 418. Interestingly, Fox does not accept that the force arranging all of the coincidences is necessarily God. Fox, *Character and Ideology*, p. 247.

6 Levenson, *Esther*, p. 95.

7 Many writers who rely on this distinction between natural and divine causation would also agree that in the Bible it is God who has initiated the sequence of natural causes and devised the laws that govern them. But actions such as promulgating the laws of nature are said to be "general divine action," as opposed to the "special divine action" that is involved in miraculous violations of the natural order. See, for example, Alvin Plantinga, *Where the Conflict Really Lies: Science, Religion and Naturalism* (Oxford: Oxford University Press, 2011). In practice, this distinction between general and special divine action amounts to the same distinction between natural and divine causation that I am discussing, only using different names. In fact, it is just this distinction between general and special divine causation that leads to the focus on violations of the natural order as the only useful evidence of God's action in the world. Plantinga is right that in a probabilistic conception of natural laws such as arises from present-day quantum mechanical theory, it is difficult to understand what this distinction in fact amounts to. But even if quantum mechanics is replaced, the distinction between general and special divine causation will still be misguided, being based on an Aristotelian conception of the world as governed by eternal and immutable natures. The Bible knows of no such eternal and immutable natures, so there can also be no eternal and immutable divine action to be "violated" or contradicted through special divine action.

8 This story appeared in Hebrew on the *Kooker* Israeli news site on July 29, 2014. A partial English translation appears in "Iron Dome Operator: God Moved Missile We Couldn't Hit," *Israel Today* website, August 12, 2014.

9 Genesis 21.20, Genesis 39.2–3, and also 39.21, 23; 1 Samuel 18.12–14; Nehemia 2.18. Compare Joshua 6.27, 14.12; 2 Kings 18.7. Similarly, when such ingenuity is absent and one fails in battle, Scripture says that "the Lord has forsaken us." Judges 6.13.

10 The tendency to think of God in terms of the gaps in our knowledge of natural causation was already criticized in Henry Drummond, *Ascent of Man* (New York: James Pott, 1894), p. 334. The term "God of the gaps" appears in Charles Coulson, *Science and Christian Belief* (Oxford: Oxford University Press, 1955), p. 20. See also Richard Dawkins, *The God Delusion* (Boston: Houghton Mifflin, 2006), pp. 151–161.

11 At the same time, an extraordinary event can also be recognized as being from God if it is possible to see this event as contributing to the birth of justice in the world. Joseph Soloveitchik, *The Emergence of Ethical Man*, Michael Berger ed. (Jersey City: Ktav, 2005), pp. 187–188. As Soloveitchik emphasizes, the miraculous quality of such events does not reside in the fact they are extraordinary in character. An extraordinary event, if arbitrary and meaningless, is not an expression of God's action in the world any more than anything else. Rather, an event is singled out as being a wonder or a miracle, and therefore as an expression of God's rule, where we see the emergence of an alignment between the natural order and God's justice. From the perspective of the prophets, the emergence of justice is a regularity that can be observed by human beings, as Moses teaches in Exodus 20.5–6, 34.6–7 and as expressed in a great many other sources.

12 Levenson, *Esther*, p. 105. Compare Fox, *Character and Ideology*, p. 81.

13 In a famous article, Klaus Koch correctly argued that throughout the Bible, rewards and punishments are depicted as being the natural consequences of the actions from which they arise. Koch, "Is There a Doctrine of Retribution in the Old Testament?" in James Crenshaw, ed., *Theodicy in the Old Testament* (Philadelphia: Fortress Press, 1983 [1955]), pp. 57–87. However, Koch's thesis is frequently, and incorrectly, said to apply only to certain "wisdom" texts in the Bible, such as Proverbs and some Psalms, which are thought to be concerned with natural, as opposed to divine, causation. This is what stands behind the proposal that the text in Esther, which does not mention God, reflects the "influence" of texts such as this one from Proverbs – but not Exodus, for example. This division of the Bible into "wisdom literature" and non-wisdom literature is, however, a late imposition, whose purpose is to force a distinction between natural and divine causation, reason and revelation, upon the biblical corpus. Insofar as it is intended to reflect the worldview of the biblical authors, it is anachronistic and misleading. See Hazony, *Philosophy of Hebrew Scripture*, pp. 1–20 and esp. pp. 284–285, n. 26.

14 Proverbs 26.27; Levenson, *Esther*, p. 105. Note that the pit and the stone in this proverb are intended primarily as metaphors, as is evident from parallel passages such as Proverbs 28.10: "He who causes the just to stray onto evil paths, will himself fall into his own pit"; and Psalms 57.7: "They have prepared a net for my steps, my soul is bowed down. They have dug a pit for me, and have fallen into it themselves."

15 Exodus 22.21–23. See also Leviticus 24.19; Deuteronomy 19.16–19; 1 Samuel 15.23, 33.

16 This particular verse, Proverbs 26.27, appears not to refer to God only when read out of context. The collection of proverbs in which this verse is found opens by declaring that "It is the glory of God to conceal [Hebrew, *haster*] a thing, but the glory of kings to inquire into a thing." Proverbs 25.1–2. And further on in the same section, we read that "Evil men do not understand justice, but those that seek the Lord understand all things." Proverbs 28.5. The latter verse indicates, as clearly as one could want, that an understanding of the manner in which justice unfolds in the world (that is, precisely the understanding that appears instantiated in Proverbs 26.27) comes from seeking God's ways; while the opening verses tell us that God conceals his ways, but that human inquiry can reveal them. The results of such inquiry into the things that God has concealed are none other than the principles that have been laid out in this collection of proverbs, including the principle in Proverbs 26.27 that those who dig pits and set stones rolling will be damaged by their own deeds.

17 As Yehezkel Kaufmann writes concerning the story of Achan in the book of Joshua: "This is a typical biblical story. Events occur through *dual causality*, that is, through both natural causes and divine direction that determines events." Yehezkel Kaufmann, *The Book of Joshua* (Jerusalem: Kiryat Sefer Vehahevra Leheker Hamikra, 1970 [1959]), p. 163 [Hebrew]; emphasis added). Kaufmann coined the expression "dual causality" to refer to this tendency of biblical texts to recognize both God and human beings as being concurrently the cause of events. See discussion in Yairah Amit, "The Dual Causality Principle and Its Effects on Biblical Literature," *Vetus Testamentum* 37 (October 1987), pp. 385–400; Jaco Gericke, "Rethinking the Dual Causality Principle in Old Testament Research: A Philosophical Perspective," *Old Testament Exegesis* 28 (2015), pp. 86–112.

25. God and Emergence

1 The word *emergence* is used in philosophy with reference to irreducible properties appearing at higher levels of description in the sciences. The phenomenon is discussed using different terms in John Stuart Mill, *System of Logic* 3.6. The term itself is today associated with the best-known discussion of it, C.D. Broad, *The Mind and Its Place in Nature* (London: Routledge, 1925); compare Soloveitchik, *Emergence of Ethical Man*, esp. p. 14, n. 8. Emergence is not to be confused with the claim that properties at higher levels of description are fully determined by the properties of bounded collections of entities at lower levels of description (i.e., "supervenience"). In fact there is no way, even in principle, to bound and characterize a collection of entities in such a way that a complete reduction of its emergent properties could ever be performed. Consequently, my references to God's actions as emergent upon the actions of human and physical causes should in no way be taken to mean that there is a possible description of a bounded set of human and physical causes that could afford a completed account of God's action in a given instance.

2 As Jaco Gericke points out, recent studies of biblical "dual causation" seem to understand these texts in terms of Aristotelian efficient causation: Man is one efficient cause and God is another, apparently unrelated, efficient cause. Yet these causes result in the same event. See Gericke, "Dual Causality Principle," p. 97. The approach I propose here, in which God's actions are seen as emergent upon human and physical causes, offers an alternative way of thinking about dual causation in the Bible. On this view, God's actions and man's are not independent, being related to one another only in that they issue in one and the same effect. Instead, they are intimately related, since God's actions are in part constituted by human actions. Divine causation is thus dependent, in part, on the decisions and actions of the human beings who contribute to it. This is analogous to the manner in which a particular observed instance of physical causation contributes to a more general physical principle or law. A physical law can also be regarded as causing the effect in question, but it more closely resembles a formal than an efficient cause, imparting a larger purpose and meaning to an otherwise arbitrary event. See Thomas Kuhn, *The Essential Tension* (Chicago: University of Chicago Press, 1977), p. 28. The same may be said with respect to God's actions when considered as emergent properties. Divine causation in instances of biblical dual causation may be better understood as a formal rather than an efficient cause, imparting a broader purpose and meaning to a constituent event that may otherwise seem arbitrary or lacking in larger significance.

3 See Chapter 2, n. 7.

4 This reminds us of the name Moses, which means "son" in the language of the ancient Egyptians; but which in Hebrew derives from the verb *masha* ("to draw out"), referring to his being drawn out of the water by Pharaoh's daughter, as well as to his drawing Israel out of Egypt at God's behest.

5 Deuteronomy 31.18. See also 31.17, 32.20; Hullin 139b. This second, Hebrew meaning of Esther's name also echoes one of the best-known passages in the book of Proverbs, which opens with the declaration: "It is the glory of God is to conceal [*haster*] a thing." Proverbs 25.2. Here, God's glory is said explicitly to be found in the manner in which he conceals (*haster*, הסתר) the workings of the world from the understanding of men, although the great, as we are told, can through their inquiries uncover that which God has concealed. Perhaps the author of Esther, in reflecting on this name, was aware that some of the verses in Proverbs 25.1–13 seem to be concerned with issues known to us from the story of Mordechai and Esther, including its advice to "Move the wicked away from before the king, and his throne will be established in righteousness." Proverbs 25.5.

6 Ezekiel 39.26–29.

7 Even if such a Persian name was in common use, the Hebrew version in our text could easily have been transliterated in other ways.

8 On the use of parallel passages and repeating phrases as a technical language for handling ideas in the Bible, see Hazony, *Philosophy of Hebrew Scripture*, pp. 74–79; Koller, *Esther in Ancient Jewish Thought*, p. 74. Regarding this particular case, see Levenson, *Esther*, p. 81.

9 Jonah 3.5–9.

10 2 Samuel 12.16, 22.

11 Joel 2.12–14.

12 Other examples of fasting and sack and ashes to petition God include 1 Kings 21.27; Nehemia 9.1–3.

13 Some readers have drawn just this conclusion: "The author of Esther ... makes it abundantly clear not only that God is not playing a role in history, but that his place has been usurped by humans.... God is not just hidden, but he has been replaced." Koller, *Esther in Ancient Jewish Thought*, pp. 99, 101. But this reading requires us to ignore the prominent implicit references to God in the text, including Esther's name and her request that the Jews of Susa fast for her for three days – a request this is plainly more fitting to a young woman reaching out to her God, or perhaps finding her God, than to the heroine of an atheist tract.

   A more moderate view is that God's presence or absence in Esther is intended to be an irresolvable question. As Fox writes, "The author is carefully creating and maintaining uncertainty. This is why he hints at God's role, but only obliquely .... The frustration of [our] expectations must be purposive. [Esther's] religious attitude is like an optical illusion that shifts orientation when you stare at it, but which ... can temporarily be fixed in a certain orientation by the viewer's decision to see it one way or the other." This comparison of the Esther narrative to a gestalt switch diagram is important, pointing to the presence of the same emergent properties I have emphasized in my discussion here. And Fox is right, too, in suggesting that in teaching readers to shift their orientation in this way, the author of Esther wishes to give us the tools "to probe the events in our own lives in the same way." Fox, *Character and Ideology*, pp. 246–247. However, the conclusion that the author's goal is only to teach a "theology of possibility" – one in which the reader is left hanging, forever poised between the possibility of God's presence and the possibility of his absence – seems to me to fall short of the mark. In this sense, the comparison of Esther to a gestalt switch diagram perhaps does this work a disservice. For it is a characteristic of such optical illusions that one can go back and forth as many times as one likes, without end. There is no right answer as to which way to look at the illusion. Esther is not an agnostic work in this sense, any more than it is an atheist work. Esther urges us, rather, to see God's hand upon the mundane chain of political events that would otherwise claim our full attention. Having learned to see reality from the vantage point of this higher level of description, we have taken the first step in a life lived in God's presence. There is no reason for us to go back, nor is there any indication that the author of Esther would have wished for us to do so.

14 Compare to Mordechai, who similarly emerges from the palace "clothed in kingship" (Hebrew, *bilvush malchut*) after having issued the decree permitting the Jews to defend themselves (8.15). See discussion in Chapter 19.

15 This view is raised by R. Eleazar in the name of R. Hanina, Megila 15a; R. Judan and R. Levi in the name of R. Johanan, Esther Raba 3.10. See also my discussion in Chapter 23.

26. God Casts No Shadow

1   Michael Walzer, *In God's Shadow*, pp. xii–xiii, 202–203, 206. God is called a "man of war" in Exodus 15.3.

2   Jon Levenson, too, proposes that biblical figures such as Gideon and Samuel preferred that God should rule over Israel "rather than man." "Category Error," *Jewish Review of Books* (Fall 2012), pp. 11–14. This misreading is the direct result of the assumption that God's rule and human rule are mutually exclusive categories, just as God's action and human action are assumed to be mutually exclusive categories. But no such separation between divine and human rule appears in the Bible. In particular, the famous declaration of Gideon, "I will not rule over you, nor will my son rule over you, but the Lord will rule over you" (Judges 8.23), is not a proposal that God should become the political ruler instead of human beings. It is an antimonarchical declaration, whose concern is that Israel live free from the oppression and idolatry that were intrinsic to the institution of monarchy in the ancient Near East. Gideon, like others in the books of Judges and Samuel, wants no part in a human king. He contends that human political leadership should arise from among the tribal leaders of Israel as it always has, with none but God above them. See Hazony, *Philosophy of Hebrew Scripture*, pp. 144–154; Yoram Hazony, "Response to Jon Levenson," *Jerusalem Letters*, December 2, 2012, available at http://jerusalemletters.com/yoram-hazony-response-to-jon-levenson/.

3   Man's corruption of the world prior to the covenant with Israel is described in the first eleven chapters of Genesis. See especially Genesis 4.8, 23–24. The concept of the incompleteness of God's name and his throne in this ruined world is familiar, for example, from rabbinic commentary on Exodus 17.16. See Midrash Tanhuma Tetzeh 11 and Rashi's comment on this verse.

4   Joshua Berman, *Created Equal: How the Bible Broke with Ancient Political Thought* (Oxford: Oxford University Press, 2008).

5   This is evident, for instance, in the description of Joseph's command over the jail in Egypt: "The minister of the jail placed all of the prisoners who were in the jail in Joseph's hand, and everything they did there was his doing." Genesis 39.22. Here the prisoners' actions are described as being their own, and yet all of their actions are also Joseph's actions ("everything they did was his doing"). This is an instance of biblical "double causation" in which both a greater human being and a lesser human being are said to be causes of a single effect.

6   See Chapter 25.

7   Genesis 1.2.

8   Isaiah 50.2.

9   Bava Batra 12b.

10 One of many examples of God "raising up" leaders among the Israelites, or adversaries against them: "And Israel cried out to the Lord, and the Lord raised them up a savior, Ehud the son of Gera, of Benjamin, a left-handed man." God is said to save Israel by raising up Ehud, yet at the same time we are told that "Moab was

subdued that day under the hand of Israel." Judges 3.14–30. Notice the assumption of both human and divine causation.

11 Addition to the traditional Shemona Esrei prayer and grace after meals for Purim. Here, too, both human and divine causation are assumed.

12 See Introduction, n. 3.

13 Exodus 3.10, 14.21.

Index of Names

Scriptural and Rabbinic References

בִּזְמַנֵּיהֶם כַּאֲשֶׁר קִיַּם עֲלֵיהֶם מָרְדֳּכַי הַיְּהוּדִי וְאֶסְתֵּר הַמַּלְכָּה וְכַאֲשֶׁר קִיְּמוּ

עַל־נַפְשָׁם וְעַל־זַרְעָם דִּבְרֵי הַצּוֹמוֹת וְזַעֲקָתָם: וּמַאֲמַר אֶסְתֵּר קִיַּם דִּבְרֵי לב

אֲחַשְׁוֵרוֹשׁ הַפֻּרִים הָאֵלֶּה וְנִכְתָּב בַּסֵּפֶר: ‏ וַיָּשֶׂם הַמֶּלֶךְ אֲחַשְׁרֹשׁ ׀ מַס עַל־ א

הָאָרֶץ וְאִיֵּי הַיָּם: וְכָל־מַעֲשֵׂה תָקְפּוֹ וּגְבוּרָתוֹ וּפָרָשַׁת גְּדֻלַּת מָרְדֳּכַי אֲשֶׁר ב

גִּדְּלוֹ הַמֶּלֶךְ הֲלוֹא־הֵם כְּתוּבִים עַל־סֵפֶר דִּבְרֵי הַיָּמִים לְמַלְכֵי מָדַי וּפָרָס:

‏ כִּי ׀ מָרְדֳּכַי הַיְּהוּדִי מִשְׁנֶה לַמֶּלֶךְ אֲחַשְׁוֵרוֹשׁ וְגָדוֹל לַיְּהוּדִים וְרָצוּי לְרֹב ג

אֶחָיו דֹּרֵשׁ טוֹב לְעַמּוֹ וְדֹבֵר שָׁלוֹם לְכָל־זַרְעוֹ: ‏

בְּנֵי־הָמָן בִּשְׁאָר מְדִינוֹת הַמֶּלֶךְ מֶה עָשׂוּ וּמַה־שְּׁאֵלָתֵךְ וְיִנָּתֵן לָךְ וּמַה־בַּקָּשָׁתֵךְ

יג עוֹד וְתֵעָשׂ: וַתֹּאמֶר אֶסְתֵּר אִם־עַל־הַמֶּלֶךְ טוֹב יִנָּתֵן גַּם־מָחָר לַיְּהוּדִים אֲשֶׁר

בְּשׁוּשָׁן לַעֲשׂוֹת כְּדָת הַיּוֹם וְאֵת עֲשֶׂרֶת בְּנֵי־הָמָן יִתְלוּ עַל־הָעֵץ: וַיֹּאמֶר

יד הַמֶּלֶךְ לְהֵעָשׂוֹת כֵּן וַתִּנָּתֵן דָּת בְּשׁוּשָׁן וְאֵת עֲשֶׂרֶת בְּנֵי־הָמָן תָּלוּ: וַיִּקָּהֲלוּ

טו הַיְּהוּדִים אֲשֶׁר־בְּשׁוּשָׁן גַּם בְּיוֹם אַרְבָּעָה עָשָׂר לְחֹדֶשׁ אֲדָר וַיַּהַרְגוּ בְשׁוּשָׁן הַיְּהוּדִים

שְׁלֹשׁ מֵאוֹת אִישׁ וּבַבִּזָּה לֹא שָׁלְחוּ אֶת־יָדָם: וּשְׁאָר הַיְּהוּדִים אֲשֶׁר בִּמְדִינוֹת

טז הַמֶּלֶךְ נִקְהֲלוּ ׀ וְעָמֹד עַל־נַפְשָׁם וְנוֹחַ מֵאֹיְבֵיהֶם וְהָרֹג בְּשֹׂנְאֵיהֶם חֲמִשָּׁה

יז וְשִׁבְעִים אָלֶף וּבַבִּזָּה לֹא שָׁלְחוּ אֶת־יָדָם: בְּיוֹם־שְׁלֹשָׁה עָשָׂר לְחֹדֶשׁ אֲדָר וְנוֹחַ

בְּאַרְבָּעָה עָשָׂר בּוֹ וְעָשֹׂה אֹתוֹ יוֹם מִשְׁתֶּה וְשִׂמְחָה: וְהַיְּהוּדִים אֲשֶׁר־בְּשׁוּשָׁן וְהַיְּהוּדִים

יח נִקְהֲלוּ בִּשְׁלוֹשָׁה עָשָׂר בּוֹ וּבְאַרְבָּעָה עָשָׂר בּוֹ וְנוֹחַ בַּחֲמִשָּׁה עָשָׂר בּוֹ וְעָשֹׂה

יט אֹתוֹ יוֹם מִשְׁתֶּה וְשִׂמְחָה: עַל־כֵּן הַיְּהוּדִים הַפְּרוֹזִים הַיֹּשְׁבִים בְּעָרֵי הַפְּרָזוֹת הַפְּרָזִים

עֹשִׂים אֵת יוֹם אַרְבָּעָה עָשָׂר לְחֹדֶשׁ אֲדָר שִׂמְחָה וּמִשְׁתֶּה וְיוֹם טוֹב וּמִשְׁלֹחַ

כ מָנוֹת אִישׁ לְרֵעֵהוּ: וַיִּכְתֹּב מָרְדֳּכַי אֶת־הַדְּבָרִים הָאֵלֶּה וַיִּשְׁלַח סְפָרִים אֶל־כָּל־

כא הַיְּהוּדִים אֲשֶׁר בְּכָל־מְדִינוֹת הַמֶּלֶךְ אֲחַשְׁוֵרוֹשׁ הַקְּרוֹבִים וְהָרְחוֹקִים: לְקַיֵּם

עֲלֵיהֶם לִהְיוֹת עֹשִׂים אֵת יוֹם אַרְבָּעָה עָשָׂר לְחֹדֶשׁ אֲדָר וְאֵת יוֹם־חֲמִשָּׁה

כב עָשָׂר בּוֹ בְּכָל־שָׁנָה וְשָׁנָה: כַּיָּמִים אֲשֶׁר־נָחוּ בָהֶם הַיְּהוּדִים מֵאוֹיְבֵיהֶם וְהַחֹדֶשׁ

אֲשֶׁר נֶהְפַּךְ לָהֶם מִיָּגוֹן לְשִׂמְחָה וּמֵאֵבֶל לְיוֹם טוֹב לַעֲשׂוֹת אוֹתָם יְמֵי מִשְׁתֶּה

כג וְשִׂמְחָה וּמִשְׁלֹחַ מָנוֹת אִישׁ לְרֵעֵהוּ וּמַתָּנוֹת לָאֶבְיוֹנִים: וְקִבֵּל הַיְּהוּדִים אֵת

כד אֲשֶׁר־הֵחֵלּוּ לַעֲשׂוֹת וְאֵת אֲשֶׁר־כָּתַב מָרְדֳּכַי אֲלֵיהֶם: כִּי הָמָן בֶּן־הַמְּדָתָא

הָאֲגָגִי צֹרֵר כָּל־הַיְּהוּדִים חָשַׁב עַל־הַיְּהוּדִים לְאַבְּדָם וְהִפִּל פּוּר הוּא הַגּוֹרָל

כה לְהֻמָּם וּלְאַבְּדָם: וּבְבֹאָהּ לִפְנֵי הַמֶּלֶךְ אָמַר עִם־הַסֵּפֶר יָשׁוּב מַחֲשַׁבְתּוֹ הָרָעָה

כו אֲשֶׁר־חָשַׁב עַל־הַיְּהוּדִים עַל־רֹאשׁוֹ וְתָלוּ אֹתוֹ וְאֶת־בָּנָיו עַל־הָעֵץ: עַל־כֵּן

קָרְאוּ לַיָּמִים הָאֵלֶּה פוּרִים עַל־שֵׁם הַפּוּר עַל־כֵּן עַל־כָּל־דִּבְרֵי הָאִגֶּרֶת הַזֹּאת

כז וּמָה־רָאוּ עַל־כָּכָה וּמָה הִגִּיעַ אֲלֵיהֶם: קִיְּמוּ וְקִבֵּל הַיְּהוּדִים ׀ עֲלֵיהֶם ׀ וְעַל־

זַרְעָם וְעַל כָּל־הַנִּלְוִים עֲלֵיהֶם וְלֹא יַעֲבוֹר לִהְיוֹת עֹשִׂים אֵת שְׁנֵי הַיָּמִים הָאֵלֶּה

כח כִּכְתָבָם וְכִזְמַנָּם בְּכָל־שָׁנָה וְשָׁנָה: וְהַיָּמִים הָאֵלֶּה נִזְכָּרִים וְנַעֲשִׂים בְּכָל־דּוֹר

וָדוֹר מִשְׁפָּחָה וּמִשְׁפָּחָה מְדִינָה וּמְדִינָה וְעִיר וָעִיר וִימֵי הַפּוּרִים הָאֵלֶּה לֹא

כט יַעַבְרוּ מִתּוֹךְ הַיְּהוּדִים וְזִכְרָם לֹא־יָסוּף מִזַּרְעָם: וַתִּכְתֹּב אֶסְתֵּר

הַמַּלְכָּה בַת־אֲבִיחַיִל וּמָרְדֳּכַי הַיְּהוּדִי אֶת־כָּל־תֹּקֶף לְקַיֵּם אֵת אִגֶּרֶת הַפֻּרִים

ל הַזֹּאת הַשֵּׁנִית: וַיִּשְׁלַח סְפָרִים אֶל־כָּל־הַיְּהוּדִים אֶל־שֶׁבַע וְעֶשְׂרִים וּמֵאָה

לא מְדִינָה מַלְכוּת אֲחַשְׁוֵרוֹשׁ דִּבְרֵי שָׁלוֹם וֶאֱמֶת: לְקַיֵּם אֶת־יְמֵי הַפֻּרִים הָאֵלֶּה

וּמְדִינָ֣ה גָּל֔וּי לְכָל־הָ֣עַמִּ֔ים וְלִהְי֤וֹת הַיְּהוּדִים֙ עתודים לַיּ֣וֹם הַזֶּ֔ה לְהִנָּקֵ֖ם

מֵאֹיְבֵיהֶֽם: הָרָצִ֞ים רֹכְבֵ֤י הָרֶ֙כֶשׁ֙ הָֽאֲחַשְׁתְּרָנִ֔ים יָצְא֥וּ מְבֹהָלִ֖ים וּדְחוּפִ֣ים בִּדְבַ֣ר יד

הַמֶּ֑לֶךְ וְהַדָּ֥ת נִתְּנָ֖ה בְּשׁוּשַׁ֥ן הַבִּירָֽה: ⁘ וּמָרְדֳּכַ֞י יָצָ֣א ׀ מִלִּפְנֵ֣י הַמֶּ֗לֶךְ טו

בִּלְב֤וּשׁ מַלְכוּת֙ תְּכֵ֣לֶת וָח֔וּר וַעֲטֶ֤רֶת זָהָב֙ גְּדוֹלָ֔ה וְתַכְרִ֥יךְ בּ֖וּץ וְאַרְגָּמָ֑ן וְהָעִ֣יר

שׁוּשָׁ֔ן צָהֲלָ֖ה וְשָׂמֵֽחָה: ⁘ לַיְּהוּדִ֕ים הָֽיְתָ֥ה אוֹרָ֖ה וְשִׂמְחָ֑ה וְשָׂשֹׂ֖ן וִיקָֽר: טז

וּבְכָל־מְדִינָ֣ה וּמְדִינָ֗ה וּבְכָל־עִ֣יר וָעִ֔יר מְקוֹם֙ אֲשֶׁ֨ר דְּבַר־הַמֶּ֤לֶךְ וְדָתוֹ֙ מַגִּ֔יעַ יז

שִׂמְחָ֤ה וְשָׂשׂוֹן֙ לַיְּהוּדִ֔ים מִשְׁתֶּ֖ה וְי֣וֹם ט֑וֹב וְרַבִּ֞ים מֵֽעַמֵּ֤י הָאָ֙רֶץ֙ מִֽתְיַהֲדִ֔ים

כִּֽי־נָפַ֥ל פַּֽחַד־הַיְּהוּדִ֖ים עֲלֵיהֶֽם: וּבִשְׁנֵים֩ עָשָׂ֨ר חֹ֜דֶשׁ הוּא־חֹ֣דֶשׁ אֲדָ֗ר א ט

בִּשְׁלוֹשָׁ֨ה עָשָׂ֥ר יוֹם֙ בּ֔וֹ אֲשֶׁ֨ר הִגִּ֧יעַ דְּבַר־הַמֶּ֛לֶךְ וְדָת֖וֹ לְהֵעָשׂ֑וֹת בַּיּ֗וֹם אֲשֶׁ֨ר

שִׂבְּר֜וּ אֹיְבֵ֤י הַיְּהוּדִים֙ לִשְׁל֣וֹט בָּהֶ֔ם וְנַהֲפ֣וֹךְ ה֔וּא אֲשֶׁ֨ר יִשְׁלְט֧וּ הַיְּהוּדִ֛ים

הֵ֖מָּה בְּשֹׂנְאֵיהֶֽם: נִקְהֲל֨וּ הַיְּהוּדִ֜ים בְּעָרֵיהֶ֗ם בְּכָל־מְדִינוֹת֙ הַמֶּ֣לֶךְ אֲחַשְׁוֵר֔וֹשׁ ב

לִשְׁלֹ֣חַ יָ֔ד בִּמְבַקְשֵׁ֖י רָֽעָתָ֑ם וְאִישׁ֙ לֹא־עָמַ֣ד לִפְנֵיהֶ֔ם כִּֽי־נָפַ֥ל פַּחְדָּ֖ם עַל־כָּל־

הָֽעַמִּֽים: וְכָל־שָׂרֵ֨י הַמְּדִינ֜וֹת וְהָאֲחַשְׁדַּרְפְּנִ֣ים וְהַפַּח֗וֹת וְעֹשֵׂ֤י הַמְּלָאכָה֙ ג

אֲשֶׁ֣ר לַמֶּ֔לֶךְ מְנַשְּׂאִ֖ים אֶת־הַיְּהוּדִ֑ים כִּֽי־נָפַ֥ל פַּֽחַד־מָרְדֳּכַ֖י עֲלֵיהֶֽם: כִּֽי־ ד

גָד֤וֹל מָרְדֳּכַי֙ בְּבֵ֣ית הַמֶּ֔לֶךְ וְשָׁמְע֖וֹ הוֹלֵ֣ךְ בְּכָל־הַמְּדִינ֑וֹת כִּֽי־הָאִ֥ישׁ מָרְדֳּכַ֖י

הוֹלֵ֥ךְ וְגָדֽוֹל: וַיַּכּ֤וּ הַיְּהוּדִים֙ בְּכָל־אֹ֣יְבֵיהֶ֔ם מַכַּת־חֶ֥רֶב וְהֶ֖רֶג וְאַבְדָּ֑ן וַיַּֽעֲשׂ֥וּ ה

בְשֹׂנְאֵיהֶ֖ם כִּרְצוֹנָֽם: וּבְשׁוּשַׁ֣ן הַבִּירָ֗ה הָרְג֤וּ הַיְּהוּדִים֙ וְאַבֵּ֔ד ⁘ חֲמֵ֥שׁ מֵא֖וֹת ו

אִֽישׁ: וְאֵ֧ת ׀ ז

פַּרְשַׁנְדָּ֖תָא וְאֵ֧ת ׀

דַּֽלְפ֖וֹן וְאֵ֧ת ׀

אַסְפָּ֑תָא וְאֵ֧ת ׀ ח

פּוֹרָ֖תָא וְאֵ֧ת ׀

אֲדַלְיָ֖א וְאֵ֧ת ׀

אֲרִידָ֑תָא וְאֵ֧ת ׀ ט

פַּרְמַ֖שְׁתָּא וְאֵ֧ת ׀

אֲרִיסַ֖י וְאֵ֧ת ׀

אֲרִדַ֖י וְאֵ֧ת ׀

וַיְזָֽתָא: עֲשֶׂ֖רֶת ⁘ י

בְּנֵ֨י הָמָ֧ן בֶּֽן־הַמְּדָ֛תָא צֹרֵ֥ר הַיְּהוּדִ֖ים הָרָ֑גוּ וּבַ֨בִּזָּ֔ה לֹ֥א שָׁלְח֖וּ אֶת־יָדָֽם: בַּיּ֣וֹם יא

הַה֗וּא בָּ֣א מִסְפַּ֧ר הַֽהֲרוּגִ֛ים בְּשׁוּשַׁ֥ן הַבִּירָ֖ה לִפְנֵ֣י הַמֶּֽלֶךְ: וַיֹּ֨אמֶר הַמֶּ֜לֶךְ לְאֶסְתֵּ֣ר יב

הַמַּלְכָּ֗ה בְּשׁוּשַׁ֣ן הַבִּירָ֡ה הָרְגוּ֩ הַיְּהוּדִ֨ים וְאַבֵּ֜ד חֲמֵ֧שׁ מֵא֣וֹת אִ֗ישׁ וְאֵת֙ עֲשֶׂ֣רֶת

ח הַמַּלְכָּה כִּי רָאָה כִּי־כָלְתָה אֵלָיו הָרָעָה מֵאֵת הַמֶּלֶךְ: וְהַמֶּלֶךְ שָׁב מִגִּנַּת
הַבִּיתָן אֶל־בֵּית ׀ מִשְׁתֵּה הַיַּיִן וְהָמָן נֹפֵל עַל־הַמִּטָּה אֲשֶׁר אֶסְתֵּר עָלֶיהָ
וַיֹּאמֶר הַמֶּלֶךְ הֲגַם לִכְבּוֹשׁ אֶת־הַמַּלְכָּה עִמִּי בַּבָּיִת הַדָּבָר יָצָא מִפִּי הַמֶּלֶךְ

ט וּפְנֵי הָמָן חָפוּ: וַיֹּאמֶר חַרְבוֹנָה אֶחָד מִן־הַסָּרִיסִים לִפְנֵי הַמֶּלֶךְ גַּם הִנֵּה־הָעֵץ
אֲשֶׁר־עָשָׂה הָמָן לְמָרְדֳּכַי אֲשֶׁר דִּבֶּר־טוֹב עַל־הַמֶּלֶךְ עֹמֵד בְּבֵית הָמָן גָּבֹהַּ
חֲמִשִּׁים אַמָּה וַיֹּאמֶר הַמֶּלֶךְ תְּלֻהוּ עָלָיו: וַיִּתְלוּ אֶת־הָמָן עַל־הָעֵץ אֲשֶׁר־הֵכִין

י לְמָרְדֳּכָי וַחֲמַת הַמֶּלֶךְ שָׁכָכָה: בַּיּוֹם הַהוּא נָתַן הַמֶּלֶךְ אֲחַשְׁוֵרוֹשׁ

ח א לְאֶסְתֵּר הַמַּלְכָּה אֶת־בֵּית הָמָן צֹרֵר הַיְּהוּדִיים וּמָרְדֳּכַי בָּא לִפְנֵי הַמֶּלֶךְ כִּי־ הַיְּהוּדִים
הִגִּידָה אֶסְתֵּר מַה הוּא־לָהּ: וַיָּסַר הַמֶּלֶךְ אֶת־טַבַּעְתּוֹ אֲשֶׁר הֶעֱבִיר מֵהָמָן וַתֹּסֶף
ב וַיִּתְּנָהּ לְמָרְדֳּכָי וַתָּשֶׂם אֶסְתֵּר אֶת־מָרְדֳּכַי עַל־בֵּית הָמָן:
ג אֶסְתֵּר וַתְּדַבֵּר לִפְנֵי הַמֶּלֶךְ וַתִּפֹּל לִפְנֵי רַגְלָיו וַתֵּבְךְּ וַתִּתְחַנֶּן־לוֹ לְהַעֲבִיר
ד אֶת־רָעַת הָמָן הָאֲגָגִי וְאֵת מַחֲשַׁבְתּוֹ אֲשֶׁר חָשַׁב עַל־הַיְּהוּדִים: וַיּוֹשֶׁט הַמֶּלֶךְ
ה לְאֶסְתֵּר אֵת שַׁרְבִט הַזָּהָב וַתָּקָם אֶסְתֵּר וַתַּעֲמֹד לִפְנֵי הַמֶּלֶךְ: וַתֹּאמֶר אִם־
עַל־הַמֶּלֶךְ טוֹב וְאִם־מָצָאתִי חֵן לְפָנָיו וְכָשֵׁר הַדָּבָר לִפְנֵי הַמֶּלֶךְ וְטוֹבָה
אֲנִי בְּעֵינָיו יִכָּתֵב לְהָשִׁיב אֶת־הַסְּפָרִים מַחֲשֶׁבֶת הָמָן בֶּן־הַמְּדָתָא הָאֲגָגִי
ו אֲשֶׁר כָּתַב לְאַבֵּד אֶת־הַיְּהוּדִים אֲשֶׁר בְּכָל־מְדִינוֹת הַמֶּלֶךְ: כִּי אֵיכָכָה
אוּכַל וְרָאִיתִי בָּרָעָה אֲשֶׁר־יִמְצָא אֶת־עַמִּי וְאֵיכָכָה אוּכַל וְרָאִיתִי בְּאָבְדַן
ז מוֹלַדְתִּי: וַיֹּאמֶר הַמֶּלֶךְ אֲחַשְׁוֵרֹשׁ לְאֶסְתֵּר הַמַּלְכָּה וּלְמָרְדֳּכַי
הַיְּהוּדִי הִנֵּה בֵית־הָמָן נָתַתִּי לְאֶסְתֵּר וְאֹתוֹ תָּלוּ עַל־הָעֵץ עַל אֲשֶׁר־שָׁלַח
ח יָדוֹ בַּיְּהוּדִיים: וְאַתֶּם כִּתְבוּ עַל־הַיְּהוּדִים כַּטּוֹב בְּעֵינֵיכֶם בְּשֵׁם הַמֶּלֶךְ וְחִתְמוּ בַּיְּהוּדִים
בְּטַבַּעַת הַמֶּלֶךְ כִּי־כְתָב אֲשֶׁר־נִכְתָּב בְּשֵׁם־הַמֶּלֶךְ וְנַחְתּוֹם בְּטַבַּעַת הַמֶּלֶךְ
ט אֵין לְהָשִׁיב: וַיִּקָּרְאוּ סֹפְרֵי־הַמֶּלֶךְ בָּעֵת־הַהִיא בַּחֹדֶשׁ הַשְּׁלִישִׁי הוּא־חֹדֶשׁ
סִיוָן בִּשְׁלוֹשָׁה וְעֶשְׂרִים בּוֹ וַיִּכָּתֵב כְּכָל־אֲשֶׁר־צִוָּה מָרְדֳּכַי אֶל־הַיְּהוּדִים וְאֶל
הָאֲחַשְׁדַּרְפְּנִים וְהַפַּחוֹת וְשָׂרֵי הַמְּדִינוֹת אֲשֶׁר ׀ מֵהֹדּוּ וְעַד־כּוּשׁ שֶׁבַע וְעֶשְׂרִים
וּמֵאָה מְדִינָה מְדִינָה וּמְדִינָה כִּכְתָבָהּ וְעַם וָעָם כִּלְשֹׁנוֹ וְאֶל־הַיְּהוּדִים כִּכְתָבָם
י וְכִלְשׁוֹנָם: וַיִּכְתֹּב בְּשֵׁם הַמֶּלֶךְ אֲחַשְׁוֵרֹשׁ וַיַּחְתֹּם בְּטַבַּעַת הַמֶּלֶךְ וַיִּשְׁלַח
יא סְפָרִים בְּיַד הָרָצִים בַּסּוּסִים רֹכְבֵי הָרֶכֶשׁ הָאֲחַשְׁתְּרָנִים בְּנֵי הָרַמָּכִים: אֲשֶׁר
נָתַן הַמֶּלֶךְ לַיְּהוּדִים ׀ אֲשֶׁר ׀ בְּכָל־עִיר וָעִיר לְהִקָּהֵל וְלַעֲמֹד עַל־נַפְשָׁם
לְהַשְׁמִיד וְלַהֲרֹג וּלְאַבֵּד אֶת־כָּל־חֵיל עַם וּמְדִינָה הַצָּרִים אֹתָם טַף וְנָשִׁים
יב וּשְׁלָלָם לָבוֹז: בְּיוֹם אֶחָד בְּכָל־מְדִינוֹת הַמֶּלֶךְ אֲחַשְׁוֵרוֹשׁ בִּשְׁלוֹשָׁה עָשָׂר
יג לְחֹדֶשׁ שְׁנֵים־עָשָׂר הוּא־חֹדֶשׁ אֲדָר: פַּתְשֶׁגֶן הַכְּתָב לְהִנָּתֵן דָּת בְּכָל־מְדִינָה

ספֶר הַזִּכְרֹנוֹת דִּבְרֵי הַיָּמִים וַיִּהְיוּ נִקְרָאִים לִפְנֵי הַמֶּלֶךְ: וַיִּמָּצֵא כָתוּב אֲשֶׁר ב

הִגִּיד מָרְדֳּכַי עַל־בִּגְתָנָא וָתֶרֶשׁ שְׁנֵי סָרִיסֵי הַמֶּלֶךְ מִשֹּׁמְרֵי הַסַּף אֲשֶׁר בִּקְשׁוּ

לִשְׁלֹחַ יָד בַּמֶּלֶךְ אֲחַשְׁוֵרוֹשׁ: וַיֹּאמֶר הַמֶּלֶךְ מַה־נַּעֲשָׂה יְקָר וּגְדוּלָּה לְמָרְדֳּכַי ג

עַל־זֶה וַיֹּאמְרוּ נַעֲרֵי הַמֶּלֶךְ מְשָׁרְתָיו לֹא־נַעֲשָׂה עִמּוֹ דָּבָר: וַיֹּאמֶר הַמֶּלֶךְ מִי ד

בֶחָצֵר וְהָמָן בָּא לַחֲצַר בֵּית־הַמֶּלֶךְ הַחִיצוֹנָה לֵאמֹר לַמֶּלֶךְ לִתְלוֹת אֶת־מָרְדֳּכַי

עַל־הָעֵץ אֲשֶׁר־הֵכִין לוֹ: וַיֹּאמְרוּ נַעֲרֵי הַמֶּלֶךְ אֵלָיו הִנֵּה הָמָן עֹמֵד בֶּחָצֵר ה

וַיֹּאמֶר הַמֶּלֶךְ יָבוֹא: וַיָּבוֹא הָמָן וַיֹּאמֶר לוֹ הַמֶּלֶךְ מַה־לַּעֲשׂוֹת בָּאִישׁ אֲשֶׁר ו

הַמֶּלֶךְ חָפֵץ בִּיקָרוֹ וַיֹּאמֶר הָמָן בְּלִבּוֹ לְמִי יַחְפֹּץ הַמֶּלֶךְ לַעֲשׂוֹת יְקָר יוֹתֵר

מִמֶּנִּי: וַיֹּאמֶר הָמָן אֶל־הַמֶּלֶךְ אִישׁ אֲשֶׁר הַמֶּלֶךְ חָפֵץ בִּיקָרוֹ: יָבִיאוּ לְבוּשׁ ח

מַלְכוּת אֲשֶׁר לָבַשׁ־בּוֹ הַמֶּלֶךְ וְסוּס אֲשֶׁר רָכַב עָלָיו הַמֶּלֶךְ וַאֲשֶׁר נִתַּן כֶּתֶר

מַלְכוּת בְּרֹאשׁוֹ: וְנָתוֹן הַלְּבוּשׁ וְהַסּוּס עַל־יַד־אִישׁ מִשָּׂרֵי הַמֶּלֶךְ הַפַּרְתְּמִים ט

וְהִלְבִּישׁוּ אֶת־הָאִישׁ אֲשֶׁר הַמֶּלֶךְ חָפֵץ בִּיקָרוֹ וְהִרְכִּיבֻהוּ עַל־הַסּוּס בִּרְחוֹב

הָעִיר וְקָרְאוּ לְפָנָיו כָּכָה יֵעָשֶׂה לָאִישׁ אֲשֶׁר הַמֶּלֶךְ חָפֵץ בִּיקָרוֹ: וַיֹּאמֶר הַמֶּלֶךְ י

לְהָמָן מַהֵר קַח אֶת־הַלְּבוּשׁ וְאֶת־הַסּוּס כַּאֲשֶׁר דִּבַּרְתָּ וַעֲשֵׂה־כֵן לְמָרְדֳּכַי

הַיְּהוּדִי הַיּוֹשֵׁב בְּשַׁעַר הַמֶּלֶךְ אַל־תַּפֵּל דָּבָר מִכֹּל אֲשֶׁר דִּבַּרְתָּ: וַיִּקַּח הָמָן יא

אֶת־הַלְּבוּשׁ וְאֶת־הַסּוּס וַיַּלְבֵּשׁ אֶת־מָרְדֳּכָי וַיַּרְכִּיבֵהוּ בִּרְחוֹב הָעִיר וַיִּקְרָא

לְפָנָיו כָּכָה יֵעָשֶׂה לָאִישׁ אֲשֶׁר הַמֶּלֶךְ חָפֵץ בִּיקָרוֹ: וַיָּשָׁב מָרְדֳּכַי אֶל־שַׁעַר יב

הַמֶּלֶךְ וְהָמָן נִדְחַף אֶל־בֵּיתוֹ אָבֵל וַחֲפוּי רֹאשׁ: וַיְסַפֵּר הָמָן לְזֶרֶשׁ אִשְׁתּוֹ יג

וּלְכָל־אֹהֲבָיו אֵת כָּל־אֲשֶׁר קָרָהוּ וַיֹּאמְרוּ לוֹ חֲכָמָיו וְזֶרֶשׁ אִשְׁתּוֹ אִם מִזֶּרַע

הַיְּהוּדִים מָרְדֳּכַי אֲשֶׁר הַחִלּוֹתָ לִנְפֹּל לְפָנָיו לֹא־תוּכַל לוֹ כִּי־נָפוֹל תִּפּוֹל לְפָנָיו:

עוֹדָם מְדַבְּרִים עִמּוֹ וְסָרִיסֵי הַמֶּלֶךְ הִגִּיעוּ וַיַּבְהִלוּ לְהָבִיא אֶת־הָמָן אֶל־ יד

הַמִּשְׁתֶּה אֲשֶׁר־עָשְׂתָה אֶסְתֵּר: וַיָּבֹא הַמֶּלֶךְ וְהָמָן לִשְׁתּוֹת עִם־אֶסְתֵּר ז א

הַמַּלְכָּה: וַיֹּאמֶר הַמֶּלֶךְ לְאֶסְתֵּר גַּם בַּיּוֹם הַשֵּׁנִי בְּמִשְׁתֵּה הַיַּיִן מַה־שְּׁאֵלָתֵךְ ב

אֶסְתֵּר הַמַּלְכָּה וְתִנָּתֵן לָךְ וּמַה־בַּקָּשָׁתֵךְ עַד־חֲצִי הַמַּלְכוּת וְתֵעָשׂ: וַתַּעַן ג

אֶסְתֵּר הַמַּלְכָּה וַתֹּאמַר אִם־מָצָאתִי חֵן בְּעֵינֶיךָ הַמֶּלֶךְ וְאִם־עַל־הַמֶּלֶךְ טוֹב

תִּנָּתֶן־לִי נַפְשִׁי בִּשְׁאֵלָתִי וְעַמִּי בְּבַקָּשָׁתִי: כִּי נִמְכַּרְנוּ אֲנִי וְעַמִּי לְהַשְׁמִיד ד

לַהֲרוֹג וּלְאַבֵּד וְאִלּוּ לַעֲבָדִים וְלִשְׁפָחוֹת נִמְכַּרְנוּ הֶחֱרַשְׁתִּי כִּי אֵין הַצָּר שֹׁוֶה

בְּנֵזֶק הַמֶּלֶךְ:   וַיֹּאמֶר הַמֶּלֶךְ אֲחַשְׁוֵרוֹשׁ וַיֹּאמֶר לְאֶסְתֵּר הַמַּלְכָּה ה

מִי הוּא זֶה וְאֵי־זֶה הוּא אֲשֶׁר־מְלָאוֹ לִבּוֹ לַעֲשׂוֹת כֵּן: וַתֹּאמֶר אֶסְתֵּר אִישׁ ו

צַר וְאוֹיֵב הָמָן הָרָע הַזֶּה וְהָמָן נִבְעַת מִלִּפְנֵי הַמֶּלֶךְ וְהַמַּלְכָּה: וְהַמֶּלֶךְ קָם ז

בַּחֲמָתוֹ מִמִּשְׁתֵּה הַיַּיִן אֶל־גִּנַּת הַבִּיתָן וְהָמָן עָמַד לְבַקֵּשׁ עַל־נַפְשׁוֹ מֵאֶסְתֵּר

יב נִקְרֵאתִי לָבוֹא אֶל־הַמֶּלֶךְ זֶה שְׁלוֹשִׁים יוֹם: וַיַּגִּידוּ לְמָרְדֳּכַי אֵת דִּבְרֵי אֶסְתֵּר:

יג וַיֹּאמֶר מָרְדֳּכַי לְהָשִׁיב אֶל־אֶסְתֵּר אַל־תְּדַמִּי בְנַפְשֵׁךְ לְהִמָּלֵט בֵּית־הַמֶּלֶךְ

יד מִכָּל־הַיְּהוּדִים: כִּי אִם־הַחֲרֵשׁ תַּחֲרִישִׁי בָּעֵת הַזֹּאת רֶוַח וְהַצָּלָה יַעֲמוֹד לַיְּהוּדִים מִמָּקוֹם אַחֵר וְאַתְּ וּבֵית־אָבִיךְ תֹּאבֵדוּ וּמִי יוֹדֵעַ אִם־לְעֵת כָּזֹאת

טו הִגַּעַתְּ לַמַּלְכוּת: וַתֹּאמֶר אֶסְתֵּר לְהָשִׁיב אֶל־מָרְדֳּכָי: לֵךְ כְּנוֹס אֶת־כָּל־הַיְּהוּדִים הַנִּמְצְאִים בְּשׁוּשָׁן וְצוּמוּ עָלַי וְאַל־תֹּאכְלוּ וְאַל־תִּשְׁתּוּ שְׁלֹשֶׁת יָמִים לַיְלָה וָיוֹם גַּם־אֲנִי וְנַעֲרֹתַי אָצוּם כֵּן וּבְכֵן אָבוֹא אֶל־הַמֶּלֶךְ אֲשֶׁר לֹא־כַדָּת

יז וְכַאֲשֶׁר אָבַדְתִּי אָבָדְתִּי: וַיַּעֲבֹר מָרְדֳּכָי וַיַּעַשׂ כְּכֹל אֲשֶׁר־צִוְּתָה עָלָיו אֶסְתֵּר:

ה א וַיְהִי ׀ בַּיּוֹם הַשְּׁלִישִׁי וַתִּלְבַּשׁ אֶסְתֵּר מַלְכוּת וַתַּעֲמֹד בַּחֲצַר בֵּית־הַמֶּלֶךְ הַפְּנִימִית נֹכַח בֵּית הַמֶּלֶךְ וְהַמֶּלֶךְ יוֹשֵׁב עַל־כִּסֵּא מַלְכוּתוֹ בְּבֵית הַמַּלְכוּת

ב נֹכַח פֶּתַח הַבָּיִת: וַיְהִי כִרְאוֹת הַמֶּלֶךְ אֶת־אֶסְתֵּר הַמַּלְכָּה עֹמֶדֶת בֶּחָצֵר נָשְׂאָה חֵן בְּעֵינָיו וַיּוֹשֶׁט הַמֶּלֶךְ לְאֶסְתֵּר אֶת־שַׁרְבִיט הַזָּהָב אֲשֶׁר בְּיָדוֹ וַתִּקְרַב

ג אֶסְתֵּר וַתִּגַּע בְּרֹאשׁ הַשַּׁרְבִיט: וַיֹּאמֶר לָהּ הַמֶּלֶךְ מַה־לָּךְ אֶסְתֵּר הַמַּלְכָּה

ד וּמַה־בַּקָּשָׁתֵךְ עַד־חֲצִי הַמַּלְכוּת וְיִנָּתֵן לָךְ: וַתֹּאמֶר אֶסְתֵּר אִם־עַל־הַמֶּלֶךְ

ה טוֹב יָבוֹא הַמֶּלֶךְ וְהָמָן הַיּוֹם אֶל־הַמִּשְׁתֶּה אֲשֶׁר־עָשִׂיתִי לוֹ: וַיֹּאמֶר הַמֶּלֶךְ מַהֲרוּ אֶת־הָמָן לַעֲשׂוֹת אֶת־דְּבַר אֶסְתֵּר וַיָּבֹא הַמֶּלֶךְ וְהָמָן אֶל־הַמִּשְׁתֶּה

ו אֲשֶׁר־עָשְׂתָה אֶסְתֵּר: וַיֹּאמֶר הַמֶּלֶךְ לְאֶסְתֵּר בְּמִשְׁתֵּה הַיַּיִן מַה־שְּׁאֵלָתֵךְ

ז וְיִנָּתֵן לָךְ וּמַה־בַּקָּשָׁתֵךְ עַד־חֲצִי הַמַּלְכוּת וְתֵעָשׂ: וַתַּעַן אֶסְתֵּר וַתֹּאמַר

ח שְׁאֵלָתִי וּבַקָּשָׁתִי: אִם־מָצָאתִי חֵן בְּעֵינֵי הַמֶּלֶךְ וְאִם־עַל־הַמֶּלֶךְ טוֹב לָתֵת אֶת־שְׁאֵלָתִי וְלַעֲשׂוֹת אֶת־בַּקָּשָׁתִי יָבוֹא הַמֶּלֶךְ וְהָמָן אֶל־הַמִּשְׁתֶּה אֲשֶׁר

ט אֶעֱשֶׂה לָהֶם וּמָחָר אֶעֱשֶׂה כִּדְבַר הַמֶּלֶךְ: וַיֵּצֵא הָמָן בַּיּוֹם הַהוּא שָׂמֵחַ וְטוֹב לֵב וְכִרְאוֹת הָמָן אֶת־מָרְדֳּכַי בְּשַׁעַר הַמֶּלֶךְ וְלֹא־קָם וְלֹא־זָע מִמֶּנּוּ וַיִּמָּלֵא

י הָמָן עַל־מָרְדֳּכַי חֵמָה: וַיִּתְאַפַּק הָמָן וַיָּבוֹא אֶל־בֵּיתוֹ וַיִּשְׁלַח וַיָּבֵא אֶת־אֹהֲבָיו

יא וְאֶת־זֶרֶשׁ אִשְׁתּוֹ: וַיְסַפֵּר לָהֶם הָמָן אֶת־כְּבוֹד עָשְׁרוֹ וְרֹב בָּנָיו וְאֵת כָּל־אֲשֶׁר

יב גִּדְּלוֹ הַמֶּלֶךְ וְאֵת אֲשֶׁר נִשְּׂאוֹ עַל־הַשָּׂרִים וְעַבְדֵי הַמֶּלֶךְ: וַיֹּאמֶר הָמָן אַף לֹא־הֵבִיאָה אֶסְתֵּר הַמַּלְכָּה עִם־הַמֶּלֶךְ אֶל־הַמִּשְׁתֶּה אֲשֶׁר־עָשָׂתָה כִּי אִם־

יג אוֹתִי וְגַם־לְמָחָר אֲנִי קָרוּא־לָהּ עִם־הַמֶּלֶךְ: וְכָל־זֶה אֵינֶנּוּ שֹׁוֶה לִי בְּכָל־עֵת

יד אֲשֶׁר אֲנִי רֹאֶה אֶת־מָרְדֳּכַי הַיְּהוּדִי יוֹשֵׁב בְּשַׁעַר הַמֶּלֶךְ: וַתֹּאמֶר לוֹ זֶרֶשׁ אִשְׁתּוֹ וְכָל־אֹהֲבָיו יַעֲשׂוּ־עֵץ גָּבֹהַּ חֲמִשִּׁים אַמָּה וּבַבֹּקֶר ׀ אֱמֹר לַמֶּלֶךְ וְיִתְלוּ אֶת־מָרְדֳּכַי עָלָיו וּבֹא עִם־הַמֶּלֶךְ אֶל־הַמִּשְׁתֶּה שָׂמֵחַ וַיִּיטַב הַדָּבָר לִפְנֵי הָמָן

ו א וַיַּעַשׂ הָעֵץ: בַּלַּיְלָה הַהוּא נָדְדָה שְׁנַת הַמֶּלֶךְ וַיֹּאמֶר לְהָבִיא אֶת־

אֲחַשְׁוֵרוֹשׁ יֶשְׁנוֹ עַם־אֶחָד מְפֻזָּר וּמְפֹרָד בֵּין הָעַמִּים בְּכֹל מְדִינוֹת מַלְכוּתֶךָ
וְדָתֵיהֶם שֹׁנוֹת מִכָּל־עָם וְאֶת־דָּתֵי הַמֶּלֶךְ אֵינָם עֹשִׂים וְלַמֶּלֶךְ אֵין־שֹׁוֶה
לְהַנִּיחָם׃ אִם־עַל־הַמֶּלֶךְ טוֹב יִכָּתֵב לְאַבְּדָם וַעֲשֶׂרֶת אֲלָפִים כִּכַּר־כֶּסֶף ט
אֶשְׁקוֹל עַל־יְדֵי עֹשֵׂי הַמְּלָאכָה לְהָבִיא אֶל־גִּנְזֵי הַמֶּלֶךְ׃ וַיָּסַר הַמֶּלֶךְ אֶת־ י
טַבַּעְתּוֹ מֵעַל יָדוֹ וַיִּתְּנָהּ לְהָמָן בֶּן־הַמְּדָתָא הָאֲגָגִי צֹרֵר הַיְּהוּדִים׃ וַיֹּאמֶר יא
הַמֶּלֶךְ לְהָמָן הַכֶּסֶף נָתוּן לָךְ וְהָעָם לַעֲשׂוֹת בּוֹ כַּטּוֹב בְּעֵינֶיךָ׃ וַיִּקָּרְאוּ סֹפְרֵי יב
הַמֶּלֶךְ בַּחֹדֶשׁ הָרִאשׁוֹן בִּשְׁלוֹשָׁה עָשָׂר יוֹם בּוֹ וַיִּכָּתֵב כְּכָל־אֲשֶׁר־צִוָּה הָמָן
אֶל אֲחַשְׁדַּרְפְּנֵי־הַמֶּלֶךְ וְאֶל־הַפַּחוֹת אֲשֶׁר ׀ עַל־מְדִינָה וּמְדִינָה וְאֶל־שָׂרֵי
עַם וָעָם מְדִינָה וּמְדִינָה כִּכְתָבָהּ וְעַם וָעָם כִּלְשׁוֹנוֹ בְּשֵׁם הַמֶּלֶךְ אֲחַשְׁוֵרֹשׁ
נִכְתָּב וְנֶחְתָּם בְּטַבַּעַת הַמֶּלֶךְ׃ וְנִשְׁלוֹחַ סְפָרִים בְּיַד הָרָצִים אֶל־כָּל־מְדִינוֹת יג
הַמֶּלֶךְ לְהַשְׁמִיד לַהֲרֹג וּלְאַבֵּד אֶת־כָּל־הַיְּהוּדִים מִנַּעַר וְעַד־זָקֵן טַף וְנָשִׁים
בְּיוֹם אֶחָד בִּשְׁלוֹשָׁה עָשָׂר לְחֹדֶשׁ שְׁנֵים־עָשָׂר הוּא־חֹדֶשׁ אֲדָר וּשְׁלָלָם לָבוֹז׃
פַּתְשֶׁגֶן הַכְּתָב לְהִנָּתֵן דָּת בְּכָל־מְדִינָה וּמְדִינָה גָּלוּי לְכָל־הָעַמִּים לִהְיוֹת יד
עֲתִדִים לַיּוֹם הַזֶּה׃ הָרָצִים יָצְאוּ דְחוּפִים בִּדְבַר הַמֶּלֶךְ וְהַדָּת נִתְּנָה בְּשׁוּשַׁן טו
הַבִּירָה וְהַמֶּלֶךְ וְהָמָן יָשְׁבוּ לִשְׁתּוֹת וְהָעִיר שׁוּשָׁן נָבוֹכָה׃ וּמָרְדֳּכַי א ד
יָדַע אֶת־כָּל־אֲשֶׁר נַעֲשָׂה וַיִּקְרַע מָרְדֳּכַי אֶת־בְּגָדָיו וַיִּלְבַּשׁ שַׂק וָאֵפֶר וַיֵּצֵא
בְּתוֹךְ הָעִיר וַיִּזְעַק זְעָקָה גְדֹלָה וּמָרָה׃ וַיָּבוֹא עַד לִפְנֵי שַׁעַר־הַמֶּלֶךְ כִּי אֵין ב
לָבוֹא אֶל־שַׁעַר הַמֶּלֶךְ בִּלְבוּשׁ שָׂק׃ וּבְכָל־מְדִינָה וּמְדִינָה מְקוֹם אֲשֶׁר דְּבַר־ ג
הַמֶּלֶךְ וְדָתוֹ מַגִּיעַ אֵבֶל גָּדוֹל לַיְּהוּדִים וְצוֹם וּבְכִי וּמִסְפֵּד שַׂק וָאֵפֶר יֻצַּע
וַתָּבוֹאנָה לָרַבִּים׃ ותבואינה נַעֲרוֹת אֶסְתֵּר וְסָרִיסֶיהָ וַיַּגִּידוּ לָהּ וַתִּתְחַלְחַל הַמַּלְכָּה ד
מְאֹד וַתִּשְׁלַח בְּגָדִים לְהַלְבִּישׁ אֶת־מָרְדֳּכַי וּלְהָסִיר שַׂקּוֹ מֵעָלָיו וְלֹא קִבֵּל׃
וַתִּקְרָא אֶסְתֵּר לַהֲתָךְ מִסָּרִיסֵי הַמֶּלֶךְ אֲשֶׁר הֶעֱמִיד לְפָנֶיהָ וַתְּצַוֵּהוּ עַל־מָרְדֳּכָי ה
לָדַעַת מַה־זֶּה וְעַל־מַה־זֶּה׃ וַיֵּצֵא הֲתָךְ אֶל־מָרְדֳּכָי אֶל־רְחוֹב הָעִיר אֲשֶׁר ו
לִפְנֵי שַׁעַר־הַמֶּלֶךְ׃ וַיַּגֶּד־לוֹ מָרְדֳּכַי אֵת כָּל־אֲשֶׁר קָרָהוּ וְאֵת ׀ פָּרָשַׁת הַכֶּסֶף ז
בַּיְּהוּדִים אֲשֶׁר אָמַר הָמָן לִשְׁקוֹל עַל־גִּנְזֵי הַמֶּלֶךְ ביהודיים לְאַבְּדָם׃ וְאֶת־פַּתְשֶׁגֶן ח
כְּתָב־הַדָּת אֲשֶׁר־נִתַּן בְּשׁוּשָׁן לְהַשְׁמִידָם נָתַן לוֹ לְהַרְאוֹת אֶת־אֶסְתֵּר וּלְהַגִּיד
לָהּ וּלְצַוּוֹת עָלֶיהָ לָבוֹא אֶל־הַמֶּלֶךְ לְהִתְחַנֶּן־לוֹ וּלְבַקֵּשׁ מִלְּפָנָיו עַל־עַמָּהּ׃
וַיָּבוֹא הֲתָךְ וַיַּגֵּד לְאֶסְתֵּר אֵת דִּבְרֵי מָרְדֳּכָי׃ וַתֹּאמֶר אֶסְתֵּר לַהֲתָךְ וַתְּצַוֵּהוּ י ט
אֶל־מָרְדֳּכָי׃ כָּל־עַבְדֵי הַמֶּלֶךְ וְעַם־מְדִינוֹת הַמֶּלֶךְ יֹדְעִים אֲשֶׁר כָּל־אִישׁ וְאִשָּׁה יא
אֲשֶׁר־יָבוֹא אֶל־הַמֶּלֶךְ אֶל־הֶחָצֵר הַפְּנִימִית אֲשֶׁר לֹא־יִקָּרֵא אַחַת דָּתוֹ
לְהָמִית לְבַד מֵאֲשֶׁר יוֹשִׁיט־לוֹ הַמֶּלֶךְ אֶת־שַׁרְבִיט הַזָּהָב וְחָיָה וַאֲנִי לֹא

הֱיוֹת לָהּ כְּדָת הַנָּשִׁים שְׁנֵים עָשָׂר חֹדֶשׁ כִּי כֵּן יִמְלְאוּ יְמֵי מְרוּקֵיהֶן שִׁשָּׁה

יג חֳדָשִׁים בְּשֶׁמֶן הַמֹּר וְשִׁשָּׁה חֳדָשִׁים בַּבְּשָׂמִים וּבְתַמְרוּקֵי הַנָּשִׁים: וּבָזֶה הַנַּעֲרָה בָּאָה אֶל־הַמֶּלֶךְ אֵת כָּל־אֲשֶׁר תֹּאמַר יִנָּתֵן לָהּ לָבוֹא עִמָּהּ מִבֵּית

יד הַנָּשִׁים עַד־בֵּית הַמֶּלֶךְ: בָּעֶרֶב ׀ הִיא בָאָה וּבַבֹּקֶר הִיא שָׁבָה אֶל־בֵּית הַנָּשִׁים שֵׁנִי אֶל־יַד שַׁעֲשְׁגַז סְרִיס הַמֶּלֶךְ שֹׁמֵר הַפִּילַגְשִׁים לֹא־תָבוֹא עוֹד אֶל־הַמֶּלֶךְ

טו כִּי אִם־חָפֵץ בָּהּ הַמֶּלֶךְ וְנִקְרְאָה בְשֵׁם: וּבְהַגִּיעַ תֹּר־אֶסְתֵּר בַּת־אֲבִיחַיִל ׀ דֹּד מָרְדֳּכַי אֲשֶׁר לָקַח־לוֹ לְבַת לָבוֹא אֶל־הַמֶּלֶךְ לֹא בִקְשָׁה דָּבָר כִּי אִם אֶת־אֲשֶׁר יֹאמַר הֵגַי סְרִיס־הַמֶּלֶךְ שֹׁמֵר הַנָּשִׁים וַתְּהִי אֶסְתֵּר נֹשֵׂאת חֵן בְּעֵינֵי כָּל־רֹאֶיהָ:

טז וַתִּלָּקַח אֶסְתֵּר אֶל־הַמֶּלֶךְ אֲחַשְׁוֵרוֹשׁ אֶל־בֵּית מַלְכוּתוֹ בַּחֹדֶשׁ הָעֲשִׂירִי

יז הוּא־חֹדֶשׁ טֵבֵת בִּשְׁנַת־שֶׁבַע לְמַלְכוּתוֹ: וַיֶּאֱהַב הַמֶּלֶךְ אֶת־אֶסְתֵּר מִכָּל־ הַנָּשִׁים וַתִּשָּׂא־חֵן וָחֶסֶד לְפָנָיו מִכָּל־הַבְּתוּלוֹת וַיָּשֶׂם כֶּתֶר־מַלְכוּת בְּרֹאשָׁהּ

יח וַיַּמְלִיכֶהָ תַּחַת וַשְׁתִּי: וַיַּעַשׂ הַמֶּלֶךְ מִשְׁתֶּה גָדוֹל לְכָל־שָׂרָיו וַעֲבָדָיו אֵת

יט מִשְׁתֵּה אֶסְתֵּר וַהֲנָחָה לַמְּדִינוֹת עָשָׂה וַיִּתֵּן מַשְׂאֵת כְּיַד הַמֶּלֶךְ: וּבְהִקָּבֵץ

כ בְּתוּלוֹת שֵׁנִית וּמָרְדֳּכַי יֹשֵׁב בְּשַׁעַר־הַמֶּלֶךְ: אֵין אֶסְתֵּר מַגֶּדֶת מוֹלַדְתָּהּ וְאֶת־עַמָּהּ כַּאֲשֶׁר צִוָּה עָלֶיהָ מָרְדֳּכָי וְאֶת־מַאֲמַר מָרְדֳּכַי אֶסְתֵּר עֹשָׂה כַּאֲשֶׁר

כא הָיְתָה בְאָמְנָה אִתּוֹ: בַּיָּמִים הָהֵם וּמָרְדֳּכַי יֹשֵׁב בְּשַׁעַר־הַמֶּלֶךְ קָצַף בִּגְתָן וָתֶרֶשׁ שְׁנֵי־סָרִיסֵי הַמֶּלֶךְ מִשֹּׁמְרֵי הַסַּף וַיְבַקְשׁוּ לִשְׁלֹחַ יָד בַּמֶּלֶךְ

כב אֲחַשְׁוֵרֹשׁ: וַיִּוָּדַע הַדָּבָר לְמָרְדֳּכַי וַיַּגֵּד לְאֶסְתֵּר הַמַּלְכָּה וַתֹּאמֶר אֶסְתֵּר לַמֶּלֶךְ

כג בְּשֵׁם מָרְדֳּכָי: וַיְבֻקַּשׁ הַדָּבָר וַיִּמָּצֵא וַיִּתָּלוּ שְׁנֵיהֶם עַל־עֵץ וַיִּכָּתֵב בְּסֵפֶר דִּבְרֵי הַיָּמִים לִפְנֵי הַמֶּלֶךְ: אַחַר ׀ הַדְּבָרִים הָאֵלֶּה גִּדַּל הַמֶּלֶךְ אֲחַשְׁוֵרוֹשׁ ג א

אֶת־הָמָן בֶּן־הַמְּדָתָא הָאֲגָגִי וַיְנַשְּׂאֵהוּ וַיָּשֶׂם אֶת־כִּסְאוֹ מֵעַל כָּל־הַשָּׂרִים

ב אֲשֶׁר אִתּוֹ: וְכָל־עַבְדֵי הַמֶּלֶךְ אֲשֶׁר־בְּשַׁעַר הַמֶּלֶךְ כֹּרְעִים וּמִשְׁתַּחֲוִים לְהָמָן

ג כִּי־כֵן צִוָּה־לוֹ הַמֶּלֶךְ וּמָרְדֳּכַי לֹא יִכְרַע וְלֹא יִשְׁתַּחֲוֶה: וַיֹּאמְרוּ עַבְדֵי הַמֶּלֶךְ

ד אֲשֶׁר־בְּשַׁעַר הַמֶּלֶךְ לְמָרְדֳּכָי מַדּוּעַ אַתָּה עוֹבֵר אֵת מִצְוַת הַמֶּלֶךְ: וַיְהִי באמרם כְּאָמְרָם אֵלָיו יוֹם וָיוֹם וְלֹא שָׁמַע אֲלֵיהֶם וַיַּגִּידוּ לְהָמָן לִרְאוֹת הֲיַעַמְדוּ דִּבְרֵי

ה מָרְדֳּכַי כִּי־הִגִּיד לָהֶם אֲשֶׁר־הוּא יְהוּדִי: וַיַּרְא הָמָן כִּי־אֵין מָרְדֳּכַי כֹּרֵעַ

ו וּמִשְׁתַּחֲוֶה לוֹ וַיִּמָּלֵא הָמָן חֵמָה: וַיִּבֶז בְּעֵינָיו לִשְׁלֹחַ יָד בְּמָרְדֳּכַי לְבַדּוֹ כִּי־ הִגִּידוּ לוֹ אֶת־עַם מָרְדֳּכָי וַיְבַקֵּשׁ הָמָן לְהַשְׁמִיד אֶת־כָּל־הַיְּהוּדִים אֲשֶׁר

ז בְּכָל־מַלְכוּת אֲחַשְׁוֵרוֹשׁ עַם מָרְדֳּכָי: בַּחֹדֶשׁ הָרִאשׁוֹן הוּא־חֹדֶשׁ נִיסָן בִּשְׁנַת שְׁתֵּים עֶשְׂרֵה לַמֶּלֶךְ אֲחַשְׁוֵרוֹשׁ הִפִּיל פּוּר הוּא הַגּוֹרָל לִפְנֵי הָמָן מִיּוֹם ׀ לְיוֹם

ח וּמֵחֹדֶשׁ לְחֹדֶשׁ שְׁנֵים־עָשָׂר הוּא־חֹדֶשׁ אֲדָר: וַיֹּאמֶר הָמָן לַמֶּלֶךְ

וַיֹּאמֶר מְמוּכָן לִפְנֵי אֶת־מַאֲמַר הַמֶּלֶךְ אֲחַשְׁוֵרוֹשׁ בְּיַד הַסָּרִיסִים:

הַמֶּלֶךְ וְהַשָּׂרִים לֹא עַל־הַמֶּלֶךְ לְבַדּוֹ עָוְתָה וַשְׁתִּי הַמַּלְכָּה כִּי עַל־כָּל־הַשָּׂרִים

וְעַל־כָּל־הָעַמִּים אֲשֶׁר בְּכָל־מְדִינוֹת הַמֶּלֶךְ אֲחַשְׁוֵרוֹשׁ: כִּי־יֵצֵא דְבַר־הַמַּלְכָּה

עַל־כָּל־הַנָּשִׁים לְהַבְזוֹת בַּעְלֵיהֶן בְּעֵינֵיהֶן בְּאָמְרָם הַמֶּלֶךְ אֲחַשְׁוֵרוֹשׁ אָמַר

לְהָבִיא אֶת־וַשְׁתִּי הַמַּלְכָּה לְפָנָיו וְלֹא־בָאָה: וְהַיּוֹם הַזֶּה תֹּאמַרְנָה ׀ שָׂרוֹת

פָּרַס־וּמָדַי אֲשֶׁר שָׁמְעוּ אֶת־דְּבַר הַמַּלְכָּה לְכֹל שָׂרֵי הַמֶּלֶךְ וּכְדַי בִּזָּיוֹן וָקָצֶף:

אִם־עַל־הַמֶּלֶךְ טוֹב יֵצֵא דְבַר־מַלְכוּת מִלְּפָנָיו וְיִכָּתֵב בְּדָתֵי פָרַס־וּמָדַי וְלֹא

יַעֲבוֹר אֲשֶׁר לֹא־תָבוֹא וַשְׁתִּי לִפְנֵי הַמֶּלֶךְ אֲחַשְׁוֵרוֹשׁ וּמַלְכוּתָהּ יִתֵּן הַמֶּלֶךְ

לִרְעוּתָהּ הַטּוֹבָה מִמֶּנָּה: וְנִשְׁמַע פִּתְגָם הַמֶּלֶךְ אֲשֶׁר־יַעֲשֶׂה בְּכָל־מַלְכוּתוֹ כִּי

רַבָּה הִיא וְכָל־הַנָּשִׁים יִתְּנוּ יְקָר לְבַעְלֵיהֶן לְמִגָּדוֹל וְעַד־קָטָן: וַיִּיטַב הַדָּבָר

בְּעֵינֵי הַמֶּלֶךְ וְהַשָּׂרִים וַיַּעַשׂ הַמֶּלֶךְ כִּדְבַר מְמוּכָן: וַיִּשְׁלַח סְפָרִים אֶל־כָּל־

מְדִינוֹת הַמֶּלֶךְ אֶל־מְדִינָה וּמְדִינָה כִּכְתָבָהּ וְאֶל־עַם וָעָם כִּלְשׁוֹנוֹ לִהְיוֹת

כָּל־אִישׁ שֹׂרֵר בְּבֵיתוֹ וּמְדַבֵּר כִּלְשׁוֹן עַמּוֹ: אַחַר הַדְּבָרִים הָאֵלֶּה

כְּשֹׁךְ חֲמַת הַמֶּלֶךְ אֲחַשְׁוֵרוֹשׁ זָכַר אֶת־וַשְׁתִּי וְאֵת אֲשֶׁר־עָשָׂתָה וְאֵת אֲשֶׁר־

נִגְזַר עָלֶיהָ: וַיֹּאמְרוּ נַעֲרֵי־הַמֶּלֶךְ מְשָׁרְתָיו יְבַקְשׁוּ לַמֶּלֶךְ נְעָרוֹת בְּתוּלוֹת

טוֹבוֹת מַרְאֶה: וְיַפְקֵד הַמֶּלֶךְ פְּקִידִים בְּכָל־מְדִינוֹת מַלְכוּתוֹ וְיִקְבְּצוּ אֶת־

כָּל־נַעֲרָה־בְתוּלָה טוֹבַת מַרְאֶה אֶל־שׁוּשַׁן הַבִּירָה אֶל־בֵּית הַנָּשִׁים אֶל־יַד

הֵגֶא סְרִיס הַמֶּלֶךְ שֹׁמֵר הַנָּשִׁים וְנָתוֹן תַּמְרוּקֵיהֶן: וְהַנַּעֲרָה אֲשֶׁר תִּיטַב בְּעֵינֵי

הַמֶּלֶךְ תִּמְלֹךְ תַּחַת וַשְׁתִּי וַיִּיטַב הַדָּבָר בְּעֵינֵי הַמֶּלֶךְ וַיַּעַשׂ כֵּן: אִישׁ־

יְהוּדִי הָיָה בְּשׁוּשַׁן הַבִּירָה וּשְׁמוֹ מָרְדֳּכַי בֶּן יָאִיר בֶּן־שִׁמְעִי בֶּן־קִישׁ אִישׁ

יְמִינִי: אֲשֶׁר הָגְלָה מִירוּשָׁלַיִם עִם־הַגֹּלָה אֲשֶׁר הָגְלְתָה עִם יְכָנְיָה מֶלֶךְ־

יְהוּדָה אֲשֶׁר הֶגְלָה נְבוּכַדְנֶצַּר מֶלֶךְ בָּבֶל: וַיְהִי אֹמֵן אֶת־הֲדַסָּה הִיא אֶסְתֵּר

בַּת־דֹּדוֹ כִּי אֵין לָהּ אָב וָאֵם וְהַנַּעֲרָה יְפַת־תֹּאַר וְטוֹבַת מַרְאֶה וּבְמוֹת אָבִיהָ

וְאִמָּהּ לְקָחָהּ מָרְדֳּכַי לוֹ לְבַת: וַיְהִי בְּהִשָּׁמַע דְּבַר־הַמֶּלֶךְ וְדָתוֹ וּבְהִקָּבֵץ

נְעָרוֹת רַבּוֹת אֶל־שׁוּשַׁן הַבִּירָה אֶל־יַד הֵגַי וַתִּלָּקַח אֶסְתֵּר אֶל־בֵּית הַמֶּלֶךְ

אֶל־יַד הֵגַי שֹׁמֵר הַנָּשִׁים: וַתִּיטַב הַנַּעֲרָה בְעֵינָיו וַתִּשָּׂא חֶסֶד לְפָנָיו וַיְבַהֵל

אֶת־תַּמְרוּקֶיהָ וְאֶת־מָנוֹתֶהָ לָתֵת לָהּ וְאֵת שֶׁבַע הַנְּעָרוֹת הָרְאֻיוֹת לָתֶת־לָהּ

מִבֵּית הַמֶּלֶךְ וַיְשַׁנֶּהָ וְאֶת־נַעֲרוֹתֶיהָ לְטוֹב בֵּית הַנָּשִׁים: לֹא־הִגִּידָה אֶסְתֵּר

אֶת־עַמָּהּ וְאֶת־מוֹלַדְתָּהּ כִּי מָרְדֳּכַי צִוָּה עָלֶיהָ אֲשֶׁר לֹא־תַגִּיד: וּבְכָל־יוֹם

וָיוֹם מָרְדֳּכַי מִתְהַלֵּךְ לִפְנֵי חֲצַר בֵּית־הַנָּשִׁים לָדַעַת אֶת־שְׁלוֹם אֶסְתֵּר וּמַה־

יֵּעָשֶׂה בָּהּ: וּבְהַגִּיעַ תֹּר נַעֲרָה וְנַעֲרָה לָבוֹא ׀ אֶל־הַמֶּלֶךְ אֲחַשְׁוֵרוֹשׁ מִקֵּץ

מגילת
אסתר

א וַיְהִי בִּימֵי אֲחַשְׁוֵרוֹשׁ הוּא אֲחַשְׁוֵרוֹשׁ הַמֹּלֵךְ מֵהֹדּוּ וְעַד־כּוּשׁ שֶׁבַע וְעֶשְׂרִים

ב וּמֵאָה מְדִינָה: בַּיָּמִים הָהֵם כְּשֶׁבֶת ׀ הַמֶּלֶךְ אֲחַשְׁוֵרוֹשׁ עַל כִּסֵּא מַלְכוּתוֹ אֲשֶׁר

ג בְּשׁוּשַׁן הַבִּירָה: בִּשְׁנַת שָׁלוֹשׁ לְמָלְכוֹ עָשָׂה מִשְׁתֶּה לְכָל־שָׂרָיו וַעֲבָדָיו חֵיל ׀

ד פָּרַס וּמָדַי הַפַּרְתְּמִים וְשָׂרֵי הַמְּדִינוֹת לְפָנָיו: בְּהַרְאֹתוֹ אֶת־עֹשֶׁר כְּבוֹד מַלְכוּתוֹ

ה וְאֶת־יְקָר תִּפְאֶרֶת גְּדוּלָּתוֹ יָמִים רַבִּים שְׁמוֹנִים וּמְאַת יוֹם: וּבִמְלוֹאת ׀ הַיָּמִים

הָאֵלֶּה עָשָׂה הַמֶּלֶךְ לְכָל־הָעָם הַנִּמְצְאִים בְּשׁוּשַׁן הַבִּירָה לְמִגָּדוֹל וְעַד־קָטָן

ו מִשְׁתֶּה שִׁבְעַת יָמִים בַּחֲצַר גִּנַּת בִּיתַן הַמֶּלֶךְ: חוּר ׀ כַּרְפַּס וּתְכֵלֶת אָחוּז

בְּחַבְלֵי־בוּץ וְאַרְגָּמָן עַל־גְּלִילֵי כֶסֶף וְעַמּוּדֵי שֵׁשׁ מִטּוֹת ׀ זָהָב וָכֶסֶף עַל רִצְפַת

ז בַּהַט־וָשֵׁשׁ וְדַר וְסֹחָרֶת: וְהַשְׁקוֹת בִּכְלֵי זָהָב וְכֵלִים מִכֵּלִים שׁוֹנִים וְיֵין מַלְכוּת

ח רָב כְּיַד הַמֶּלֶךְ: וְהַשְּׁתִיָּה כַדָּת אֵין אֹנֵס כִּי־כֵן ׀ יִסַּד הַמֶּלֶךְ עַל כָּל־רַב בֵּיתוֹ

ט לַעֲשׂוֹת כִּרְצוֹן אִישׁ־וָאִישׁ:   גַּם וַשְׁתִּי הַמַּלְכָּה עָשְׂתָה מִשְׁתֵּה נָשִׁים

י בֵּית הַמַּלְכוּת אֲשֶׁר לַמֶּלֶךְ אֲחַשְׁוֵרוֹשׁ: בַּיּוֹם הַשְּׁבִיעִי כְּטוֹב לֵב־הַמֶּלֶךְ בַּיָּיִן

אָמַר לִמְהוּמָן בִּזְּתָא חַרְבוֹנָא בִּגְתָא וַאֲבַגְתָא זֵתַר וְכַרְכַּס שִׁבְעַת הַסָּרִיסִים

יא הַמְשָׁרְתִים אֶת־פְּנֵי הַמֶּלֶךְ אֲחַשְׁוֵרוֹשׁ: לְהָבִיא אֶת־וַשְׁתִּי הַמַּלְכָּה לִפְנֵי הַמֶּלֶךְ

בְּכֶתֶר מַלְכוּת לְהַרְאוֹת הָעַמִּים וְהַשָּׂרִים אֶת־יָפְיָהּ כִּי־טוֹבַת מַרְאֶה הִיא:

יב וַתְּמָאֵן הַמַּלְכָּה וַשְׁתִּי לָבוֹא בִּדְבַר הַמֶּלֶךְ אֲשֶׁר בְּיַד הַסָּרִיסִים וַיִּקְצֹף הַמֶּלֶךְ

יג מְאֹד וַחֲמָתוֹ בָּעֲרָה בוֹ:   וַיֹּאמֶר הַמֶּלֶךְ לַחֲכָמִים יֹדְעֵי הָעִתִּים כִּי־

יד כֵן דְּבַר הַמֶּלֶךְ לִפְנֵי כָּל־יֹדְעֵי דָּת וָדִין: וְהַקָּרֹב אֵלָיו כַּרְשְׁנָא שֵׁתָר אַדְמָתָא

תַרְשִׁישׁ מֶרֶס מַרְסְנָא מְמוּכָן שִׁבְעַת שָׂרֵי ׀ פָּרַס וּמָדַי רֹאֵי פְּנֵי הַמֶּלֶךְ הַיֹּשְׁבִים

טו רִאשֹׁנָה בַּמַּלְכוּת: כְּדָת מַה־לַעֲשׂוֹת בַּמַּלְכָּה וַשְׁתִּי עַל ׀ אֲשֶׁר לֹא־עָשְׂתָה